"Book of the year."   Leonard Feather, *Los Angeles Times*

"Recommended to everyone. It's an invaluable aid to both those who are deeply involved in the music and those who would take the plunge."

Richard C. Walls, *Creem*

"Giddins shows off his musical and literary skills. He reports on various encounters with Cecil Taylor and on a Sarah Vaughan concert series; affectionately eulogizes Ethel Waters, Joe Venuti, and Charles Mingus; displays his knack for revealing the essence of his subjects in interviews (especially the hilarious Red Rodney article) or in more personal reflections (like those on Art Pepper and Frank Sinatra's *Trilogy*). He is also willing to plead the case of the under-appreciated and the forgotten, and his profiles of such figures as Otis Blackwell, Jack Teagarden, and Donald Lambert are among the finest in the book. . . . This larger vision, looking beyond single artists and performances, provides a thematic coherence one rarely finds in anthologies."

Bob Blumenthal, *Boston Phoenix*

"These reports and reviews are the work of a brilliant young writer who clearly regards jazz as a fine art that requires the highest critical standards, and yet the pieces are as entertaining as they are serious and insightful. They also reveal a rare appreciation of the interrelationship of jazz, folk music, and pop music."

Albert Murray, author of *Stomping the Blues*

RIDING ON A BLUE NOTE

RIDING
ON A
BLUE NOTE

Jazz and American Pop

GARY GIDDINS

DA CAPO PRESS

Library of Congress Cataloging in Publication Data on file

First Da Capo Press Edition 2000

Most of the material in this book appeared in somewhat different form in *The Village Voice*. "It's Dizzy Again" appeared in somewhat different form in *The New York Times Sunday Magazine*. Grateful acknowledgment is made to Col. R. L. Sweeney for permission to quote from Scott Joplin's *Treemonisha*.

"Good Morning Blues" by Count Basie, James Rushing, and Ed Durham © 1938 by Bregman, Vocco & Conn, Inc. Copyright renewed 1965. All Rights Reserved. Used by Permission.

Published by Da Capo Press
A Member of the Perseus Books Group
http://www.dacapopress.com

1 2 3 4 5 6 7 8 9 10——03 02 01 00 99

For S.M.R.

Jazz is based on the sound of our native heritage. It is an American idiom with African roots—a trunk of soul with limbs reaching in every direction, to the frigid North, the exotic East, the miserable, swampy South, and the swinging Wild West.

—*Duke Ellington*

Jazz is only what you are.

—*Louis Armstrong*

I say play your own way. Don't play what the public wants—you play what you want and let the public pick up on what you are doing—even if it does take them 15, 20 years.

—*Thelonious Monk*

"Jazz" is only a word and really has no meaning . . . I don't know how such great extremes as now exist can be contained under the one heading.

—*Duke Ellington*

Eh, eef, gaff, mmff, dee-bo, deedle-la-bahm,
Rip-rip, de-doo-de-doo, dee-doo-de-doo, da-de-da-da-do,
Ba-do-de-do-do-doo, ba-ro-be-do-be-do, dat,
Geef, gaf, gee-bap-be-da-de-do, de-da-de,
Rip-dip-do-dum, so come on down, do that dance,
They call the heebie jeebies dance, sweet mama,
Papa's got to do the heebie jeebies dance.

—*Louis Armstrong*

Contents

Preface to the Da Capo Edition

Looking back at my first book, after 20 years, I am relieved to find the perpendicular pronoun in relatively short supply, because in many other respects *Riding on a Blue Note* seems to me strangely autobiographical: a working out of youthful obsessions by an energetic writer whom I recall but dimly, with a mixture of bemusement, affection, chagrin, and surprise. This guy had a lot on his mind and apparently believed that by putting it on paper he could alter the world, or at least its musical habits.

The poor sap. Writing to his own generation, the first to disavow seniors—people over thirty—in the name of sex, drugs, and rock and roll, he aspired to pave a thoroughfare between pop and jazz, though handicapped by his own disinclination to travel both directions. For if he was convinced that nothing more than exposure was required to make numberless Ellington and Parker converts, he was obliged to admit he could not have distinguished Led Zeppelin from Moody Blues had his life hung in the balance. He chose as a theme the ubiquity of the blue note, yet discussed pop chiefly as a tangent to jazz, his examples of the former invariably predating 1960. Note that he resisted the then current phenomenon of fusion or jazz-rock, hoping time would echo his disdain. I wish I could fly back to tell him the good news, but then I would also have to alert him to the greater pestilence of jazz lite.

What really interested him about tracking the synchronous paths of jazz and pop were issues of style, repertory, rhythm, and other mutualities of expression that flourished when both idioms could not help but enjoy each other. Perhaps in frontloading the book with five essays about classic pop, urban blues, and rock and roll, he figured he was demonstrating a liberalism that would disarm open-minded pop fans before luring them into his jazz web. Personally, I doubt that such an idea ever crossed his mind, but who knows? Unmistakable, however, is his messianic obsession with jazz and his belief that he could contribute to its recognition and acceptance. You can see the result: Twenty years later, jazz's share of the marketplace is akin to that of an unpopped kernal in a bag of popcorn.

Happily, he was relentlessly consistent in trying to tie together the sprawling estate of jazz, taking it whole from Teagarden to Taylor, Joplin to AACM. On this subject, I am on intimate terms with the writer; indeed, we are two peas in a very lonely pod—but, alas, in the minority. When *Riding on a Blue Note* appeared in 1981, the writer felt impelled to demand respect for this much maligned art that evolved without commerical consideration for most of the century, and to confidently predict that the Establishment would have no recourse but to eventually welcome it with open arms, gates, and purses. That came to pass with gratifying rapidity, but you can see the result: Uptown arts centers offer mainstream music while downtown radicals shroud themselves in bohemianism, and major record companies ignore them both.

And yet the jazz audience regenerates itself, rediscovering classics and encouraging newcomers. Jazz history is very much in the making. A listener coming to it in 1999 might have the chance to see such historic—even legendary—figures as Sonny Rollins, Benny Carter, Cecil Taylor, John Lewis, Ornette Coleman, Lee

Konitz, Dave Brubeck, James Moody, Wayne Shorter, and Muhal Richard Abrams. Many of the younger players discussed in *Riding on a Blue Note* are now themselves acknowledged masters, including David Murray, Arthur Blythe, Henry Threadgill, James Ulmer, and Willem Breuker. In one arena things have taken a dramatic upturn for the better: Jazz singing seemed moribund in 1980, but has made an explosive comeback in the '90s, with such artists as Cassandra Wilson, Denise Jannah, Carla Cook, Diana Krall, Alan Harris, Jeanne Bryson, Kevin Mahogany, Paula West, Ian Shaw, and others. There is no point in listing a few of the dozens of gifted instrumentalists who have come along in the past twenty years; the well shows no signs of drying up. Jazz is a music you count out at your own peril.

Riding on a Blue Note, which was largely constructed from essays written for *The Village Voice* between 1975 and 1980, had a jolting birth. The original editor liked the completed manuscript enormously, or so she said, before taking a maternity leave; her boss, into whose lap it fell, declared the work "unpublishable" and demanded the return of his trifling advance. The redoubtable Sheldon Meyer at Oxford University Press, with whom I had discussed other projects, came to the rescue, and published it for fifteen years. At the end of that time I was finishing my fourth book for him, *Visions of Jazz: The First Century*, and Sheldon encouraged me to cannibalize the earlier volumes for material I considered essential to the more comprehensive work. Revising as I went along, I chose a paragraph from Elvis, most of Mingus, Ellington, and Ethel Waters, and scattered sentences here and there. Still, the duplications amount to little, and I am pleased that Da Capo is republishing this book as it initially appeared, with no second guessing. The picture presented here reflects a transitional period as experienced by a jazz critic in the trenches, containing several essays I could no longer write but none I can't approve.

One section requires an addendum. "Adventures of the Red Arrow" caused much comment back in 1975, and even talk of a movie treatment. Subsequent to its publication, Red was arrested on some of the charges for which the statute of limitations had not lapsed. He wrote me from prison telling me what an easy time he was having, working with the Jewish men's association and cleaning a dozen or so nurses' uniforms, assuring me he did not regret the article and hoped I didn't feel guilty. When he was released, he married well and bought a new set of teeth that allowed him to play with his old strength and technical prowess. During the following decade, the best of his career, he co-led a marvelous band with Ira Sullivan (see *Rhythm-a-ning*) and a bruising quintet with Gary Dial and the then unknown Chris Potter. As we grew friendly, it became evident that however much of a rogue he had once been, he was still a spinner of tall tales. When I asked why he told another writer something patently untrue, Red explained with the weariness of an old con, "Gary, sometimes you have to tell them what they want to hear."

That was before I learned of the possibility that I had been one of his more credulous marks. Shortly before Red died, a journalist set out to write his biography. On returning from a trip to Nevada, he told me—to our mutual dismay—that he was unable to verify Red's account of robbing the Atomic Energy Commission. Was the AEC unwilling to concede it had been conned by a junkie musician? Was the episode a figment of Red's imagination? Then a question arose as to whether he had pulled his Albino Red ruse on more than a single occasion (mere skepticism did not stop Clint Eastwood from using it in his film, *Bird*). Until further evidence is uncovered to the contrary, I am determined to accept every word in "Adventures of the Red Arrow" as gospel, just as I am determined to believe jazz is going to make a terrific incursion into mainstream America, any minute now.

Gary Giddins
November 1999

Introduction to the 1981 Edition

Sidney Lanier defined music as "love in search of a word," but those of us who search for words to express our love of music aren't operating in an entirely loving milieu. With jazz, you have to take into account the ignorance and consequent indifference of the public, and the disdain of an arts establishment still chasing the illusion of European respectability. Forced to compete with pop music in the marketplace, and snubbed by public institutions that consider American precocity—especially when exemplified by blacks—an insufficient pedigree, jazz has been effectively segregated from the mainstream of American life. Despite an internationally celebrated tradition of nearly a century, blues music (in Albert Murray's catholic phrase) is a mystery to the natives, and the question asked most frequently of a jazz critic is "How did you become interested in it?"

Prejudice and misconception are inevitable when cultural traditions are subsumed in the contest for a proper name. The battleground between jazz and the academy is often a semantic one. Even as jazz became the world's first ecumenical music, the dictionary definition of classical music changed from "having permanent interest and value" to "music in the educated European tradition." The 1972 supplement to the *Oxford English*

Dictionary added a new definition: "opp. JAZZ," followed by three quotations that establish jazz as something other than classical. Jazz criticism has always been hobbled by semantic imprecision—"swing" defies definition, "blues" has too many definitions; "jazz," a hopelessly ragged umbrella that never kept out as much rain as the purists hoped, is as loose a term as "classical music" or "serious music" or "pop," and perhaps that's the way it should be. These words are conveniences and are useful as such. Problems arise when they are turned into weapons. By permitting semantics to obscure comprehensive standards of excellence, we've produced cultural institutions— newspapers, record companies, radio, television, the Pulitzer music committee, the National Academy of Recording Arts & Sciences, government funding projects—that fail to properly recognize, document, and support our homegrown genius.

Still, there's no reason to expunge that magical word "jazz." It's worked too hard to get out of the gutter (does any American word have wider currency?), and people all over the world recognize in it not only a way of playing music, but a categorical expression of spontaneity, innovation, resilience, and freedom—in Blaise Cendrars's words, "a new reason for living." In the myopic late '60s, it was fashionable to say that jazz was dead; the observation is made whenever jazz is mutating. The '70s brought a resurgence in its popularity, a cooling down of the pioneering fevers of the avant-garde, an often cynical indulgence in stylistic fusions. For the first time in its history, jazz was without a leader, real or symbolic. Suddenly, the recently departed Armstrong and Ellington were renewed sources of pride, and in the absence of a pathfinder, the entire jazz tradition was renewed as an unplundered text. New standards had to be invoked, and the obvious places to look for those standards were the jazz past (from ragtime to extreme modernism) and neighboring musics (rock, Europe, the third world, etc.).

This collection is a product of that decade, when we were listening beyond categories and trying to make connections. It's

called *Riding on a Blue Note,* after Duke Ellington's 1938 recording, because the illusory blue note is all that the artists I've
chosen to discuss have in common. The blue note is endemic in
jazz, blues, and gospel, and has settled in every corner of American music, from Tin Pan Alley to Nashville and from sympho-
nies to New Wave rock. Yet it is invisible in Western musicol-
ogy: a microtone—a wavering pitch between, say, a third and a
flat third—can't be notated. In recent years, musicologists have
comforted themselves by redefining the blue note as a flat third,
flat fifth, and flat seventh. Even so, the blue note remains elusive, appreciable only in relation to another note. But we know
it when we hear it, and we hear it constantly. Each of these
thirty-odd artists pursued the blue note and the pulsating rhythm
that usually accompanies it, and each attempted to steer it into
a form of personal expression. The black performers were raised
on it, and the white performers were transformed by it. The
reader deserves a warning, however: Although a quarter of the
book is concerned with artists who were only tangentially related to jazz, their music is studied from the always partisan
viewpoint of a jazz critic.

The first section is devoted to singers, and nowhere else is the
generic incest between jazz, pop, blues, rhythm and blues, gospel, rock and roll, and country music more apparent. The discussion of a cycle of concerts by Sarah Vaughan addresses a
problem that is all too prevalent in jazz ventures—a great artist's ambitious undertaking sabotaged by inadequate production values. Two inimitable singers, Professor Longhair and
Jack Teagarden, are included with the instrumentalists in Section 2—an assemblage of mavericks. The third section is devoted to composers, from the primeval dawn of Joplin and
Berlin through a taste of Ellington's immense accomplishment
to two shapers of the modernist impulse; it concludes with two
examples of a phenomenon of the '70s, the musical collective—
one that emerged from an American inner city, the other from
Europe. The final section consists of portraits of seven promi-

nent musicians, based in all but two instances on interviews. Because most of these men came of age in the '30s and '40s, three themes are asserted repeatedly—the impact of Charlie Parker, the devastating postwar presence of heroin, and the difficulties of surviving without compromising one's music. I'm grateful to Dizzy Gillespie, Red Rodney, Dexter Gordon, George Benson, and Cecil Taylor for the time they gave me. Art Pepper and Wes Montgomery are the subjects of a reverie and a polemic, respectively.

With two exceptions, these pieces were selected from the criticism I've written for the *Village Voice* since 1973. All have been revised considerably, for reasons of concision, elaboration, accuracy, stylistic vanity, and, in two or three instances, to amend opinions. I owe thanks to many people, not least the friends, colleagues, and musicians whose conversation has been a constant source of ideas, clues, and challenges. In particular, the writings of Dan Morgenstern, who drafted me for *Down Beat* nearly ten years ago, and Martin Williams, who asked me to participate in an enlightening seminar at the Smithsonian and encouraged the publication of this book, tutored me in listening to and evaluating American music. Their encouragement has been fortification. One of the best things about the Smithsonian seminar was the chance to meet Albert Murray, who is as spellbinding a conversationalist as he is a writer.

Much of the writing in this volume would not have been done without the blessings of Susan Rogers. None of it would have found its present form without the numerous kindnesses of Alice and Leo Giddins, and Donna and Paul Rothchild. I owe thanks to Lee Tovah for her inspiration; to Sheri Robbins for her keen editorial judgment and support; to Ken Emerson for asking me to write the Dizzy Gillespie story for the *New York Times Sunday Magazine*; to Emilie Jacobson for being my agent; and to Sheldon Meyer for being my editor and salvation. I owe an immense debt to my editors, colleagues, fact checkers, photographers, interns, and even publishers at the *Village Voice:* Diane Fisher brought me into the paper; Richard Goldstein, Jill Goldstein, M. Mark, and John Pareles originally prepared some of these pieces for publication. Most of them were originally prepared by the *Voice's* indefatigable music editor, Robert Christgau, the Dean of American Rock Critics, who taught me much about writing and criticism, and is responsible for more than an occasional felicity in what follows.

New York
July 1980

G.G.

Note: The epigrams come from: Duke Ellington's *Music Is My Mistress;* a liner note by Hugues Panassie; a Thelonious Monk interview with Grover Sales; and a transcription by Neil Leonard (revised slightly by myself) of Louis Armstrong's scat vocal on "Heebie Jeebies."

1

Singers

The Mother of Us All

Ethel Waters had been living in California for some time when she died there on September 1, 1977, but the obituary sent out by the Los Angeles office of the Associated Press was perfunctory and misguided. In one paper, it bore the headline ETHEL WATERS DIES 80 AND PENNILESS, and claimed, "She made an art form of singing the blues." The same thing had been said of her in 1921, when she cut her first big records with mostly blues-tinged material; the journalistic sophism that makes all black singers blues singers is apparently deathless. The *New York Times* did better, even beginning its story on the front page, yet neglected her singing in favor of her Broadway and Hollywood successes, furthering the prevailing notion that she is a historical figure remembered chiefly for her acting.

Waters's singing has long been in eclipse, although many of her records are presently available on Columbia and Biograph anthologies. If you were born after the Second World War, you probably remember her as Berenice Sadie Brown in *Member of the Wedding;* you may dimly recall her television series, *Beulah;* and you may have been aware that she was a frequent participant in Billy Graham's crusades. She was also a radiant jewel of "the jazz age"—a brilliantly witty, sassy, and subtle singer of pop songs—and one of the most fascinating aspects of her career is that the vaudeville trouper and the evangelist in her continually vied for dominance. Much of her art seems to have been forged in extreme rebounds between a bitter rebelliousness that she traced back to her loveless childhood and a refined gentility that she once girlishly coveted in the much admired white ladies of vaudeville. As an actress, she faced down the conflict between her spiritual and secular selves; and as a singer, she recognized her ambivalence about being black.

It isn't difficult to understand why she's treated peripherally in histories of American music. She was not a jazz singer, though she influenced many jazz singers and a few jazz musicians (Bix Beiderbecke was an enraptured fan); nor was she a blues singer, though she had an unprecedented impact on popularizing the blues among white audiences. So it's not surprising that jazz and blues writers have concentrated on Bessie Smith while cursorily acknowledging Waters's coequal influence in the '20s. Contemporary pop writers, on the other hand, confine themselves to rock; lineages, when they are bothered with at all, are traced to blues and country roots at the expense of the pop tradition itself; and, as a result, that tradition is forever being recycled as unevaluated nostalgia.

Waters, in many respects, was the mother of modern popular singing, the transitional figure who combined elements of white stars such as Nora Bayes, Fannie Brice, and Sophie Tucker with black rhythms, repertoire, and instrumentation. If this sounds analogous to an idea included in just about every obituary written about Elvis Presley, the comparison is unavoidable. Presley adapted a black aesthetic to a white image; Waters adapted white theatrical styles to a black image. Presley made rhythm and blues a workable form for whites; Waters opened the world of high-toned white entertainment to blacks. She was a source of inspiration for black singers who had no inclination toward the blues, and for black comics and actors who had little affinity with the characterizations inherited from minstrelsy (as exemplified by Bill Robinson, Butterbeans and Susie, and Bert Williams, the only black performer to get top billing in a white theater before Waters). She was equally inspiring to white singers who wished to sing jazz, blues, and pop but lacked the burnished sonorities of Bessie Smith or Ma Rainey. They admired her unpretentious but finely tuned dramatic style, her energy, and her perfect phrasing. By the late '20s, she had developed such rigorous standards for the delivery of pop songs that even Sophie Tucker, older by twelve years, paid her for singing lessons. Waters's influence, whether direct or indirect, is discernible in the work of numerous vocalists of varied styles, including Adelaide Hall, Mildred Bailey, Ivie Anderson, Bing Crosby, Lee Wiley, Bill Kenny, Lena Horne, Una Mae Carlisle, Connee Boswell, Frances Wayne, Pearl Bailey, Mel Torme, Bobby Short, Barbra Streisand, and Maria Muldaur.

The ease with which she made the transition from a blues-oriented repertoire to Tin Pan Alley even had its effect on such individualists as Bessie Smith and Billie Holiday. Although Waters began recording two years before Smith, Bessie was the older and more established performer; yet it was almost certainly Waters's phenomenal success that encouraged Bessie to record as much pop material as she did. I suspect, too, that the popularity of Waters's 1928 "My Handy Man" fostered Smith's 1929 "Kitchen Man" session, as well as countless other double-entendre blues records. (Andy Razaf was commissioned to write both of those songs, and Smith's rolled "r" in the "Kitchen Man" verse was as unusual for her as it was characteristic of Waters.) Billie Holiday attributed her style exclusively to Bessie and Louis Armstrong, but it is Waters we hear on the first Holiday record, "My Mother's Son-in-Law." And there is an unmistakable harbinger of Billie's mature style in Waters's 1928 "My Baby Sure Knows How To Love"—listen to the way she phrases the lines "He plays my ukelele / Likes to strum it daily."

There's little doubt that Billie found her "Love is like a faucet / It turns off and on" chorus (from "Fine and Mellow") in Waters's 1923 "Ethel Sings 'Em."

Waters did not much care for genuine blues singers; she called them "shouters," and was thrilled to eventually earn the epithet "the Ebony Nora Bayes," for Bayes—the composer of "Shine On, Harvest Moon," who billed herself as "The Greatest Single Woman Singing Comedienne in the World"—never, in Waters's words, "gave out with any unladylike shouts and growls." Yet Waters boasted in her vivid and unsparing autobiography, *His Eye Is on the Sparrow* (1951), of her own vulgar tongue, violent disposition, and lonely toughness. Born October 31, 1896, the illegitimate child of a thirteen-year-old rape victim, she grew up in the red-light district of a suburb of Philadelphia. She suggests her childhood ambivalence over color in describing the way she mistreated her stepsister: " 'Yaller dog' and 'yaller puppy' were my favorite names for Genevieve. But I'd warn her, 'I'll kill you if you ever say I'm dark. Don't you ever dare say I'm blacker than you.' " A practiced thief and gang leader, she discovered religion when her grandmother enrolled her in a Catholic school for black and white kids. She was astonished by the nuns' patience and especially by the fact that you could call them "sister"—a common term of familiarity in black neighborhoods—instead of "ma'am." Significantly, her best subject was elocution.

Buffeted between the warmth of her religious citadel and the brutish world of her childhood, fiercely proud of her blackness yet envious of sophisticated white women, she somehow synthesized these contradictions in her art. Her worldly cynicism led her to parody the very performers she idolized; her imagination and sincerity enabled her to adapt their talents to a modern sensibility. Of course, the same contradictions were operating at large when she began touring the southern black vaudeville circuit as Sweet Mama Stringbean, and when she was given the chance to record. By 1920, when Mamie Smith became the first black woman singer to record, blues singers had long been tempering their music with musical and showmanship borrowings from minstrelsy—not because they wanted to reach white audiences (which was largely unthinkable), but to express their own aspirations in the emerging show-business climate. There was another motive: at a time when record companies were threatened with boycotts if they recorded black singers, compromises were unavoidable.

In 1921, the clarity of Ethel Waters's diction, the lilting gaiety of her voice, and the relative whiteness of her style impressed the ambitious Harry Pace, cofounder with W. C. Handy of Black Swan records. The company was more ambivalent about blackness than Waters was; here's how a 1923 ad read: "Only bona fide Racial Company making talking machine records. All stockholders are Colored, all artists are Colored, all employers are Colored. Only company using Racial Artists in making *high class* song records. This company made the only Grand Opera Records ever made by Negroes. All others confine this end of their work to blues, rags, comedy numbers, etc." There was a discussion over whether Waters would sing popular or classical numbers, but she knew exactly what she wanted to do and what kind of accompaniment she needed. Her first sides, "Down Home Blues" and "Oh Daddy," sold 500,000 copies in six months and brought the company out of the red. More important, the record sold to blacks and whites alike; she was acclaimed "Queen of the Blues," though the record was a vivacious minstrel-like interpretation of the blues, complete with a spoken chorus à la Jolson. The Black Swan house pianist was Fletcher Henderson, then a chemistry student with classical leanings. Waters made him study the piano rolls of James P. Johnson, and his accompaniments improved markedly (hear him on Bessie Smith's "Any Woman's Blues"). Henderson organized a band to accompany her on a tour of the South, where they became the first blacks heard on radio. Following the tour, she was advised to make it on "white time," while Henderson abandoned chemistry to start a regular band (which debuted at the Nora Bayes Theater).

Those early collaborations are wonderfully eager and spirited—Waters was more the scintillating entertainer out to kill the audience than the jazz singer inviting the audience into her own emotional sanctum. She was inclined to tell the story rather than swing the song; by jazz standards, she didn't really swing at all (though a case could be made for some records, like "Heebie Jeebies"), but her rhythmic sensitivity and buoyancy were acute. There's a touch of Al Jolson on "Oh Joe, Play That Trombone"; the brightness with which she invests the line "I'm goin' down to the levy" on "One Man Nan," and the polished bravura of "Sweet Man" are her own; "Georgia Man" is replete with minstrel histrionics, but the phrasing is impeccable and that high note in the middle of the first chorus is still exciting.

In 1925, she replaced the legendary Florence Mills at the Plantation Club and introduced "Dinah"; in 1927, she appeared in a Broadway revue, *Africana*. She made her first film in 1929, playing herself in *On with the Show*—here we can appreciate her compelling stage presence as she sings "Birmingham Bertha" and (dressed as a cotton-picker) "Am I Blue?"; she's lovely and her voice beguiling. The "jazz age" was in full gear, though jazz itself was still underground. Ballrooms sprouted all over the country, and everyone wanted to foxtrot to the syncopated sounds of Paul Whiteman and the like. Black music, however diluted, best captured the sensual stance of rebellious youth; traditionalists found it a heart of darkness, and accused it of undermining the nation's morals. Without meaning to—the divisions in her temperament mirrored the divisions in the nation—Waters played both sides against the middle. She was irrepressibly erotic at one moment, and abundantly high toned the next. She was now recording for Columbia, and her accompaniments varied from lone pianists to studio orchestras. Her theatrical characterizations matured as she perfected a conversational delivery in which the subordinate notes in a phrase were half-spoken and half-sung. She became an expert parodist, occasionally dropping quick-witted asides from the corner of her mouth. She "took off on" Ethel Barrymore on "You Can't Do What My Last Man Did," and Rudy Vallee on "You're Lucky To Me." On the hilarious "Come and See Me Sometime," she begins as Waters and concludes as Mae West.

Sometimes it's difficult to tell when she's kidding and when she's playing it straight. One presumes she was hamming it up on "When Your Lover Has Gone," with its stressed vowels, rolled consonants, and cracking voice, but there are ballad performances from 1929–30 that are simply dreadful. The subtlety of her diction and intonation is such that her attitude toward a song sometimes seems to change from line to line. In a recording of "My Special Friend Is Back in Town," she strikes a dazzling balance between singing, talking, and joking, and recalls, in her comedic personality and assurance, Fannie Brice. Ironically, her last session for Columbia took place on November 27, 1933, with the accompaniment of Benny Goodman's band; that same afternoon, Goodman recorded a couple of titles under his own name that introduced an eighteen-year-old Billie Holiday. Waters had dominated pop singing in the early '30s—even Bessie Smith had fallen out of favor—but the Holiday debut foreshadowed the coming of the great jazz singers who would make her own records date prematurely. Broadway was beckoning.

Waters's career is rather neatly packaged in decades—she was a recording star in the '20s, a Broadway actress and personality in the '30s, a film star in the '40s, and the architect and victim of her own myth in the '50s. Her earliest Broadway performances were in musical revues, but even then she thought of acting as something deadly serious. She would not accept roles she couldn't relate to or admire. The ambivalences she resolved as a sophisticated chanteuse stormed into open combat when she mounted the stage. In a sense, the theater for her became a churchlike edifice, and she was never frivolous in it, whether belting the show-stopping "Heat Wave" in *As Thousands Cheer*, or emoting "Stormy Weather" in the *Cotton Club Show of Spring, 1933:* "Your imagination can carry you just so far," she wrote. "Only those who have been hurt deeply can understand what pain is or humiliation. Only those who are being burned know what fire is like. I sang 'Stormy Weather' from the depths of the private hell in which I was being crushed and suffocated." She turned down *Porgy and Bess* because it wasn't "quite true to life to me," but she jumped at the chance to play Hagar in the 1939 *Mamba's Daughters*, her first dramatic role. In Hagar—"a lumbering, half-crazy colored woman with a single passion: seeing that her beautiful daughter Lissa has a better life than she's known"—she recognized her mother: "All my life I'd burned to tell the story of my mother's despair and long defeat. . . ." She was the first black actress to star on Broadway, and the highest-paid woman in show business. She considered opening night the most important in her life, "except for when I found God."

Her Hollywood experience was less fulfilling, at least in the beginning. Whatever her talent, she was black—so she was relegated to playing cooks and maids. In her middle forties and having gained too much weight, she was equipped to move in on the Mammy monopoly controlled by Louise Beavers (more than sixty films between 1929 and the early '60s) and Hattie McDaniel (thirty-eight films between 1934 and 1949), who had recently won an Oscar for portraying the super-Mammy in *Gone with the Wind.* The situation was worse for young, attractive, light-skinned women, since Hollywood would not allot them love-interest roles, unless the story concerned a doomed mulatto; and with people like Jeanne Crain and Mel Ferrer playing light-skinned Negroes, not even those parts could be counted on. For young, dark-skinned actresses, the situation was hopeless. Waters, in just a handful of basically stereotypical roles, made a crucial difference.

She played opposite Paul Robeson in a segment of *Tales of*

Manhattan, which Robeson considered so vile that he left Hollywood, never to return. In 1943, she re-created her role in the stage hit *Cabin in the Sky,* after demanding that the part be rewritten to suit her religious convictions. She did full justice to the best songs in the splendid Vernon Duke–John LaTouche score—"Happiness Is Just a Thing Called Joe," "Taking a Chance on Love," "Cabin in the Sky"—and symbolically re-enacted the polarities of her personality by first outpraying and outsinging, and then outvamping and outdancing, everyone in the picture (no mean feat in a cast that included Lena Horne and John Bubbles). Yet the set was a stormy one. She earned the reputation for being "difficult" and was, she claimed, blacklisted from Hollywood for the next six years—the nadir of her career. During that bleak time, she sang occasionally, but Ella Fitzgerald had come on the scene, and Waters felt inferior. She ached for another dramatic role. In 1949, Hollywood responded to postwar moralizing with no less than four it's-all-right-to-be-a-Negro movies: *Home of the Brave, Lost Boundaries, Intruder in the Dust,* and *Pinky,* the story of a light-skinned girl passing for white. John Ford was set to direct; and Ward Bond, an old fan of Waters, recommended her for the part of the girl's grandmother.

During the enforced years away from Hollywood, Waters came to understand the extent to which she was caught between two cultures. Her hotel room became "like the walls of a cell," and she spent more and more time in Harlem—"But I quickly learned there are great disadvantages when you are prominent and try to live in a humble place. . . . All I wanted was to be with the kind of people I'd grown up with, but I discovered you can't go back to them and be one of them again, no matter how hard you try." Shortly before getting the offer to do *Pinky,* she was asked to star in the Broadway production of Carson McCullers's *Member of the Wedding.* She assumed both roles with a vengeance. McCullers had to assure her personally that she could interpret the character of Berenice as she chose, and John Ford was replaced by Elia Kazan on *Pinky* because of his disagreement with her concept of the part. Darryl F. Zanuck was quoted as saying, "Ford's Negroes were like Aunt Jemima characters."

Pinky was a timorous social-conscience movie, but there was nothing half-stated about Waters. She played Jeanne Crain's grandmother, a laundress, with urgency and the suggestion of infinite personal reserve. If the Mammy figure had been cartoon simple in the Beavers-McDaniel films, Waters exposed the long-repressed complexities behind the mask. As Donald Bogle suggests in his book *Toms, Coons, Mulattoes, Mammies, & Bucks*, she used this part and the one in the film version of *Member of the Wedding* to demolish one of Hollywood's iron-clad clichés.

Before *Member* was filmed, she signed for a TV season as Beulah, the happy domestic originated by McDaniel on radio and subsequently taken over from Waters by Beavers. She also published *His Eye Is on the Sparrow*, which became a best seller. In it, she emerged as a tough survivor of mythic resilience: cantankerous, naturally gifted, suspicious, deeply religious, ungiving, loving, smart, naïve, vulgar, refined—a tangle of paradoxes cut through only by her mother's love (which arrives climactically on the last page). Some who read it cried when they saw her performance of Berenice Sadie Brown in *Member*, certain that she was playing herself. To a degree, she was; Berenice's relationship with the white girl, Frankie, parallels Waters's relationship with her grandmother. "All my life I been wanting things I ain't been getting," Berenice/Waters says stoically, and you can no more imagine the part played differently than you can Brando's Terry Molloy in *On the Waterfront*. In this crowning achievement, she once again gave us both sides of Ethel Waters—the spiritually comforted, infinitely patient earth mother, and the earthier, comfortless woman whose best years had passed.

But America extracts great prices from its mythical figures, and Waters's decline was cruel. Having turned the Mammy caricature into a figure of strength and depth, while still offering the broadest shoulders ever made to dry white tears, she found herself in a cul-de-sac. She didn't make another film for seven years, when she played Dilsey in an idiotic version of Faulkner's *The Sound and the Fury.* Worse, there had been the humiliation of appearing on a TV quiz show, "Break the Bank," in a widely publicized attempt to win the money she owed in back taxes. From being earth mother she became queen for a day. There was a final one-woman show on Broadway, and a memorable role as a jazz singer in an episode of *Route 66* on television, but her forty-year career in the lively arts was pretty much over. The church, which had provided her only solace as a girl, became a haven to her again, and she began years of touring with Billy Graham; her second volume of autobiography, published in 1973, was called *To Me It's Wonderful.*

Yet the records are still there, and the movies are infrequently shown, and the first book continues to be reprinted. Through them, especially the records, she shows that popular art can survive the fashions that spawn it and triumph over those that dismiss it. The records fairly sparkle with her talent, with her knowing, seductive wisdom. She doesn't belong to history exclusively, but to us as well.

October 1977

Bing for the Millions

It seems almost an impertinence to discuss **Bing Crosby**, the most widely admired American show-biz icon of the last half-century, in terms of the specifics of his singing. Never mind that his final appearance in New York, at the Uris Theatre, was frequently a bore, that the vast majority of his records are dated and out of print, that his sentimental aura is rebuffed by the baby-boom generation. Great pop stars aren't meant to survive their own lives—only the very best, a handful, can even sustain lifelong careers. Maybe only the contemporaries of a pop artist—those whose taste en masse has made his or her popularity possible in the first place—are in a position to judge. The rest of us have only inherited Crosby.

In the '60s, there was a brief magazine-art-directors' fad in which current pop stars were depicted as they might look in middle age. The old sensibility was accustomed to enduring public figures. There was a show-biz hierarchy of entertainers whose sheer persistence transcended the media that spawned them. Whether singers, comics, dancers, or actors, they eventually became all of those during the long haul from vaudeville to radio to movies to television. Al Jolson, Eddie Cantor, Crosby, George Burns, Bob Hope, Jack Benny, Groucho Marx, and the others embodied a challenge to upcoming performers. In fantasizing Bob Dylan with wrinkles, we were questioning our own ability to endure. Dylan was as much a product of the '60s as Crosby was of the '20s, but would Dylan transcend the era of his apotheosis as completely as his predecessors, whose commitment was exclusively to mass taste?

The strength of the old sensibility was so powerful in the early '60s that the most ambitious rock-and-roll singers imagined themselves locked not in a minuet with their immediate audience but in a struggle for acceptance from their elders. Bobby Darin challenged Sinatra as audaciously as Mailer challenged Hemingway; when he recorded his first "adult" album, he protected his flank with a follow-up called *For Teenagers Only*. Singers as variable as Jackie Wilson, Bobby Rydell, and Lloyd Price were recording tributes to Jolson, Crosby, and Sinatra. It took the Beatles in 1964 to show them how completely they had miscalculated. Darin spent the rest of his life deciding whether to wear a tuxedo or a pair of jeans to his next gig. There may never be another generation of entertainment venerables like those Lenny Bruce imagined occupying Show-Biz Heaven. One reason is the increasing accuracy of audience targeting, and the consequent dissolution of family entertainment. At the turn of the century, the only alternative to family entertainment, represented by vaudeville, was the risqué derivation of burlesque. Bing Crosby (and, less dramatically, Rudy Vallee) embodied an aesthetic of the '20s that was decidedly youth oriented. Benny Goodman and Frank Sinatra revitalized the youth market at a time when Crosby had settled into a middle-American safety clutch. Youth in Crosby's generation meant college aged; Sinatra's mystique invaded the high schools. Goodman once told me he was shocked to see the target audiences of pop performers decreasing in age, decade by decade, so that in the '70s the mass taste is defined by fourteen-year-olds.

Elvis Presley was a decisive turning point, but Presley, Sinatra, Crosby, and Jolson—the four most influential white pop idols of the century—had much in common. For one thing, they are connected by a lineage of influence. Crosby's first inspirations—before he heard Ethel Waters, Louis Armstrong, and the Whiteman jazz stars—were Jolson, John McCormack, Harry Lauder, and Cliff Edwards. He consciously imitated Jolson; in listening to some of the radio transcriptions they made together in 1947, we sense the unmistakable impact of the veteran minstrel on the matinee-idol crooner. At one point, Crosby is speaking in tones so low and singsong that Jolson parodies him with an Amos-'n'-Andyism, calling him "Kingfish." Crosby, for all his early fascination with jazz—he has called Louis Armstrong "the beginning and the end of music in America"—was more deeply embedded in the minstrel tradition than is generally recognized. Many of the recordings he made with Whiteman in the late '20s and early '30s, like "Mississippi Mud," "Cabin in the Cotton," and especially the "Southern Medley," must be embarrassments to him now. But as late as 1947, he broadcast a "Philco Radio Time" show that was an effort to revisit the "golden, romantic era of the American theater and revive the melody, romance, and gaiety of the good old minstrel days" (in the words of the show's announcer). Crosby, Jolson, and John Charles Thomas were cast as the "end men and fun makers," and the dialect was replete with "dat," "dese," "gwine," "dem."

It's not my intention to impugn Crosby with the suggestion of racism, though one might find him guilty of naïveté, but rather to show how strongly the minstrel tradition continued to linger. Minstrelsy was not part of Sinatra's immediate frame of reference; he began by imitating Crosby for his modern attributes—his way with a microphone, the canny informality of his phrasing. Presley, who was more profoundly affected by Jolson and Crosby than by the younger, Sinatra-influenced pop singers, updated the notion of minstrelsy to include the white mimicking of rhythm-and-blues conventions. (For a curious harbinger of Presley's style, listen to the way Crosby sings the second chorus in his recording of "Sunshine Cake," from the mid-

'40s.) Which points to the other bond of influence tying them together. Jolson, Crosby, Sinatra, and Presley operated against the annealing influence of the black-music continuum. Each responded to the black images and styles of his respective decade, so that Crosby's admiration of Jolson was crucially tempered by his idolization of Armstrong, Beiderbecke, and Waters; Sinatra's debt to Crosby was mitigated by his involvement with Billie Holiday and Tommy Dorsey; Presley's response to the white pop tradition was shaped by his involvement with blues and rhythm and blues. Which is not to derogate the minstrel impulse as a purely negative phenomenon. Minstrelsy is not an aberration but a continuing tradition in popular American culture. Economically and socially, minstrelsy is more often than not unjust; aesthetically, it is the key with which some of our more intelligent white performers unlocked the doors to their own individualities.

It's interesting to note that the ever skeptical jazz audience has kept more Crosby recordings in print than have his middle-of-the-road adulators. All you can find of the more than twenty years he spent with Decca is a couple of collections of Irish ballads (clearly for a specialized audience) and a best-of collection with the songs and novelties of the war years. There are several sets documenting the '20s and '30s, when Crosby was more self-consciously a singer and when he infused his material with a commitment that seems surprising in light of his later work. If the best of the early recordings are more affected than the later ones, they are also more involving. Crosby's infatuation with jazz did not extend to the evenly trampling 4/4 of swing; he was a Dixieland man to the bone. There is still something irresistible about these early up-tempo jazz sides with his cleverly rhythmic interpolations, like "My Honey's Lovin' Arms," "Sweet Georgia Brown," and "One More Time." If the success of a popular singer's work can be measured in terms of the emotional authenticity with which he invests even the most banal lyrics, then his heartfelt interpretations of "Street of Dreams,"

"Just a Gigolo," and "I Surrender, Dear" must be accounted remarkable performances.

Perhaps the turning point in Crosby's career as a singer came in 1934, when he signed a long-term contract with the fledgling Decca record company and underwent the Jack Kapp treatment. Kapp, who founded Decca, believed that singers should sing everything, that they should please all the people at one time or another. He had his artists perform with each other in an unending incest of guest appearances, and he favored novelty songs of staggering idiocy. The character of the company can be summed up by the example of Jascha Heifetz, who signed with Decca in a brief sabbatical from RCA, and dutifully recorded "White Christmas." Ella Fitzgerald spent the first twenty years of her career on the Decca plantation, and the percentage of the 300 sides she made that remain palatable is pitifully low. Crosby, however, was a natural for such a rigorous recording program. He recorded Hawaiian songs, Irish ballads, novelties, and even an occasional jazz session. (At one such session with Eddie Condon, when Kapp asked trumpeter Wild Bill Davison to tone down his expressive effects, Crosby handled the producer with characteristic even-tempered wit: "You go back to the board of directors if you make one more remark," he told Kapp. "I've flown these boys in at great expense. Eddie flew in without a plane.")

In these "White Christmas" years, Crosby became a minstrel in the old sense of a wandering songster. His singing was smoother, the tones were richer, and the cry and the youthful emotion were gone. It wasn't that his renditions were any less believable, but that the material itself didn't require much belief. Almost as a symbolic enactment of his new role, Crosby made a film in 1936, *Pennies from Heaven,* in which he played a wandering singer, with guitar, haircut, and imperturbable outlook. What was perhaps most endearing about the wartime Crosby was that the singing reflected the genuine insouciance of the man. Cool crooning replaced the torchy ballads because that's what the era demanded.

German soldiers affectionately called him Der Bingle when they heard the creamed-corn baritone of the Groaner—which is what he called himself—on their foxhole radios. It was the voice of hometown decency, however indolent—friendly, unassuming, melodious, and irrefutably American. On the home front, that voice, as enchanting in speech as in song, and that presence, Hollywood's top box-office draw throughout the mid-'40s, was a national security blanket. There were the "Kraft Music Hall" and "Philco Radio Time," and there were *Holiday Inn* (featuring "White Christmas") and *Going My Way*, for which he won an Academy Award as best actor. There were the largely trivial songs committed to little more than the necessities of nostalgia and constancy, and the genuine, easy wit, and the unruffled personality. It was simply impossible to dislike Bing Crosby.

Just how irresistible Crosby could be was demonstrated at the rehearsal before his opening at the Uris. His ad libs, which I thought would turn up during the actual performance, were apparently genuine ad libs. Also, he did not display a performer's persona as distinguished from the image he presented offstage. His wife, Kathryn, a beautiful, untalented woman in black skin-tight leather pants, unconsciously pointed up his naturalness with her own stage face—the plastic smile and studied posture that means "I'm on." Crosby, the true minstrel, was never off. He reminded me of a line in an old Carl Reiner–Mel Brooks routine about a pop singer, Fabiola, who says of his audience, "I am them, they are me, we are all singing, I have the mouth." He moved on a stage as though it was his living room. Everyone else was frantic. Son Harry was tuning his guitar, and Mom called him over to get his floor cue. Bing: "He's tuning his guitar." Kathryn (impatiently): "Well, you have to come here." Harry: "What color am I?" Kathryn: "Blue." Bing suddenly sang "Am I Blue?"—". . . ahhh, Ethel Waters," he reminisced, then walked over to Hank Jones at the piano and asked, "Remember Buck and Bubbles?" He told a story about hearing John Bubbles sing "Am I Blue?"

The actual show was smooth but limp. The jokes were unworthy of him—the usual Bob Hope-type TV-gag witticisms that only a soundtrack can laugh at. Rosemary Clooney joined him for a sprightly "Slow Boat to China"—which proved to be the highlight of the evening—and then sang some old numbers well, though her high notes were strained. Crosby sat down to sing "Send in the Clowns," and his habitual detachment turned the song into an undistinguished croon. When Sinatra appeared at the Uris the previous year, it was the same song that enabled him to shuffle off his absurd posturing in favor of the lyric's irony. Crosby was just going through the motions—expertly, of course, but without the personal resonance that someone who knew him best from the pre-Decca recordings might have expected.

After intermission, he introduced the Joey Bushkin Quartet with that ineffable number from *High Society* "Now You Have Jazz." Bushkin is a distinctively lyrical pianist—for a while Capitol tried to package him as a keyboard Bobby Hackett—but he had been away from the piano and sounded it; his chordal improvisations and arpeggiated flourishes were obvious and frivolous. Milt Hinton and Jake Hanna made a fine rhythm team, and it was nice to see the elusive guitarist Johnny Smith. The Crosby family—Mom plus Larry, Moe, and Curley Joe—followed. The only one with stage poise is the youngest, Nathaniel, who was stuck singing a round; Harry played a surface-action serenade on the guitar; daughter Mary Francis kicked up her legs; and Kathryn, who should have been playing Major Bowes with a cane, dueted with her husband on "My Cup Runneth Over."

Finally, Crosby announced he would sing some old stuff (applause) and he fed everyone's nostalgia with nearly four dozen song excerpts in medley fashion, accompanied by the Bushkin quartet. The audience was hungry, applauding the first measure of every ditty, most of them rather ephemeral. Johnny Smith's obbligato was clever, and at one point his rippling through a series of minor chords caused Crosby to laugh in acknowledgment. On several songs, the audience joined in. And why not? We weren't there to hear Bing Crosby the legendary singer, but to pay homage to the ultimate pop icon whose very presence gave cohesion to several generations of American feelings. He was not there to move us, but to remind us. He was us, and we were him, only he had the mouth.*

December 1976

---

* Crosby died on October 14, 1977, while playing golf. He was seventy-three, if you believed the singer, who said his birth date was 1904, or seventy-six, if you believed his brother, who said it was 1901.

Placing the Dominoes

During the last couple of years, an uneasy tolerance has characterized rock writing about jazz (and, less frequently, jazz writing about rock). Maybe it's an aftermath of '60s battle fatigue, and maybe it's an unstated alliance against middle-of-the-road fusing of any sort, but rock critics who once stigmatized jazz are now listening to it. Some even borrow prestige from it—for example, the *Rolling Stone* writer who offered the ludicrous but provocative opinion that honking tenor-sax records were the "missing link" between bebop and rock and roll. If only links were so neat, the history of American music could be studied as a game of dominoes.

The most surprising aspect of this new interest is the rediscovery of the modern jazz of the '40s, saddled forever with the onomatopoeic name bebop. Charlie Parker records are being reissued by the carload, and not only by independents and bootleggers. No major label would record Parker when he was alive, but his music is now issuing forth in lush packages from Columbia, Verve, Warners, and Savoy. It's been a long time coming. Most music of the 1950s—in jazz, pop, rhythm and blues, and rock and roll—implied a specific disavowal of bop and the whole notion of hip or cool or reticent or intellectual musicianship. This was to be expected. Bop had eschewed four qualities essential to early rock and roll (and a great deal of America's successfully commercial music): sentimental material, bordering at times on morbid self-pity; an unwavering dance beat; vocal harmonies not far removed from their antecedents in the barbershop quartet; and readily accessible melody. In the field of jazz, the reaction to bop was inevitable; the music became earthier, tempos were modified, and harmonies were edited. Chords, the blueprints and nutriments of bop, were replaced with modes or done way with altogether, leading at first to the feared avantgarde and later to a compromised, popular jazz. Rock and roll, on the other hand, simply dismissed most of bop's implications, and found much of its source material in the swing-influenced pop styles of the '30s. The southern pioneers of rock, both the white rockabillies at Sun and such black singer-writers as Little Richard, Fats Domino, and Chuck Berry, managed to avoid some of the sentimentality and novelty gimmicks that plagued their northern counterparts. A closeness to rural elements was one reason; the reversion to even earlier pop styles was another.

The renewed popularity of Al Jolson in the late '40s, sparked by his film biography, and of Eddie Cantor, through television, provided models for a new age of fevered, heart-on-outstretched-arms *performing*. At the same time, two seminal crossovers were taking place. Whites were largely preoccupied with blending white and black styles (as were a few blacks); blacks were chiefly concerned with mixing secular and religious musics. King Records, founded in Cincinnati in 1944 by Sydney Nathan, was one of the most successful independents of the '50s; its catalogue is a microcosm in which the diverse antibop forces are modified and blended into rock and roll, even though the label avoided rock and roll per se. King recorded country singers (Cowboy Copas, the Delmore Brothers), rhythm-and-blues shouters (Wynonie Harris) and balladeers (Bullmoose Jackson), back-beat-oriented jazz musicians who rejected bop and continued to play for dancing (Lucky Millinder, Earl Bostic, Tiny Bradshaw, Bill Doggett), and vocal groups ranging from the mundane (an unfortunate edition of the Ink Spots, the early Platters) to the raucous (Hank Ballard and the Midnighters). The evolution from blues and slick jazz to rock and roll and soul, with gospel inflections absorbed along the way, is traceable in the work of the Nat Cole-inspired Ray Charles, the B. B. King-inspired Freddie King, Clyde McPhatter, Jackie Wilson, Little Willie John, and James Brown—all King artists.

A Nashville distribution company (Gusto Records) has implemented a program of King reissues with a dozen albums, including four by the Dominoes (where McPhatter and Wilson got their starts), which help to place in perspective that influential and neglected group. The Dominoes were founded and led by pianist Billy Ward, a classically trained composer who chose its members from among his students. The son of a Baptist minister, he was one of the first to make the then courageous crossover that wedded rhythm and blues to gospel—at least a year before Ray Charles abandoned his Nat Cole trio stylings. In considering the group's name, it should be noted that a domino is a clergyman's cape. But a great difference exists between the ways in which Ward and Charles went about adapting church ritual to pop singing, one that reflects the difference between the theatrical presentation of spirituals as introduced by the Fisk Jubilee Singers in the 1870s and a genuine, Holy Roller service. Although the difference between "a sacred or holy as opposed to a secular or profane movement," as delineated by Albert Murray in *Stomping the Blues,* was "a matter of very delicate nuance," the acknowledged barrier between the two was rigid. Ward recognized the commercial viability of bringing church fevers to rhythm and blues, but knew also that it would be condemned as a sacrilege. Not surprisingly, he originally modeled the Dominoes after the Ink Spots, and the lead tenors he employed—first McPhatter, then Wilson (both trained in gospel)—were energetic but sweet singers; the gospel electricity was released in small doses. The lead vocals seem timid indeed when compared with the whooping and moaning of Ray Charles; the ink-bespotted crooning of the backup singers is far removed from the congregational chanting of the Raelets.

A substantial two-record set could have been edited to dramatize the virtues of the Dominoes, and its value as a transitional group that introduced three notable singers (McPhatter, Wilson, and bass Bill Brown), but there isn't enough good material to fill out four albums. Most of the selections benefit from the presence of a competent guitarist and a honking tenor saxophonist, yet the choice of standard material betrays the sentimentality at the core of much transitional rhythm and blues. McPhatter, who was seventeen when he joined the Dominoes, often favored an ersatz torch singing that makes one long for the healthy hermaphroditic piping of Bill Kenny, the tenor lead with the original Ink Spots. "These Foolish Things," for example, meets the mushy fate from which numerous jazz musicians (especially Billie Holiday and Lester Young) saved it, and has the obligatory talking bass vocal, which was a trademark of the Ink Spots in the late '30s. The Dominoes even revive such hopeless Ink Spots material as "When the Swallows Come Back to Capistrano" (which Bobby Day, of "Rockin' Robin" fame, also resurrected; one recalls that Dee Clark saw fit to revive the Spots' even loonier "Whispering Grass"). Ward's "The Bells" is a surreal threnody—"I know why they're ringing / They're ringing out for me"—reduced to bathos by McPhatter's sobbing.

When the group performed Ward's earthier material, however, it came alive, and the church training resounded, as on the spirited blues "Have Mercy Baby," where the Dominoes shadow McPhatter's every expert phrase; the similarly arranged, thirty-two bar "That's What You're Doing to Me"; and "I'd Be Satisfied," on which McPhatter strangely anticipates Wilson. If frequent musical allusions to the Ink Spots suggested an alliance with the black pop music of the '30s, the arrival of Jackie Wilson as the group's new lead in 1953 solidified its continuity with vaudeville. Wilson was all showman. Impeccably coiffed and dressed, he would twirl his coat overhead, jump into the air for a perfect split, sing trite ballads on bended knee as though they were minstrel arias, roll consonants, hurdle large intervals into his astonishing falsetto, and turn rocking chants— of a type that came to be associated with him ("Talk That Talk," "I'll Be Satisfied," "Am I the Man")—into lavish production numbers with choirs, tympani, piccolos, organ, full jazz band, and strings. Not for nothing did he program one of his early albums, *You Ain't Heard Nothin' Yet,* as homage to Al Jolson. But all of this came after his first success as a single in 1957 with the dazzling blues "Reet Petite."

While a member of the Dominoes, Wilson was more restrained, though not much more restrained. His tearful emoting runs to excess on these early sides, and he isn't always sure where best to use melisma, but his contagious energy vitalizes the group; a few selections—not "Rags to Riches," which enabled him to leave the Dominoes—are among his best ever, including "Love Me Now," "Jacob's Ladder" (a spiritual with secular lyric), a melodramatic "St. Louis Blues," and "You Can't Keep a Good Man Down." He does fairly well with "Until the Real Thing Comes Along," which would later be salvaged by Dexter Gordon and John Coltrane, but which in the early '50s was still associated with Pha Terrell (of Andy Kirk's band) and the Ink Spots. He is defeated soundly by such ephemera as "Three Coins in a Fountain" and an unspeakable sop to white teenage girls, "Bobby Sox Baby."

Bill Brown, one of the four best bass singers in that enduring genre of black vocal groups (the others being Orville Jones with the original Spots, Jimmy Ricks with the Ravens, and Will Jones with the Coasters), is heard on "Sixty Minute Man," "Pedal Pushin' Papa," and "Chicken Blues"—all among the better sides by the Dominoes. Billy Ward's work is indicative of an uncertain period when America was desperate for a popular dance music to fill the gap left by the dissolution of the big bands; when the relationship between blacks and whites was redefined by a Supreme Court decision; and when a few adventurous individuals of both races knew that only an injection of black music could cure the sickly state of the hit parade. Ward was smart enough to look to the church for the answer, but not inspired enough to break completely with the stifling pop orthodoxies of the day. Still, his most ingenious recordings are lively and entertaining period pieces, deserving of more than a footnote in a recounting of the obstetrics of rock and roll.

November 1977

Just How Much
Did Elvis Learn
from Otis Blackwell?

Rock criticism has been so absorbed in the personality-biased enthusiasms of the fan that there has been comparatively little research into the specifics of how the first wave of rock-and-roll successes broke. Much has been written about the transition from black blues to white rock, and little about whatever originality and quality exist in songs like "Don't Be Cruel," "Down in Mexico," "What'd I Say," and "Lawdy Miss Clawdy," which suggested the vitality of the new movement before star performers arrived to give it dimension. Similarly, a cult of the producer has developed, while virtually nothing has been said about the impact of demos (demonstration records produced by songwriters for publishing companies), which played a role in early rock unprecedented in popular music. On another level, few of the backup musicians who created "the big beat" have even been acknowledged.

Rock and roll was a businessman's music from the beginning. Music-publishing battles, in and out of court, over composer credits were the result of a palm-greasing environment as iniquitous as anything uncovered in the payola scandals. But that was backstage stuff: the youth-directed product was built around the lone image of the performer, pristine and unencumbered by collaborators. Which was all right with the collaborators—most of them were embarrassed by their contributions to a fad they didn't expect to outlast the decade. So a lot of stories haven't been told, a lot of credit unfairly distributed on speculation. One such story involves a relationship unlike any other I know of in music: Elvis Presley, white, born in Mississippi in 1935, rock and roll's most explosively successful performer, and Otis Blackwell, black, born in Brooklyn in 1932, rock and roll's most influential songwriter. His songs include "Don't Be Cruel," "All Shook Up," "Return to Sender," "Great Balls of Fire," "Fever," "Hey Little Girl," "Handy Man," "Make Me Know It," "Just Keep It Up," and "Breathless." From 1956 through the early '60s, they fed off each other's talent, sharing a close musical affinity and, more incredibly, a vocal style so similar as to be eerie. They never once met.

I had never given any thought to Otis Blackwell until I sat across the aisle from Panama Francis on a plane. Panama had garnered impressive credentials as a jazz drummer (with Roy Eldridge, Lucky Millinder, Cab Calloway, et al.) before he rather reluctantly earned a reputation as *the* session drummer for pop records in the '50s. From 1953 to 1963 he laid down the rhythm for numerous hits cut by La Vern Baker, Jackie Wilson, Buddy Holly, Dinah Washington, and many others. Wincing in pain at the memory, he described an afternoon when Fabian sang forty-one takes of "Tiger"—"and he never did get it right." Surprised at my interest in the subject, he asked if I had ever heard of a little guy named Otis Blackwell, who made demos for Presley, which were copied, note for note, by Presley's musicians. "If you compare the demos with the records, you'll see that Presley's vocals were practically an exact copy." Noticing my skepticism, he promised to play one for me when he returned from a long gig out of town.

A week later the *Voice* had an ad for an upcoming engagement at the Other End by one "Otis Blackwell, the Man Who Made Elvis Presley and Jerry Lee Lewis." Intrigued, and confused as to whether the demos had been made for the publishing company or the record company, I went up to RCA to see if anyone knew anything about Blackwell. There was some disbelief at the story, but I was told that the only one who would know was Grelun Landon, now RCA's manager of press and information in Los Angeles, who had worked with the Colonel (Tom Parker, Presley's fabled manager) and the song publishers in the '50s. A call to Landon revealed that yes, Presley's musicians had to copy the Blackwell arrangements off the demos because they couldn't read music. But did Blackwell actually influence Presley's singing? "Well, Elvis learned how to deliver the songs from Otis." He paused. "I remember Otis always wore a hat and he wouldn't take it off until he warmed up to you. He was an *extreme* talent, an original. I wish I could tell you more about him; he was very much respected."

When Blackwell opened at the Other End on a Saturday night, the place was nearly full. It was the first time in twenty years that he had sung for an audience. Barely five feet, he ascended the stage while a loud rhythm section went into "Don't Be Cruel." He has large round eyes and a gap-toothed smile, and moved loosely, as though each limb were tied to a marionette's string. The shock was in the voice: the high notes had Presley's cutting tenor edge; he rode the beat with broken syllables—"We-el do-on't be-e cruel-l"—and on the longer, strained notes there was the Presleyan quiver, receding into a faint whirr. On quieter songs, like "Return to Sender" and "Love Me Tender," the similarity was equally apparent, and the audience seemed to respond as much to the novelty of a middle-aged black man who sounded like Elvis as to anything else. He acknowledged his friend and colleague Doc Pomus in the audience and sang a medley of Pomus songs, beginning with "Save the Last Dance for Me." He sang "Handy Man," without the falsetto screeching that was Jimmy Jones's trademark. (The Jones record had actually been a Blackwell-produced demo that M-G-M decided to release.) In response to the ovation for his stomping "Great Balls of Fire," he said, "Yeah, I think I'll stay around for a while."

Otis didn't want to do an interview until after the gig, so I called Doc Pomus, a large, heavily bearded white man, confined to a wheelchair, whose songwriting activities have ranged from a blues for Ray Charles, "Lonely Avenue," to Dion's "Teenager in Love." Today, he has a patriarchal physical presence somewhere between Orson Welles and William Gaines, but thirty years ago, he and Otis performed in joints for five dollars a night, until Otis got into songwriting and encouraged Pomus to follow. He had tried to convince Blackwell to perform several years ago and was excited about the opening night. "He's a complete original. You can't think of anyone who did the kind of things he did before; no one ever wrote songs like 'Don't Be Cruel' or conceived them in that way. He's as close to a genius as anyone I've ever met in this business. The totality— as a songwriter and performer—is his genius. He has an originality of phrasing and a voice quality . . . I'll tell you this, on the second set he sang my 'Suspicion' and he did it better than Elvis or anyone else. It's an incredible thing to me."

Pomus and his cowriter Mort Schuman had also done demos for Presley where the arrangements were copied. "Presley is an extraordinary talent, the first white singer to get real recognition for the blues, and he could sing *anything*. He's an original— always Presley—but on certain things—fast tempos—he comes from Otis." As a songwriter, Pomus names Leiber and Stoller and Blackwell as influences: "Jerry and Mike in terms of structure, and Otis in the sense of originality and spontaneity." I asked him about the assumption, prevalent in Presley criticism, that Elvis created head arrangements on his best records, that he was in effect the producer. "This is absolutely untrue. Elvis did not create those sounds, and I can tell you that he managed to get his name on songs he had nothing to do with writing. One thing I can assure you is that his singing was significantly influenced by Otis. If you compare the demos, you will find it incredible how close Presley copied them, especially the *sound* of Otis's voice."

On Sunday, the day after opening, Blackwell rehearsed for five or six hours and blew out his voice. I went back Wednesday and found him recuperated, concentrating on the fast numbers, but not quite as sure as on opening night. After the set, he said he had heard the backup group, Grand Union, when they opened for Billy Swan several months back. Doc Pomus had urged Otis to come down and hear Swan. Otis sat in, smoked the place, and dug the sweet glare of the spotlight. He had been trying to get a backup for some time but could never find the musicians he wanted. He suggested that Grand Union get a drummer and rehearse with him for three weeks. "And this is what happened. I like it, it feels good 'cause I haven't done it in *so* long." He wasn't playing piano, he explained, because "I play in flats and they don't."

In 1822, an English music-hall performer named Charles Matthews was visiting America, observing Negro music and dialect. He got the idea of blacking himself up and becoming an interpreter of "Ethiopian" melodies. Robert C. Toll, in his instructive book *Blacking Up*, pinpoints that moment as the beginning of minstrelsy, the most widespread and influential medium for American popular culture in the nineteenth century.

Minstrelsy is said to have died at the hands of vaudeville, but it was a death in form, not spirit. Its images abound in contemporary life, from the indelible memory of Tim Moore's Kingfish to the witticisms of Earl Butz. The Aunt Jemima–Uncle Ned darky, solicitous of massa and scornful of the abolitionists who would wreck their joyful plantations, was implanted in the American mind to such an extent that even black minstrels, in the antebellum years, were expected to enact the familiar stereotypes memorialized by minstrel composers like Stephen Foster. There was triple-edged irony here: minstrelsy provided unprecedented opportunity for gifted black performers, among them Bert Williams and Ma Rainey, but only if they could adapt the ludicrous precepts of white "Ethiopian imitators"; the blacks were so good, so "authentic," that white minstrel troupes were soon put out of business; the minstrel form was then replaced by a new kind of entertainment nourished by Tin Pan Alley tunesmiths who had found their initial success by appropriating a black sound called ragtime.

The process of whites stealing from blacks is also the process of osmosis by which whites allowed black music to enter the commercial mainstream. In this regard, the most influential of modern minstrels have been Al Jolson, Bing Crosby, and Elvis Presley. Jolson, a protégé of minstrel Lew Dockstader, seriously believed he was bringing the Negro sound to Broadway when he crooned "Mammy" on bended knee. He was confident enough of his authenticity to suggest that *Porgy and Bess*—an opera by the same man who had given Jolson "Swanee"—be staged in blackface with Jolson in the lead. (Perhaps Sophie Tucker would have played Bess.) Bing Crosby's distillation of black song in the '20s was relatively sophisticated, causing Jolson's performing brilliance to seem quite suddenly out of date. But it wasn't until the Presley revolution that Jolson's style became untenable: Jolson still sold a lot of records even in the years immediately following his death in 1950.

In Jolson, theatrical show-biz schmaltz was mated with an irresistible vitality—maudlin sentiment was the flip side of snappy eye-rolling rhythms. He had much in common with Presley: each came from lower-class, culturally alienated environments (immigrant Jewish and southern poor white); each was something of a rebel—Jolson, the son of a cantor, left home in adolescence to travel the country singing in music halls, and Presley, also from a religious family, found himself in Negro blues. Each was an obsessive mother-lover; each chose to live in isolation at the peak of his career. In *Feel Like Going Home*, Jerry Lee Lewis tells Peter Guralnick, "I loved Al Jolson, I still got all of his records. Even back when I was a kid I listened to him all the time." Elvis's first record for the Sun label, "I Love You Because," was a thinly disguised rewrite of a melody that Jolson never recorded but that rebellious Asa Yoelson sings repeatedly during the first half hour of *The Jolson Story*, released in 1946 (when Presley was eleven), a song called "When You Were Sweet Sixteen." Presley remained true to Jolson's schmaltz even as his best work eclipsed that of "the jazz singer." What would Jolson have made of a white boy with a pompadour as high as a Negro conk, bumping like a stripper and singing "Heartbreak Hotel" on national television? He probably would have been a lot less shocked than many of his contemporaries. For Jolson's pelvis swiveled much the same way, as can be seen in his performance of "Toot Toot Tootsie" in the 1927 film *The Jazz Singer*.

Bing Crosby might have empathized with Presley, for they made similar leaps. True enough that Crosby chose omnipresent asexuality as his mature show-business persona, in contrast to Presley's unavailable metasexuality. But Crosby was once the carousing, would-be jazz singer of the jazz age whose ultimate success came in delivering a "White Christmas" to every American turntable. For him, Presley's willingness to become Hollywood's teddy bear must have seemed inevitable; nor could he have been much surprised to learn of Presley's nonexistent personal relationship with Blackwell, as it somewhat parallels Crosby's rather aloof relationships with his black idols, Louis Armstrong and Ethel Waters. Jolson was palatable for about thirty years (1919–50), Crosby for about thirty-five (1926–60). By palatable, I mean capable of renewing their audiences generationally rather than depending on antiquarians. Presley had been a star for over twenty years when he died on August 16, 1977; it would have been interesting to see how far he could go in the long stretch.

The nature of Presley's minstrelsy assumes particularly bizarre overtones if one imagines him secretly imitating Blackwell vocals. Imitation, however, was tempered by Presley's own considerable abilities (which were perhaps more strikingly evident on ballads than on rockers; he could put over a song like "Loving You" with all the purring emotionalism of Edith Piaf), and by the relationship's mutual usefulness. Blackwell wrote songs ideally suited to Presley's rocking style, and Presley gave them the widest possible exposure. Since their voices and vocal styles were remarkably alike, Blackwell's demos provided Presley with delivery cues that didn't force him appreciably to alter his own impulses, while Blackwell could hear his material performed almost exactly as he imagined it. Otis twice avoided opportunities to meet Elvis, out of a superstitious fear that their working relationship might crumble if Presley did not measure up to his preconceptions. He estimates that Presley's records are "90 percent exact copies" of the demos. His respect for Presley is absolute; he even hopes to record a collection of Presley tunes he *didn't* write, as homage.

Which is not to say that there weren't shady dealings. Otis's office, in what used to be known as the Brill Building, is decorated with a huge color poster of Elvis and sheet-music covers of songs he wrote for Elvis, Del Shannon, Pat Boone, Johnnie Ray, and Jerry Lee Lewis. The Presley songs are credited to both Blackwell and the singer. There are also two plaques on the wall: one is a "Citation of Achievement" from BMI to Otis Blackwell for "Fever"; the other is a "Special Citation of Achievement" from BMI to John Davenport for the same song.

Otis originally used Davenport, his stepfather's name, as the pseudonym on "Fever" because he wrote it for Little Willie John of King Records, while contracted to another publishing company. When he got into serious tax troubles, he made a deal whereby the song was given to Henry Glover, who owned King. The BMI plaque notwithstanding, Otis's name is no longer listed on the song. The presence of Presley's name on songs like "Don't Be Cruel" simply indicated business-as-usual in the music-publishing business. One remembers Irving Mills sharing the credit for Duke Ellington songs, Ed Kirkeby taking

credit from Fats Waller, and Benny Goodman getting credit
for several tunes he cheerfully admits he did not write.

Otis Blackwell started performing in amateur shows in
Brooklyn in the '40s. Willie Saunders of the *Amsterdam News*
took him on one of his traveling shows with a shake dancer,
and, while making the rounds, Blackwell met Doc Pomus, who
was also singing the blues. (Otis names as his main influences
Larry Donnell, who had a big record with "I'll Get Along
Somehow," and the better-known Chuck Willis.) In 1949 and
1950 Otis recorded a few sides for Davis records, including a
fairly successful track called "Daddy Rolling Stone." They were
subsequently issued as an LP, along with a few sides he made
for RCA. On Christmas Eve 1955, he went to Shalimar Music
with seven songs, including "Don't Be Cruel." A month later,
the head of the company called to tell him about a guy named
Elvis Presley who was going to be very big.

"Well, you know, there had to be a deal, share this and that.
I said no at first, but they said Elvis is gonna turn the business
around, so I said okay, and they put it on the other side of
'Hound Dog.' It turned out we sounded alike, had the same
groove, so I began doing demos for other publishers for Presley—'Teddy Bear,' 'All Shook Up,' 'Easy Question,' 'Don't Drag
the String Around.' The cat was hot, that's why his name is on
the songs. Why not? That's the way the business is anyway."

It was a good deal for Otis. He wasn't interested in being a
performer; he loved the way Elvis sang the songs, and Elvis did
something no black singer could have achieved at that time.
"Everything was in categories and all black artists were classi-
fied as blues, so if you wanted to make money with a song like
'Don't Be Cruel,' you had to have a white singer. A lot of sta-
tions wouldn't play the black rocks until after they started playing the white rocks." One disc jockey who did take a chance
and made a difference, according to Otis, was Martin Block of
WNEW's "Make-Believe Ballroom," in New York, who surprised people by pushing two of Johnny Ace's records.

Otis's first demos were just piano and overdubbed vocal. After the success with Presley, he could hire rhythm sections and make the demos complete. The musicians who played on them regularly included guitarists Kenny Burrell and Mickey Baker, bassist Milt Hinton, and drummers Panama Francis, Pretty Purdie, and Sticks Evans. The Colonel asked Otis to appear in the Presley movie *Girls, Girls, Girls,* for which he had written "Return to Sender," but the superstition about meeting Elvis kept him from accepting. An earlier movie offer had more significant results.

Otis was asked to choose the additional talent for a low-budget musical with the odd cast of Julius LaRosa and Count Basie. He spent a day in a Brooklyn record store listening to everything he could, until he heard Jerry Lee Lewis's "Whole Lotta Shakin'." "I grabbed it and ran, told them there's a cat on Sun records who's gonna be a big man." The record hadn't become a hit yet, but the movie people wanted only songs they could control, so Otis wrote "Great Balls of Fire." Lewis never appeared in the film—Otis doesn't remember the name of the movie or why—but he soon wrote a follow-up hit for Lewis, "Breathless." "I thought, man, I got it made. I got a Presley and a Jerry Lee. But then he got into that trouble and they stopped playing his records." He met Jerry Lee at one of Allen Freed's Brooklyn Paramount shows. "You can get along with him because he boogies, man. He's beautiful people."

Jerry Lee also copied the demos closely, but Dee Clark didn't. Otis wrote "Just Keep It Up" and "Hey Little Girl" for Clark, but Calvin Carter of Vee-Jay did arrangements on them. Then there were records he produced for Mahalia Jackson and Connie Francis. One assignment he brought off, despite absurd obstacles, was making a hit record for Sal Mineo. "They said he's gonna be a big movie star, so they wanted a record. I went to his house five times to teach him. He was no singer, but he was a young, nice-looking kid and the record ["Start Movin"] made it."

In the mid-'60s, there were problems, first with the IRS, and then with drink. "Everything I wrote sounded like garbage." Otis made two albums that never got off the shelves. Now he's writing again—"It used to take a half-hour to do a song; now it takes a couple of days"—and wants to continue singing. And when I spoke with him, he was ready, at long last, to meet Elvis. In the summer of 1976, he was in Nashville and sent Presley a telegram consisting mostly of song titles. "The guy who reads his mail thought it was a prank and threw it away. Later Elvis wrote a letter apologizing." Asked to assess his career, he said, "I got a real kick out of it because it was what I wanted to do. It wasn't just the money; there were some damned good songs. I mostly enjoyed working with unknowns, because I felt there was part of me coming through, like Mineo, Jimmy Jones, Elvis. Everyone said Elvis was just a flash, but I knew he'd be around a long time because he'd try *any* kind of song that was given him. Now I'd like to meet him."*

October 1976

---

* He never did—Elvis was dead within ten months of our talk.

Bobby Blue Bland
Meets the White Folks

It took twenty years, but in light of the successful marketing of B. B. King, his mentor, it was inevitable that Bobby Blue Bland would be detoured out of the race circuit for a confrontation with white America. The first step was to wash the conk out of his hair—King had capitulated around '67, making Bland the last holdout—and get him such modish duds as the ostentatious caps he sports on the covers of the four records he's made for ABC. The whitening of King had entailed a series of records designed to belie his talent: the most monstrous of them, *Friends,* was presented to him as a fait accompli, like a music-minus-one exercise, with spaces for him to overdub his "parts." But in live performance, King has maintained his integrity with inspiring fortitude. Bland, however, was never as spontaneous as King. He was an icon from the beginning, placed on a pedestal by music directors, advisers, image makers, and a closed, tradition-minded audience. When he made a rare New York appearance in 1975, at a discotheque called Barney Google's, I wondered if he would reflect the new, bland Bland of the slick records or sustain the hard-won urban-blues image that had allowed him to be introduced, with a drum roll and a brass flour-

ish, as the DYNAMIC, INCOMPARABLE, SENSATIONAL
BOBBY . . . BOBBY BLAND!

No problem. The capacity audience at Google's was predomi-
nantly black—for all the press it received, the one-nighter might
have been a trade secret—and Bobby was right at home: no cap,
no new songs.

I first saw him at a concert in Iowa about seven years before.
He arrived ahead of the band bus in a mile-long car and wore a
gold suit. His processed hair was pulled tight on the sides and
puffed up on top. He sang his most famous songs exactly as he
sang them on records, and it was startling to watch him sing one
of his vengeance numbers while his cheeks parted for a satanic
smile. Musically, little had changed for the Google's performance. Lyrically, his songs still deliver the schizoid scenario of
undying devotion and zealous contempt. He continues to be
boyish and macho at the same time, just as his voice can be
sweet and ferocious in the same phrase.

Bland walks with a drawl. Through the open stage door, you
can see him meticulously quash his cigarette; as he ambles out,
he buttons his jacket and betrays the slightest shyness at the
boldness of the spotlights. The audience is tuned to every mannerism—this is what it paid to see, right down to the entrance
walk and the subtle flinch.

The songs and arrangements are time tested, as are the responses of the knowing audience, and the ritual is nostalgic in
a positive way. It is a shared experience in the present, that refers to the past: Where were you when you first heard "I'll
Take Care of You" or "Drifting"? The jazz singer is in constant
search for new material, but the blues singer is concerned with
the compilation of hits to be celebrated endlessly. The jazz audience expects progress and innovation from its artists; the
blues audience demands that they satisfy the tradition. The key
phrase shouted throughout Bland's performance was "Take
your time, baby!"—we know where the climaxes are, so just
take your time in getting there.

He begins with a shouting promise, "Ain't That Loving You," and the women are screaming. He accentuates the theme of security with a crawling "I'll Take Care of You." "Take your time, baby!" someone yells. Soon he is warning his wayward woman about "Your Friends," an exquisitely sung blues, before indulging the restrained brutality of "I Pity the Fool." He is resigned and philosophical in "That's the Way Love Is," with its "Stormy Monday" type lyrics, and when he actually goes into the more passionate "Stormy Monday," he walks out onto the dance floor and falls on bended knee. "Lord have mercy," he implores. Take your time, baby. "LORD HAVE MERCY," he growls with such ferocity it's as though the sound were carving rivulets in his throat to get out. The horns have departed from the stage: only the guitarist remains to provide sympathetic dialogue. Bland walks over to him and commiserates with his solo. "Take your time, baby," he says. The band comes back for "Driftin'," and he drifts off for good. No encore. A pretty good, short (about forty minutes) set by Bobby Bland.

For some reason, it came together in W. C. Handy's town, Memphis. The blues lineages of Texas, Oklahoma, and Kansas City to the west, and Mississippi, New Orleans, and Georgia in the east, fused there like a laser beam and a disparate group of teenagers banded together in its intensity. B. B. King was the oldest, though they were all born around 1925–30. King came to Memphis in 1948, as a disc jockey, the same year Bobby Bland was getting pointers in singing from Roscoe Gordon and pianist Billy "Red" Love. A year later, Bland was singing in Adolph Duncan's band: the pianist was Johnny Ace. Junior Parker, Earl Forrest, and Gatemouth Moore were also there, and when they all worked together, they called themselves the Beale Streeters. Chicago had become the center for the urbanization of rural blues, but the Beale Streeters were out to modernize that urbanization. They were more sophisticated. King knew about Django Reinhardt as well as T-Bone Walker and Scrapper Blackwell; Bland had grown up listening to country music before he was seduced by gospel; Ace knew the pop singers as well as Joe Turner.

Most of all, there was B.B. himself, already an encouraging and guiding influence on the others. He brought Bland to Modern records in Los Angeles, though little came of it. I once asked King if he really started Bland and others recording. He said, "I wouldn't say I actually started him but I would say that I was a big influence. I would say I influenced most of the guys my age or younger because . . . well, Bobby Bland used to ride around with me. Junior Parker was the same way. I knew Magic Sam, I knew most of the guys long before they were recording."

And B.B. was conscious of the hybridization in blues roots, the cross-pollination of influences: "It's a funny thing, like I'm from Mississippi but very few of the guys I used to listen to were from Mississippi. Blind Lemon [Jefferson] and T-Bone Walker were from Texas; Lowell Fulson's from Oklahoma. I would hear those people in the delta of Mississippi and I guess the same thing was true of Muddy Waters and John Lee Hooker, 'cause we were all from Mississippi. Now when you get to England, everybody thinks that everybody playing blues is from Chicago. Are there *any* blues singers really from Chicago?"

Bland had just enough time to hear King's first hit record, "Three O'Clock Blues," before getting drafted in 1951. He served in the same outfit as Eddie Fisher—he's always claimed to have been influenced by white pop singers—and on being discharged, signed with Duke records in Houston. A few months later, Duke's biggest star, Johnny Ace, lost a game of Russian roulette on Christmas eve 1954 and failed to see "Pledging My Love" hit the charts. Within a year, "It's My Life" established Bobby Bland as a distinctive blues balladeer with a smooth, jaunty style that contrasted with King's strident grit. A prolific string of singles followed, accompanied by successful tours and the painstaking development of the Bobby Bland show.

But while the Beale Streeters went on to enjoy considerable success, they remained invisible to white folks. King and Bland could fill huge auditoriums in a procession of one-nighters year after year but the only likelihood of press was in *Ebony,* and record distribution was restricted. Some of their contemporaries made breakthroughs—Little Willie John, Fats Domino, Little Richard, Chuck Berry—but they were identified with the first frantic wave of rock and roll. Later the vogue switched, not surprisingly, to cool, sweet soul—Sam Cooke, the Drifters, Marvin Gaye. James Brown alone retained some of the nastiness of the blues, but in attitude rather than lyrical substance. In the early '60s, despite the "rediscovery" of rural bluesmen, no one talked about the contemporary blues singers. When I was prepubescent, my parents had a teenage black girl help take care of my sister and me. She turned me on to Little Richard, Jackie Wilson, Dee Clark, and B. B. King, and I could never understand why B.B. alone was never heard on the radio.

Ray Charles paved the way for the Memphis boys. He had vision and genius in programming concepts as well as arrangements. With "I Can't Stop Loving You," he put a record atop the soul, pop, and country charts simultaneously, and proved the compatability of standard gospel and blues techniques with the exigencies of pop music. In 1967, after thirty albums and 225 singles, B. B. King was discovered by white America. The discovery was not cheap. ABC thought he should be playing with studio hacks rather than his own band, and B.B., who appreciated the money and fame, resigned himself. The process had been transferred from his head to his recordings. ABC tapped Bobby Bland in 1973, but he had always been a more malleable performer than King—no stranger to the sterile task of overdubbing vocals on otherwise completed records, he had been molded with great deliberateness, both musically and iconographically, by his advisers—and if he had yet to crash through the race barrier, it was not for lack of trying.

On the liner notes to one of his Duke albums—which is plastered, incidentally, with notices not from critics and colleagues, but from distributors and press flacks, testifying to the fact that our boy Bobby *sells*, is nothing if not a star—an English writer compares him to Billie Holiday and Bessie Smith. This is precisely the wrong comparison. It was Holiday who wrote, "I can't stand to sing the same song the same way two nights in succession . . . if you can, then it ain't music, it's close-order drill or exercise or yodeling or something, not music." By jazz standards, that is a common attitude, but "close-order drill" is not an unfair description of the Bland recording session Charles Keil reported in his book *Urban Blues;* here is a singer whose every phrase is coached and coaxed by his music director. The classic Bland performances are perfect, but they are also unchanging.

He is not an intuitive singer, but rather a master at employing a cache of techniques for the optimum expression of a song's lyric. His voice is unique, rimmed with a soft peach fuzz, capable of gullying low like a cello, and ranging high with gargled *waaaaaahhh*s and long melismatic moans. He's a screamer without being a shouter, in the Rushing-Turner sense, but he is always in control, never crackling into a desperate B. B. King yell. In this regard, he is really a pop singer working with a blues palette. He has superb time and knows where the drama in a song lies, when to climax and when to constrain himself. But he does not take overt chances; to do so might imply that his mastery of the tried and true is less than sufficient.

The musical genres he explored in more than fifteen years with Duke were outlined in his first album, *Blues Consolidated,* which also featured Junior Parker. In the succeeding seven albums and two best-of collections, the material continued in the same basic genres: the blues, both original and classic; blues ballads, an area in which Bland has no peers; up-tempo jump tunes, like "Turn On Your Love Light"; and his overtly commercial schlock songs, like "Care for Me," "I'm Not Ashamed," and "Playgirl" (a waltz), with trudging triplet rhythms, do-wop choirs, banal melodies and lyrics, and occasionally Latino bunny-hop charts.

If the bows to the worst conventions of rock and roll never achieved for him the "American Bandstand" status they deserved, Duke was sweetening his records in other, more rewarding directions. Strings and flutes were sometimes added; backup voices became more professional and the repertoire more challenging. In several instances, Bland took songs associated with other singers and made them incontestably his own: "Who Will the Next Fool Be?" and "Stormy Monday" sound as though Charlie Rich and Billy Eckstine had composed them for him, and his "Blues in the Night" is the most successful version of that standard since Jimmie Lunceford. Other songs defeated him. His boyish approach to "Ain't Nobody's Business" was trite compared with the storming braggadocio of Jimmy Witherspoon; his "Driftin' " is more stable, less histrionic than the definitive recording by Ray Charles, but it is also less commanding and imaginative.

His last Duke album, *Spotlighting the Man,* his most nearly perfect set since *Here's the Man,* was carefully aimed at a larger market, but not a teenage market. Excepting two trite melodies—"Wouldn't You Rather Have Me" and "Ask Me Nothing" (and he even tries to make *them* come alive)—the album suggests the areas Bland might have further explored. "Chains of Love" is the ultimate blend of expensive strings and down-in-the-alley guitar flickerings, and who would have expected him to find so much soul in "Who Can I Turn To?"? In "Rockin' in the Same Old Boat" the metrical equilibrium is given a twist by the alternation of bell-like accents on the three and the two (one two THREE four/one TWO three four). A different kind of sophistication is heard during the last chorus of "I'm On My

Way," when the guitarist accompanies him with Wes Montgomery octaves. But the key assumption of this record—that Bland is a good enough singer to deserve good material and arrangements that support rather than compete—went unheeded by his producers at ABC.

The California Album and *Dreamin'* are similar, both overarranged by Michael Omartian, a dim, ersatz blues pianist who shows little regard for Bland's gifts or tradition. With his voice layered behind the excessive, constipated charts, Bland is made to sound more Motown than Beale Street. It is less a question of updating his sound than of killing off his individuality, with the race icon smashed in favor of a more familiar persona, right down to those mod caps. On "It's Not the Spotlight," he's made to sound like Wilson Pickett.

A Bland trademark is to fall back when he seems most likely to explode; no blues singer has better understood the strength in restraint. He can't exercise this control on the ABC records, because the arrangements keep him on a treadmill, moving soft to loud. He can't take his time, baby. Musicians are assigned repetitive ostinato figures instead of being permitted some dialogue ("Goin' Down Slow"), several of the instrumental interludes are pure Muzak ("Dreamer"), and never before have Bland's dubbed vocals sounded so obvious. He is still singing well, but whatever spontaneity Joe Scott, Duke's music director, was able to inject into his early records has been squeezed out.

Another indication that Bland's assurance justified a more relaxed approach to recording was *B. B. King & Bobby Bland Together for the First Time . . . Live,* the nicest dividend of having both artists on the same label. Recorded before a claque in a studio rather than an audience in a theater, it's satisfying nonetheless, and you can't help wondering why Bland isn't recorded informally more often.

But ABC continues its musical packaging. On his new album, *Get On Down,* the artificial flavoring is country and western, and, surprisingly, the result is quite pleasant. The idea and style are both indebted to Ray Charles, obviously, but Bland has an abiding affection for country music, and the songs are mostly congenial. The syrup in "I Take It on Home" and (the very Charles-like) "You've Almost Got the Blues" is relatively harmless. On "I Hate You," Bland is subtly inflective, though, again, the catharsis is written into the arrangement instead of emanating from Bland's singing. Unfortunately, side two, excepting the very good "You're Gonna Love Yourself," is dreadful, recalling the strange unevenness of the Duke records.

Most performers insist on plugging their latest record in concert, so it is significant that Bland doesn't parade his new stuff in front of his audiences. Of course, he still doesn't have much of a white audience for live performances. Bluesmen are a fast-fading breed, and Bland's precarious tightrope walk—balancing music in one hand and image in the other—makes him look conspicuously like the last Mohican. The blues audience is diminishing, so ABC would like to concoct an image for him that may compromise his genuine talent beyond recognition. Thus far, he offers no point of identification for the largely narcissistic rock audience, and he is considered too unsophisticated by the jazz audience, which demands improvisatory risks and idiomatic technique. Bland is unlikely to attain a position from which he can dictate the musical environment he wants to inhabit. But perhaps ABC will check out some of his live performances, listen closely to the best of his recorded work, and have the decency to let Bland's talent (and the company's public-relations department) sell him. Because Bobby Blue Bland is a remarkable singer.

September 1975

Divine and Mortal

At the outset of 1979, George Wein's Festival Productions, Inc., called a press conference to announce its latest attempt to—in their phrase—make "jazz history." Sarah Vaughan would be heard at Carnegie Hall in an unprecedented cycle of three concerts, each representing (in the words of the press release) "a totally different facet of Ms. Vaughan's art and repertoire." I cringed at the "totally," but why carp at a little hyperbole; for once somebody was producing the Divine One just like the classical divas. What's more, she'd be presented with a bevy of impressive, not to mention highly significant, guests: Gerry Mulligan's big band and Mel Torme on March 21, doubtless signifying the cool, jazzified pop aspect of her career; Betty Carter and Eddie Jefferson on March 23, signifying her involvement with the modernism of the '40s; Count Basie and his Orchestra on March 30, signifying both her apprenticeship with big bands and a personal reunion. I was all atwitter.

The series was historic, I suppose, in two respects—the cycle (including a repeat performance on the first night) was completely sold out, demonstrating feasibility and providing precedent for future endeavors, and the second concert was one of the most stirring I've ever attended. By contrast, Concert III was something more than adequate and Concert I something less. The disappointment rumbling through the hall was mitigated by the usual equivocation, i.e., middling Vaughan is better than the best of anyone else. There may be some truth there, if one is out for tonal richness and accuracy of pitch and intonation. To be sure, there were great moments at all three programs, but if one is accustomed to being electrified by Vaughan, as has been the rule annually at Newport, one is not likely to be appeased by a mere buzz. Moreover, it wasn't only the singer but the concept that failed to measure up. Or was I being naïve? I interpreted the press release's promise that Vaughan would "have the privilege of working with some of her favorite artists" as indication that they would be sharing the stage. As it turned out, she encountered her guests only on the bebop evening; otherwise, they were opening acts.

Nor was the promise of a "totally different facet of Ms. Vaughan's art and repertoire" made good, unless they meant having the same arrangement of the same song performed first with a trio, then strings, then a big band. Some statistics. Vaughan sang a total of thirty-three numbers (including a spontaneous jam with Carter and Jefferson) at the three concerts, but only eighteen different songs. Four were heard three times, six twice, and eight (often the highlights) once. The thrice-told items made a kind of commercial sense—three ("I've Got the World on a String," "How Long Has This Been Going On?" and "If You Went Away") were from her current albums, and one ("Send In the Clowns") was a guaranteed audience rouser she'd been using as a closing theme. Every selection but two ("The Lord's Prayer" and a medley) was from her current repertoire, so there was no attempt at a retrospective. It wasn't really a cycle at all.

Before we get down to specifics, a word about the sponsor. Anyone who failed to notice the seventeen appearances of the Kool logo on each of the four-page programs (including a full-page ad depicting a couple in tuxedo and white evening gown, each holding a cigarette in one hand and a glass of milk in the other; no chocolate-chip cookies, though), or the massive Kool Super Nights sign twinkling from the back curtain, or the lackeys handing out cigs in the lobby, or the ads and posters that featured Kool in bolder print than Vaughan, would still know who was footing the tab from the patter onstage. The company provided its own barker at the third concert, while the first two found Wein reduced to guffawing over the cleverness of the Super Nights pun since Super Lights were "the newest member of the Kool family"—what a wholesome image, a family of carcinogens. I'm delighted when an industry chooses jazz as a mode of advertisement, but a modicum of taste could only have helped their campaign. No sponsor would have dared cheapen a classical event with so much onstage hawking. And at classical concerts, Carnegie Hall's ushers seat latecomers *between* numbers. Bumptious stragglers, competed relentlessly with the first selections every night.

Gerry Mulligan opened Concert I with Al Cohn's "Lady Chatterley's Mother," which sounds like a bebopped "Sleigh Ride" and has a fine chorus for the reeds. Four additional numbers were predictable and tired, reaching bottom with a concerto for Mulligan's piano and coming to life briefly with a few stop-time passages on "K-4 Pacific." Mel Torme entered—slick, superficial, and full of pizzazz. He shares with Vaughan a faultless intonation and, if possible, an even tighter reign on pitch, so you experience a certain luxury in listening to him—as with Vaughan, you know that no matter what he tries, he will hit the right notes. That, of course, is not sufficient; nor is jazzy cleverness. Torme hummed the chords behind Mulligan on "Bluesette," paraded "Round Midnight" in broken sylables, sang four very limpid Mulligan originals in unison with the saxophonist (matching his terminal vibrato to a T), and scatted a dozen swing and bop riffs on "Lady Be Good." His arrangement on "Blues in the Night" was the inspired idea of a mediocre musician—it changed tempo and style every eight measures, and was as arty as designer clothes.

But at least Torme beamed professionalism and energy; Vaughan was clearly uncomfortable. The program listed her trio of the past several years—Carl Schroeder, Walter Booker, Jimmy Cobb—but instead she debuted a new band. Mike Wofford, Andy Simpkins, and Roy McCurdy are all highly regarded West Coast musicians, but they were indistinct and tenuous on this night. The pianist was given one token solo, and both he and Simpkins were badly undermiked. The real culprit was McCurdy, who lagged behind the beat in a lackadaisical dream of his own; this was especially disconcerting if you were used to the brash authority of Cobb. Her fourth accompanist was trumpeter Waymon Reed, late of the Basie band and now her husband. The luscious dimensions of her voice flooded the hall on a fast, opening "I'll Remember April," but there was an immediate diminuendo in impact. "Easy Living" and "If You Went Away" were unfocused, and "Watch What Happens" and "Green Dolphin Street" throwaways. She sang a wonderfully blithe "I've Got the World on a String" and did her best with the intransigent "Over the Rainbow," beginning with the release; her legato phrasing on "How Long Has This Been Going On?" made the bossa nova arrangement less cloying than on the record.

The highlight was a sumptuous reading of Benny Golson's "I Remember Clifford," a miraculous two-part melody that suggests the beauty and drama of Clifford Brown's trumpet, but which also prepares you for a stunning brass interlude that Reed failed to capitalize on. Still, there were no pyrotechnic displays, the audience slipped through her fingers, and when she left the stage after nine songs, the usual GASO (Stanley Dance's acronym for Great American Standing Ovation) was not forthcoming. She got it for her encore, "Send In the Clowns," with an unaccompanied conceit where she sings "losing

my timing this laaate [hold it a while] in myyyyyyyyyyyy [hold
it much longer and then careen into] career." Over the cheering, she finishes the song by sobbing the refrain, an extremely
uncharacteristic aesthetic mistake. Vaughan is no more an actress than Joan Sutherland, and her crying is not only musically inept but false to the lyric's irony and her own message of
strength.

Anyone attending the first and second concerts received an
unforgettable lesson in the difference between uninspired and
inspired Vaughan. From her first measures of "There Will
Never Be Another You," there was electricity in the air. But
then, she had a couple of tough acts to follow, and if competition wasn't the motive, you tell me what turned her on.

Phil Woods imitator Richie Cole opened the program with a
short set of cocktail bop, before Eddie Jefferson, the sixty-year-
old father of jazz vocalese—the craft of putting words to jazz
solos—pranced onstage. He sang numbers long associated with
him—Duke Pearson's "Jeannine," two Charlie Parker solos, one
by Miles Davis, "Bennie's from Heaven," and "Moody's Mood"—
and he sang them at vertiginous tempos, hitting every note
square and projecting energy and excitement. He never stopped
moving, hands fluttering, feet mincing angular dance steps, and
though most of the words were unintelligible the audience
seemed to know exactly what he was doing. It was a long-
overdue coming-out party for a gifted performer whose reputation has subsisted underground for thirty years. Vaughan personally requested Jefferson and Betty Carter on the program,
and she paid additional homage to Jefferson's art by singing the
"girl's part" (actually the lyricized piano solo) on "Moody's
Mood."*

---

* Only six weeks later, Eddie Jefferson was murdered. The killing took place
in the early hours of May 9, after Jefferson finished an evening's engagement at a club in Detroit. A suspect was arrested and subsequently ac-
quitted.

Jefferson was born August 3, 1918, and became a professional dancer at
age fifteen, appearing at the Chicago World's Fair in 1933. In 1950, he was

Carter, supported by the John Hicks trio, carried the ball with equal energy, scatting "I Could Write a Book" with trombone vibrato and short, jerky arpeggios that she choreographed with her hand. She explained that Vaughan was the singer who made it possible for other singers to stretch out, said this was "one of the most memorable nights of my lifetime," and jaunted through a mesmerizing set that showed her to be more of an actress than most singers. She stalked the stage, affecting complementary sensual poses, and phrased comfortably behind the beat, making every lyric a channel of communication. Her material amounted to a resume, including a revived "My Favorite Things" and a medley of standards favored by bop instrumentalists—"If I Should Lose You," "All the Things You Are," "Just Friends," "Star Eyes," and "I Should Care." I've never seen her in better form.

Vaughan had her mojo and all other muses working for her this evening. There was a jazz orchestra to her left and a string section to her right. Presumably, the economical string arrangements were by Marty Paich, and the good sound balance allowed them to work as an unobtrusive carpet. Moreover, there were two drummers—Grady Tate played lead for McCurdy, giving a much needed panache to the rhythm. Vaughan was magnificent, relaxed, playful, elegant; she luxuriated in the glamour of her voice, and didn't need any highwire bits or a capella selections (not that they wouldn't have been appreci-

---

working with Sarah Vaughan when he met King Pleasure, who (according to Jefferson) "copped" his lyrics to James Moody's improvisation on "I'm in the Mood for Love" ("Moody's Mood for Love"). Pleasure's record was one of the biggest-selling rhythm-and-blues hits of the early '50s and ushered in a new kind of vocalese, subsequently popularized by Lambert, Hendricks & Ross. Jefferson was long overlooked as the creator of the style, although he was undoubtedly its most satisfying proponent. His intonation was thick and his pitch accurate, and he was especially skillful at simulating the accents and phrases of a saxophone. Through much of the '50s, he was James Moody's vocalist and manager, putting lyrics to solos by Charlie Parker, Miles Davis, Lester Young, Coleman Hawkins, and Moody, among others.

ated) to keep everyone alert. This time "Easy Living" and "If You Went Away" told stories, the latter more memorably than on the record. Her intervallic leaps were so natural and unstudied on "I Got It Bad" that the orchestra seemed to be following her; she concluded in the cellar of her voice. "How Long Has This Been Going On?," however, got to be trying. It's one of the lesser items on the album of that name (why did she ignore "Body and Soul" and "More Than You Know"?), and the coy show-biz ending (she scats obliviously while the horns fade out) doesn't wear well. The one attempt at contemporary material combined a soporific Roberta Flack ballad with Stevie Wonder's "All in Love Is Fair"; she sang the latter well despite evident unfamiliarity. A more rewarding medley combined seven standards in a presentation that was supposed to be autobiographical. They weren't the songs most associated with her, but it was a pleasure to hear her riding high through "Everything I Have Is Yours," "Cherokee," "Perdido," and the others. Billy Eckstine, who convinced Earl Hines to hire her in 1943 and later hired her for his own band, emerged from the wings for a bow and didn't sing. A perfectly turned "Send In the Clowns" brought the audience to its feet, and then Carter and Jefferson came out to trade blues choruses. At first they were toying, but Carter started to build two- and three-chorus units into real solos, and Vaughan picked up the challenge, first parodying and then parrying. They ended riffing, "bye bye baby bye," and it was wonderful.

The final concert was a return to normal. In 1958, Vaughan made a record with the Basie band minus Basie, called *No Count Sarah*, and in 1960, finally recorded with him. The concert was more no-Count Sarah. Basie's set was typical, starting out well enough, with a thunderbolt (Butch Miles firing every turnback with a twenty-one-cymbal salute), and then cooling down with features for his excellent young bassist, John Clayton (whose tone resembles Jimmy Blanton's), trombonist Dennis Wilson, and trumpeter Pete Minger. The best number was

Basie's own blues solo, after which his latest band singer, a Lou Rawls clone named Dennis Roland, did several numbers. For Vaughan's set, however, her trio took over the key spots with the orchestra, and Basie was never seen again. She was in fine voice, especially on the two ballads ("Misty" and "I Remember Clifford"), but there was little genuine excitement. The band was strictly a background ensemble, and while her rhythm section was much improved from the first night, the flame was low. All of the remaining selections had been heard during the previous two concerts, as had the patter ("those of you who don't know me . . . I'm Carmen McRae"), and it wasn't until she reprised "Clowns" that real tension was generated; she even played down the sobbing slightly. And then, she saved the evening with a stunning encore, "The Lord's Prayer." Vaughan got her start in the choir of Newark's Mt. Zion Baptist Church, but aside from her acclaimed 1947 recordings of "The Lord's Prayer" and "Motherless Child," she has avoided spirituals. If this cycle of concerts had really been planned to represent the varied facets of her repertoire, it would have been the perfect opportunity for her to investigate that body of work from her childhood. Her encore performance, much superior to the recording, was reason to hope she will yet. As she arched into the climax, spiraling at ever higher intervals—"For thine is the KINGdom, and the POWer, and the GLORy, forEVer. Amen."— the feeling and the beauty and the power were riveting.

A friend noted, "It's so easy for her to enrapture the audience, why doesn't she?" That's one of several questions raised by this cycle. For example, why is she so hesitant in expanding her repertoire? She has finally jettisoned "Feelings," praise the Lord, but she is still devoted to ephemera like "Watch What Happens," and too many good but hackneyed standards from the '40s. Vaughan's ability to fill concert halls without benefit of hit records is impressive, but her paltry output of first-rate albums since the early 1960s ought to be a music-biz scandal. I don't know if Vaughan is the finest living interpreter of American popular song—her playful irreverence and musicality make it clear that she regards Tin Pan Alley as a starting gate and not a shrine; I do know that she is the most creative singer working within the standard pop-song repertoire, and that her control of timbre, pitch, articulation, and dynamics, her ability to improvise harmonically, melodically, and rhythmically, and the very sound of her instrument rank her with the best jazz instrumentalists. The Super Nights suggested a stiffening in the joints. Of course, it's absurd to think she didn't know that. What she accomplished at the second concert must have been as enchanting for her as it was for everyone else.

April 1979

Betty Carter
Sings Like a Woman

To a large extent, women have dominated jazz singing. Louis Armstrong may have had the most influential vocal style in all of American music, but no male singer extended his example as ingeniously or intuitively as Billie Holiday. Most of the men—Ray Charles is the notable exception—have honed to the blues or barrel-chested crooning: only Jimmy Rushing and Joe Turner could begin to approximate the majesty of Bessie Smith; none had the range of Sarah Vaughan, the swinging energy of Ella Fitzgerald, or the passionate irreverence of Dinah Washington.

Women jazz singers usually communicate a specifically feminine sensibility. Of those mentioned above, only Fitzgerald's music has an occasionally sexless, instrumental character—you can imagine her improvisations sung by a man. The others—as well as Betty Carter, Anita O'Day, Carmen McRae, Ivie Anderson—suggest the alienation that women have experienced in the jazz world and, by extension, society. They do this less through choice of material, although that's certainly a part of it, than by using the contours of their voices to stress feminine stances, from girlishness to sensuality to fierce independence and barely contained anger. There is an element of coyness in the work of women jazz singers that is never heard in the work of their male counterparts.

The profound femininity with which Betty Carter imbues songs seems entwined with her light, agile, alternately quavering and precise voice. In her upper register she is disarmingly naïve, but the middle register is strengthened by an adult matter-of-factness, and the low notes can be provocatively intimate. As she phrases fluidly throughout her considerable range, tension results, as demonstrated in her reading of "But Beautiful"—one senses a deliberate persona play between a tender emoter and a tough improviser. An obvious correlative is the disparity between the sentimental standards and incisive originals that make up her repertoire.

"But Beautiful" can be heard on *What a Little Moonlight Can Do,* a reissue on Impulse of two rare albums. Carter has a reputation for doing things her own way, and most of her records since the late '60s were issued on her own label. In recent years, we've heard her exclusively with trios, so this reissue reminds us how well she could negotiate big production numbers. And it raises the inevitable question of why so distinguished a performer can show only ten albums for a career that is nearly thirty years old.

The earlier album collected here was originally called *Out There* when Peacock released it in 1958 with a cover photograph of a sputnik and a USAF missile. Gigi Gryce put together the small band and contributed arrangements, along with Melba Liston and Benny Golson; there are solos by Golson on tenor sax and Ray Copeland on trumpet (Kenny Dorham was on the date, but he is imperceptibly in the background), and outstanding piano accompaniment by Wynton Kelly. It includes Carter's best-known original, "I Can't Help It," a jaunty trot through "You're Getting To Be a Habit," an unusual arrangement of "Isle of May," which illustrates Carter's dual moods, a Randy Weston waltz, and a surprisingly effective

Latin vehicle, "All I've Got." Only "Something Wonderful" reveals a slackening in control.

There is much to admire in her phrasing, in the way she flings words against the rhythm, and especially in her enunciation: the lack of sibilance, the inflection she gives certain consonants such as *L*, the long notes that sound like faint yawns. These qualities are also apparent on the companion disc, originally released as *The Modern Sound of Betty Carter* in 1960 on ABC, a year before her duets with Ray Charles. There was no personnel listing on the original, and no one has bothered to ferret out details for the reissue, although there are several brief solos, a good rhythm section, and a strong pianist. The arrangements by Richard Wess are generally tasteful; on "Don't Weep for the Lady," Carter's voice is set against the strings like a diamond on black velvet. "At Sundown" gives clear indication of her full range; "My Reverie" reveals her indebtedness to Vaughan, while "Mean to Me" proves her incomparable originality.

Betty Carter's present position in jazz has a disheartening aspect—no major voice has come along to carry on her tradition. Aretha Franklin is in a state of confusion, Jeanne Lee seems committed to the esoteric, and Dee Dee Bridgewater is clearly less sure of herself than some of us thought. Carter's influence can be heard in the work of Cleo Laine, an eclectic show performer, but the great lineage of the female jazz singer from Smith to Carter appears to be in real danger. The mawkish ladies of the current cabaret circuit make Carter's heady individualism that much more valuable.

At forty-eight, Betty Carter is the youngest of the indisputably great jazz singers, and after hearing her twice at the Village Vanguard recently, I don't see how a cult-sized following can contain her much longer. In the past ten years, she has perfected her music on every front—repertoire, arrangements, and presentation—and the payoff at the Vanguard was startling. The total musicality with which she organizes a set, the lucid pacing and dynamics, has long been in evidence, but it has often been counterbalanced by a reticence in her performing style. The energy was there, but its vibrations were sometimes swamped by her fascination with texture, forcing a leap of faith from the audience—perhaps the sine qua non of a cult following. At the Vanguard, she left no room for indifference; she reached out, she entertained, she dazzled. And all the vocal mannerisms that on off-nights can get rutted in a slough of stylization were at the service of her songs, only one of which was repeated during two long sets.

Repertoire can be a revealing gauge of jazz singing, and Carter's is hard won. Like Billie Holiday, she implies a motif in her choice of songs—something like "Love is beautiful but men can't be trusted so keep swinging"—and like Holiday, she underscores it with original pieces. There the comparison ends. Carter is too eagle-eyed to be forlorn; the other side of her sensuality is satire, and she keeps her audience wondering as she flies from a fast, funny excoriation of the male species to a suspensefully slow love ballad to a soaring anthem about music itself. On ballads, she renews substantial songs in the most personal terms possible; each one is made liquid by her trebly, sighing glissandos, and whole by the drama, musical and lyrical, she wrests from its body. Interspersed among a selection that includes "Everything I Have Is Yours," "But Beautiful," "I Could Write a Book," and "Alone Together" is her sprightly version of "Music, Maestro, Please," accompanied during the first chorus by stride piano; "The Trolley Song," with the verse rippling by so fast that the words are almost unintelligible and the chorus braked by theatrical wit as she italicizes every "ding" and "dong"; and "All I've Got," where her deliberate phrasing is pinned to a brutally swinging Latin arrangement. Inevitably, her sets end with a long—too long, I think—scat routine, which she colors with note skeins that have the effect of triple tonguing.

Carter started out as an arranger and singer for Lionel Hampton, after studying at the Detroit Conservatory of Music, and her arranging skills are very much to the point in her performances with the trio. Pianist John Hicks (a rigorous, voluble accompanist), bassist Cameron Brown, and drummer Kenny Washington provide a scrim so colorful that you don't miss horns. Several times during the set the rhythm section will lay out, and Carter will sing a break or half a chorus a capella, only to rejoin the trio with unerring precision.

I can't overemphasize the contagious sense of fun she brought to the songs, and her evident relaxation as she bounced a lyric off a member of the audience, or swooped around the small stage to guide a song with body English from the shoulders, or reached for a note just below or above the one you thought she had her eye on, or laughed unself-consciously at the sheer pleasure of her music making. I've delighted in Betty Carter's singing for years, but I had the feeling at the Vanguard that she had taken another hurdle. You didn't have to be a fan to love her; you couldn't help yourself.

November 1976 and January 1979

The Once
and Future Sinatra

Frank Sinatra is the most frustrating performer in American popular music. Ambitious and brilliant and infuriating, he is at once the embodiment of good taste, garrulous vulgarity, and bourgeois mush—the Rolls-Royce of Tin Pan Alley and a polyester of trendy compromises. For forty years, Sinatra has loomed as a sovereign interpreter of what we diffidently call pop songs, which in his hands more than most endure as America's vernacular art songs. He's recorded more than a thousand, tailoring each one like a theatrical role; he divines their meanings, caresses their melodies, and bestrides their rhythms. But Sinatra is a relentlessly public figure, a collector of homages (his protestations of wanting privacy notwithstanding), and it's difficult to listen to the singer without hearing the clatter of the man. This, after all, is an artist who hires press flacks to invent sobriquets—Old Blue Eyes is back!—that weren't born of affection.

Sinatra's audacious 1979 recording, *Trilogy*, his first in five years, invited frustration. A culmination of his obsession with time (subsuming all those very good years), it presumed to turn the corner on his past, present, and future—intimating how he made it, how he held on, and how he'd like it to be told. If the result emerged not as a mere retrospective of a great entertainer, but a drama in which the singer was finally apotheosized into an eminence of mythic proportions, no one could say it wasn't expected. Sinatra has kept us fawning and flinching for decades. His intimidating ego is the other side of his consuming vulnerability. Half mensch and half punk, a virtuoso at storing wounds, he is alternately the exemplary male performer (cool, sharp, elegant) and the hapless teen idol badly in need of womanly coddling. Yet the contradictions that confound his public image are the very marrow of his art.

Sinatra proved to a generation of male singers that their profession was a manly one. Not only didn't you have to be a pansy to sell Brill Building wisdom, but it actually *helped* if you were a worldly, stand-up guy. He brought a new attitude to pop songs. People might settle for singing like Crosby while mowing the lawn, but Sinatra was how they wanted to sound to their girl friends. (At least in white America; blacks had other vicarious troubadors.) Still, for all his virility, Sinatra was profoundly, achingly vulnerable. He may have been a rogue but he was singing from his heart. His public image, and the seeming contempt for women that peeked through, was one thing, and the records something else—despite an occasional ring-a-ding-ding-all-you-chicks, they were tender and loving and decent and moving.

Other singers no less extraordinary than Sinatra plied the pop market—singers who were more creative (Louis Armstrong), versatile (Ray Charles), exciting (Jimmy Rushing), sexy (Billy Eckstine), and swinging (Nat Cole)—but they were jazz-oriented stylists, and none operated so fastidiously on the borderline between breezy recitation and unalloyed sentiment. And few kept at it as long or as well. Sinatra didn't swing impetuously like a jazz singer, but he patented a clean, amiable rhythmic charge that was true to the songs and the period (post-swing/pre-rock). Even when he subjected ballads to brutal tempos—"Dancing in the Dark," "The Song Is You"—he made you hear nuance and detail, and a sweetness at the core. His peerless phrasing, with its long, Dorsey-like vowels, subtle breathing, impeccable articulation, and minimal embellishments, was always at the service of the song; he was less a stylist than a recitalist, a strict constructionist. A jazz singer might take a standard and alter a couple of notes, substitute a few chords, retard this phrase and rush that one, and presto!—you had a new song, or at least a new way of thinking about the song. With Sinatra, you had a definitive interpretation.

But you didn't always have definitive Sinatra. The frustration he occasioned wasn't limited to the disparity between the recording angel and the public boor. He was sometimes a recording boor too. An arbiter of pop songs is dependent on songwriters, and subject to a curious kind of hubris: if a good musician can play any kind of music, a good pop singer ought to be able to sing any kind of pop songs. Sinatra came up during the Golden Age of Tin Pan Alley—heir to and master of a tradition. Suddenly, his era was over—first the big bands evaporated (a boon to his career), then his voice, then his audience. The voice and audience were never gone for long, but the Golden Age was ending, and quality material was becoming scarce. The teenage rave with the light, pretty voice who sang with Harry James and Tommy Dorsey from 1939 to 1942, went solo in '43, crooning ballads against the impenetrable strings of Axel Stordahl. Sinatra sounded good, but he was soon warring with the repertoire and the arrangements. For every "Body and Soul" or "Blue Skies" or "Nevertheless," there was an "I Went Down to Virginia" or collaborations with the Double Daters or Dagmar.

In the late '40s and early '50s, Columbia Records and Sinatra fell into the hands of the megalomaniacal Mitch Miller. It was the age of "Come on a My House," "How Much Is That Doggie in the Window?," "Que Serra," and endless gimmickry. Miller thought performers were commodities and audiences chimpanzees (he was a genuine prophet), and was proven right first by the success of the records he produced and later by a tremendously popular television series in which he conducted a choir of homely, middle-aged men singing things like "She Wore a Yellow Ribbon." Sinatra was desperate enough to go along with him to a certain extent, but to no avail—Columbia dropped him in 1952. When he made his most significant of several comebacks two years later, signing with Capitol Records on the heels of his *From Here to Eternity* film triumph, he was practically another singer.

Sinatra's best and most consistent work was recorded during the ensuing decade. He stopped sounding like a kid, and learned how to swing an orchestra. He recorded dozens of excellent songs—cramming fifteen onto his 1956 masterpiece *Songs for Swinging Lovers*—with lucid, colorful arrangements, the best of them by Nelson Riddle. Riddle used a jazz orchestra, strings, percussion, even an occasional soloist to spice the charts; and though some of them are slick, they remain generally functional and unembarrassed by the passage of time. They were almost always distinguished by a commanding rhythm section, with a strong bass line, and teasing solo comments. The best of the teasers was Harry Edison, whose solos came in three basic flavors: beep beep beep, beep beeeep beep, and b'beep'm b'beep. He turned up when least expected and never failed to be appropriate and witty. Most of the albums were programmed according to tempo—so that *Swinging Lovers* was medium, *A Swingin' Affair* was medium fast, *Come Dance with Me* was fast, and *Only the Lonely* was aw-ful-ly slow. Albums that mixed ballads and swingers, like *Come Fly with Me,* were exceptions. Gordon Jenkins wrote the effusive string arrangements (Axel Stordahl was a curmudgeon by comparison) and Billy May, the effusive brass arrangements (employing clanging pop-jazz effects echoing down from Stan Kenton's Olympus, and never giving a soloist an inch).

In 1961, Sinatra started his own label, Reprise (which, among other nice things, employed Duke Ellington as a producer), and continued to record collections of swingers and ballads. There was a splendid tribute to Tommy Dorsey with Sy Oliver (*I Remember Tommy*), but the *Swinging Brass* record showed signs of strain, and the three collaborations with Count Basie, though replete with marvelous moments, indicated that the voice was eroding: a slight tremor and pitch problems were audible. He eventually succumbed to the Top Forty, encouraged by the immense success of "Strangers in the Night." There was no Mitch Miller around telling him to record "Somewhere in Your Heart," "Forget Domani," "That's Life," and "Winchester Cathedral." No one put a gun to his head and told him to prance around Madison Square Garden croaking "Bad, Bad Leroy Brown." No, he did it his way. Except for one and a half albums with Antonio Carlos Jobim, his records became maudlin and embarrassing. He edited a retrospective called *A Man and His Music,* adding spoken comments that would redden a presenter at the Academy Awards. The liner notes, always sycophantic, turned to gas (". . . that man who stands straight on earth, sure in a universe rich with doubt"). Yet his 1978 tour (including a stop at Radio City Music Hall) was stirring. He sang the songs that reared him—Porter, Gershwin, Kern—and only a few of the contemporary ditties that he's convinced himself are as good or as worthy of his time and particular talent, and he was in magnificent voice.

The long-awaited *Trilogy* wasn't entirely satisfactory, but it was an event and a musicianly triumph. It found him singing with renewed authority and energy. The voice had changed again—becoming darker, loamier, tougher; there was not a trace of the hesitation or tremor that plagued him only a few years back. I can't think of another instance when a singer of sixty-four made so complete a recovery. The problem was repertoire. Sinatra may be obsessed with his past, but he doesn't completely trust it, and he wants to copyright the future. He's so caught up in his own myth that he seems to have lost sight of what sort of artist he is.

Trilogy is subtitled "Past Present Future," and attempts to satisfy its premise by devoting three volumes to songs of the distant past, the recent past, and the immediate past. (What else can you do without a time machine?) The results are predictably uneven—the songs become increasingly less convincing as they press home to the present—but Sinatra is so formidable that it did not require undue optimism to interpret the package as a misguided but startling new beginning. All he needs is a producer willing to delve into the ASCAP files in search of material that doesn't insult the singer's talent or the listener's intelligence. Not that the newer material won't continue to do well for him: Sinatra learned to outsentimentalize his audience in the '70s, and he undoubtedly struck a few dulled nerves here. But long-time Sinatraphiles probably don't play volumes two and three too often.

"The Past," also called "Collectibles of the Early Years" (note the patronizing tone), actually covers the first 25 years of Sinatra's career. He recorded only three of the ten selections before, in the '58-'63 period, and in every instance I prefer the new version. Billy May improved his arrangement for "The Song Is You," which, remarkably, is taken faster than in 1958; Sinatra is positively buoyant, and though he goes for the high seventh only once, he has no trouble with it. The arrangement of "Let's Face the Music" is far superior to the old one by Johnny Mandel, and "Street of Dreams" is marred only by a pointless fadeout. "But Not for Me" is done in the Tommy Dorsey–Pied Pipers style, and "I Had the Craziest Dream" has suggestions of Harry James—two bones to the nostalgiacs, yet expertly rendered. Sinatra heartily emotes the difficult release of "My Shining Hour," growls exuberantly through "All of Me," and gives two of his strongest performances in twenty years on "It Had To Be You" and "More Than You Know." Even the sorry joke—everybody starts laughing—that caps a delightful performance of "They All Laughed" works. If possible, Sinatra sounds even more urgently personal than in the '50s. He's communicating something new, maybe the revived powers of an immensely gifted performer who knows—contrary evidence be damned—that these are the songs he was made for. He fastens on the lyrics, inflates key melodic phrases, and prods the rhythms. In sum, this is a superb record.

Volume two, "The Present," is subtitled "Some Very Good Years," and in some ways, I suppose this is a more personal disc. Certainly, Sinatra has to work harder for these songs, and he's in prime shape for the thankless task. But the effect is like Fred Astaire gliding into a bed of quicksand. The material is generally the kind of middle-of-the-road sludge that passed for quality when rock seemed most excessive—the stuff for which some desperate pundit coined the term "hook." Gershwin and Kern wrote melodies; Hamlisch and Manilow write hooks— cheap two-bar geegaws that give momentary focus to unfocused songs. To compensate for melodic deficiencies, such songs pretend to deal with Big Ideas. It was a peculiarly nutty conceit of the singer-songwriter generation to think that it brought song lyrics to maturity, while Tin Pan Alley was allegedly awash in nothing but June/moon platitudes. Homilies are not necessarily preferable to platitudes: how many of the new songs transcend the rest of the '70s' mass-distributed wisdom? By contrast, the lyrics of Hart, Porter, Mercer, Gershwin, and Harburg are full of concise and witty observations that stand up quite nicely. What's more, they sing well—the lyrics rarely overwhelm the melodies, something Sinatra should know better than anyone.

Yet in "The Present," he gives his all to a typical Kris Kristofferson self-sufficiency seduction song, "For the Good Times" (Larry Hart wouldn't have penned a line like "this old world keeps a-turnin'"), with Eileen Farrell playing an operatic Tammy Wynette to Sinatra's George Jones. He does everything for Neil Diamond's disingenuous "Song Sung Blue" but drop to bended knee—though Don Costa, who arranged the session, threw in a mattress of voices just in case. You could take a bath in Costa's brief strings interlude during the Bergmans' instant-self-gratification ode, "Summer Me, Winter Me" and of course, there are a couple of look-back-in-nostalgia anthems, "You and Me" and "MacArthur Park." I liked George Harrison's "Something" when it came out—at least, I admired its use of an instrumental refrain. But it hasn't worn well; the melody works so hard to support the lyric that it collapses under, the strain, and Sinatra's attempt to toughen it—"You stick around, Jack," he exhorts, voice a-tremble—is transparent. The low point of the disc is "That's What God Looks Like": God looks like stars, wheat, moonlight reflected on snow, a garden, and lots of other things—but make no mistake, God's a He. Two songs, however, are genuinely transformed. Billy Joel's "Just the Way You Are," despite an utterly nondescript release and a distracting tempo change, becomes a convincing Sinatra swing vehicle. Kander and Ebb's "New York, New York," despite silly honkytonk piano accompaniment, is a big, chest-out, hands-in-semaphore-pattern Broadway melodrama, and Sinatra sings the hell out of it. (Why doesn't somebody write a movie musical for this guy?)

If "The Present" seems more dated than "The Past," "The Future" is the most outmoded of the three. "Reflections on the Future in Three Tenses" is a forty-minute oratorio by the indefatigable Gordon Jenkins, in which one Francis Albert Sinatra, a self-styled saloon singer, travels through space and dispenses wisdom: "Let yourself live, let yourself love, let yourself go! / I've been there . . . and I know." The temptation to quote liberally from the text must be resisted, and it wouldn't be fair anyway. Because though the words are inane (Francis finds ladies in Hades and pizza on Uranus), they come off more palatable in performance. Sinatra sounds fine—he hits the lowest notes of his life on Neptune, and sings every dumb sentiment with absolute conviction—and Jenkins is hack enough to make his pastiche consistently familiar. You know where the melodies will lead before they get there. Still, kitsch affords the poorest and cruelest sort of pleasure, and it's no fun laughing at Sinatra when he's working so well; camp amusement soon gives way to disappointment and disbelief.

So, *Trilogy* proved that Sinatra hadn't lost his voice. And it established him once again as the most ambitious and intransigent of pop singers. You can't blame him for commissioning and tackling Jenkins's "Reflections," though you can wish he'd given the assignment to someone else or at least had the decency to skim some of the self-congratulation from the libretto. Sinatra's favorite conceit about himself is that he's done it all his way and come out on top (listen to him roar "king of the hill, top of the heap" in "New York, New York"). And still he's a victim of the shibboleth that says a pop singer must keep doing contemporary material, no matter how unsuitable. He exhibits undeniable gumption in investing so much of himself in his current repertoire, but what happened to the other kind of gumption that he demonstrated in the early '50s, when he better gauged his gifts and made a commitment to excellence? Volume one of *Trilogy* was the first completely successful Sinatra record in fifteen years. It was exciting not only for what it delivered, but for the promise of glories to come. There are all kinds of songs you want to hear the new Sinatra go after. You hope he'll stop trying to be all things to all people, much less all tenses, and that subsequent records will continue to document an autumnal renaissance. In the meantime, *Trilogy* embodies all the contradictions and fosters all the frustrations. It's not about past, present, and future, but about genius, compromise, and hubris.

March 1980

Instrumentalists

The Best Trombone
Player in the World

I never saw Jack Teagarden except in films. He's always seemed
unreal to me: a sheet-white face chiseled as abruptly as a cigar-
store Indian's—some thought he was Indian, though he was actually of German descent—and a towering but modestly carried
frame. He had black slicked-back hair, and when he smiled his
eyes and mouth formed two parallel slits. You can see him perform "Basin Street Blues," which he played and sang nightly
for twenty-five years, in a Mickey Rooney film called *The Strip.*
He appears as a member of Louis Armstrong's 1951 All-Stars,
with Earl Hines and Barney Bigard. Something about his presence matches the restraint in his music. He seems shy and distant, professional but tired, pleasant but mechanical.

When Teagarden died in 1964 at the age of fifty-eight, his
place in jazz seemed assured. Leonard Feather wrote in *The
Encyclopedia of Jazz in the '60s,* "Always years ahead of his
time, the possessor of a wholly individual sound both as instrumentalist and vocalist, he ranks with Armstrong, Beiderbecke, Coleman Hawkins, and a handful of others as one of the
unquestioned titans in the history of jazz." Martin Williams, in
his *Saturday Review* obituary, placed him similarly in the "advanced guard" of the '20s. Indeed, the prose temperature he

inspired was consistently warm, patient, and frankly preju-
diced. He was the subject of possibly the only noncritical cover
ode ever published in *Jazz Review* as well as two fan bio-
discographies; in a lyrical 1962 review, the *New Yorker's* Whitney Balliett concluded, "Bless Teagarden, and may he pros-
per, too." His admirers apparently identified pretty strongly
with him.

I started listening to Teagarden shortly after his death and
became an instant enthusiast, marveling at his technique and
sound, his cool, finding in it a complete personality at the service of material, time, and place. He was nothing if not emotionally honest, and part of the reward of listening to him, especially his later work, was his detached yet vulnerable strength.
The performance level was astonishing; no matter how wretched
the material or arrangements, Teagarden's trombone was implacable. But at the same time there was something private and
wounded—that oblique sensibility, perhaps, that white jazz
fans respond to in some white jazzmen, sensing a bond of
recognition and safety in a black and exotic music. A Con-
donesque ensemble might be brimming with Dixieland cheer,
but when Teagarden's trombone attains the spotlight it evokes
another world. He was always himself regardless of the musical
setting. Teagarden's lazy time, the casual triplets percolating
unexpectedly from his warming Texas blues riffs, the technical
aplomb, the richly powerful but pliable timbre, and the forth-
rightness of his solos all served to illuminate his moods. He was
the perfect foil for Louis Armstrong, an incisively muted counterpoint to Louis's thousand wattage.

The best Teagarden anthologies (Decca 4540* and RCA
Vintage 528) are long out of print, as is Armstrong's magnificent 1947 Town Hall concert, in which Teagarden joined with
him for an inspired "Rockin' Chair" duet and then delivered
a matchless performance of "St. James Infirmary"—a quintes-

---

* Most of Decca 4540 has been reissued as *A Jazz Holiday;* see Discography.

sential three-minute summation of his accomplishments as trombone virtuoso and blues singer. Subsequent recordings were uneven. A strangely successful Dixie-swing-bop session, with Lucky Thompson and Kenny Kersey, took place in 1954, but from then on Teagarden was heard in formula Chicago-Dixie groups, or as the featured soloist against an expensive backdrop, or with one of his working bands, which were no more worthy of him than Armstrong's later bands were of Armstrong: the same tunes over and over, predictable ensembles, faceless clarinetists, and the vulgar Charlie Shavers imitations of Don Goldie. Most of the energy that didn't come from Teagarden was supplied by the pianist Don Ewell, a thumping stride tickler with few original ideas. It sometimes sounded like jazz for a Shriners' convention. But listen closely to Teagarden and there is always the shock of cogitating, feeling humanity; most of his albums offered enough freshly conceived trombone playing or singing to fan one's lingering admiration.

I had not listened much to Teagarden for a while when several reissues appeared. It's been a happy reacquaintance. Teagarden has sometimes been confused with Chicago's Austin High gang because of his involvement with Bud Freeman, Dave Tough, Eddie Condon, and the others, but he was more an influence than an associate. He remained true to blue tonalities despite an uncommon gift for harmonic improvisation, disregarding the whole-tone patterns that Bix Beiderbecke and Pee Wee Russell toyed with so impressively. Armstrong was his idol, and by the time he first recorded with him in 1929, at one of the first integrated sessions, he had adopted much of the trumpeter's architectural soundness. When he arrived in New York in 1927, his powers were immediately recognized by both black and white players. An awed Coleman Hawkins brought Jimmy Harrison, then the star trombonist of Fletcher Henderson's band and New York, to hear him. Bud Freeman remembers Pee Wee Russell calling him at 3 a.m. to come over in a hurry: "Jack Teagarden, the best trombone player in the

world, just blew into town from Oklahoma City." Two anecdotes convey the first impressions of Beiderbecke and Armstrong. Armstrong told Richard Merryman, "The time of those
riverboats, we'd just put into New Orleans and on the levee
was a cat named Jack Teagarden wanting to meet me. . . . He
was from Texas, but it was always, 'You a spade, and I'm an
ofay. We got the same soul. Let's blow'—and that's the way it
was." Beiderbecke, as Bud Freeman has written, was jealous—
"If I want to hear flute, I don't have to listen to it on a
trombone."

It's likely that if Teagarden had been black his career and
music would have gone in a different direction. Instead of
spending long years with Ben Pollack and Paul Whiteman, he
would have sat next to Harrison in the orchestra of Fletcher
Henderson, who is alleged not to have believed that Teagarden
was really white. He might even have avoided the limitations
of the Dixieland circuit in his later years. On the other hand,
while Teagarden was undoubtedly an advanced musician in the
'20s, there are few indications of radicalism. He was very much
a traditionalist: having honed a style, he stuck with it. Like
Armstrong, he had no doubts about its efficacy, and like Armstrong he had more reason to refine his singing than his instrumental style, which was sure from the start. Armstrong's singing
always dazzled ("Heebie Jeebies"), but it was not until the late
'20s and early '30s ("Star Dust," "All of Me") that it reached a
daringly imaginative peak. Teagarden was never as provocative
or versatile a vocalist as Armstrong, but he could emote as
much feeling. His early work is occasionally awkward (the original "Basin Street Blues" with Red Nichols) and frequently at
the mercy of contemptible material, but as he simplified his
phrasing and settled on a sound somewhere between a croon
and a moan, he developed a mastery of ballad interpretation,
and eventually the ability to uplift dog tunes by simply slurring
the kinks out of them.

He demonstrated vocal proficiency on such early recordings

as "Dirty Dog" and "One Hour," both included on Epic's *Jack Teagarden, King of the Blues Trombone,* which traces his progress from a 1928 session with Jimmy McHugh's Bostonians, where his solos are conspicuously well conceived, to four tracks from a notable 1940 Bud Freeman session. (Strangely, Epic bypassed a wry, genial blues from that date, called "Jack Hits the Road.") The music is woefully uneven, several of the more primitive selections being all but smothered in jazz-age camp. Even the ensembles led by Teagarden are often badly dated, but the improvisations shine through with ageless clarity. The trombonist's unfettered elegance, usually too briefly displayed, is never upstaged by the fine work from Benny Goodman, Fats Waller, Pee Wee Russell, Frank Trumbauer, and Dave Tough.

During the last decade of his career, Teagarden usually recorded with his working band or in collaboration with Bobby Hackett. The most vigorous of his encounters with the trumpeter was Capitol's 1957 *Jazz Ultimate:* the four-man rhythm section works as one, and the four-man front line is lean, lively, and direct—Peanuts Hucko (swinging brightly on tenor) and Ernie Caceres (less bright on clarinet) are amiable, while Hackett and Teagarden are sharp as diamonds. (Beware of the German Capitol reissue of this session, which uses a flawed alternate take of "Indiana.") A 1958 date with Teagarden's own band (Ewell, undistinguished clarinet and trumpet, lethargic rhythm) has several moments to raise the proceedings from period slumber, including a lovely reading of "Someday You'll Be Sorry" and a couple of slow blues. The unavailable *Mis'ry and the Blues,* recorded for Verve, was probably the best showcase for his band.

I don't know if Teagarden's audience has grown much in the years since his death. His reputation is not now as universally celebrated as seemed likely in the mid-'60s, and you have to care enough about the core of personality to get beyond the frequently mediocre wrappings of his records. His historical importance is unquestionable, and numerous solos suggest the timelessness of his conception and its undiminished pleasures, but he no longer appears as integral to the development of jazz as Armstrong or even Hawkins and Beiderbecke. Rather, he haunts the music with his individuality. He was what the clichés say a jazz musician ought to be—a player who expresses himself with honesty and immediacy every time he raises horn to lips. I wish better anthologies of his music were in print, but the available ones will serve to keep his memory alive at a time when the restrained virtuosity, easy ingenuity, and personal charm that characterize almost all of his music are temporarily eclipsed by concerns more fiery or lurid or modern or commercial.

March 1977

A Penchant for Mayhem

Joe Venuti, the great jazz violinist and notorious practical joker, died August 14, 1978, of a heart attack. Depending on which reference book you consult, he was eighty-four, eighty-two, eighty, seventy-five, seventy-four, or seventy-two. Venuti, who surely had one of the strangest senses of humor in music history, encouraged the confusion. He often insisted that he was born on the Atlantic Ocean while in steerage from Italy, but in recent years it was learned that when the boat docked Joe was ten, and already an accomplished violinist. The deception has been variously traced to Venuti's father, who hoped to speed up the naturalization process, to Joe's fear that a foreign-born jazz musician would not be taken seriously by his peers, and to his general penchant for mayhem.

He was the first important violinist in jazz and one of the most influential musicians of the '20s—especially in Europe, where several violin-guitar duos were formed in imitation of Venuti's partnership with Eddie Lang. Yet decades of obscurity followed Lang's death, and history was on the verge of positioning Venuti in a footnote when he reappeared in the late '60s, playing with staggering vitality. His tone was penetrating and bright, on ballads and original chamber-styled pieces, where he bowed with intoxicated romance, and on the fast numbers, where he soared with an aplomb that sometimes suggested hilarity. It was a joy to see him at jam sessions, swaying with contrapuntal rejoinders before wiping out the competition, or at the New York Jazz Repertory Company's tribute to Bix Beiderbecke, when he tied the hairs of the bow around the violin and sawed gusty solos of four-note chords. Venuti was built like a cement mixer. When at rest, his jowls were crepe-paper hangings, and his mouth folded into a quizzical, placid smile. When he laughed he roared, and he talked like an extortionist.

Venuti grew up in Philadelphia with Eddie Lang, a former violinist who switched to guitar. By 1921, they were working together in a hotel in Atlantic City, and within a couple of years they were firmly ensconced in the white jazz community of New York. Each was an innovator, demonstrating how an instrument on the periphery of jazz could play a larger role. Venuti's conservatory technique made him as valuable to society bands as to the hot ensembles, and he became increasingly popular as a one-man string section behind singers. He played in the bands of Jean Goldkette (sharing choruses with Bix Beiderbecke on "Clementine," Frank Trumbauer on "I'm Looking Over a Four-Leaf Clover," and Lang on "Look At the World and Smile"), Red Nichols, Paul Whiteman, Roger Wolfe Kahn, Hoagy Carmichael, and the Dorsey Brothers, and accompanied numerous singers, including Ethel Waters, the Boswell Sisters, Ukelele Ike, Chick Bullock, Smith Ballew, Steve Washington, and Bing Crosby.

Crosby came to admire Venuti and Lang when all three worked together in the Whiteman band; violin and guitar provided enviable rhythmic ambiance for the singer on "If I Had a Talking Picture of You" and "After You've Gone," where Venuti balanced his half-chorus on a characteristic double-timed two-bar break, of the sort Louis Armstrong patented. In 1930, they went to Hollywood to appear in *The King of Jazz*,

and two years later Lang accompanied Crosby's "Please" in
The Big Broadcast. In later years, Venuti was a frequent guest
on Crosby's radio show—"I rehearsed all afternoon so it'll
probably be nuttin'," he growls on one transcription. A 1949
broadcast pairs Crosby and Venuti with Armstrong and Jack
Teagarden, and Venuti's counterpoint for Armstrong makes
you wish they had recorded together formally.

Venuti's most important recordings were the trios with Lang
and a pianist, and the pioneering Blue Four and Blue Five sessions, made prolifically between 1926 and 1933, when Lang
died, and only intermittently during the rest of the '30s. These
were milestones credited with bringing the intimacy of chamber
music to jazz, much heard and copied. In a way they complement the Beiderbecke-Trumbauer sessions, to which Venuti and
especially Lang also contributed. Venuti's authoritative swing
catalyzed the sessions; he tossed syncopations around like jug-
gler's pins, and barged through the registers of the violin, alternating single notes and chords, finding unexpected harmonic
hollows, doubling and halving the tempo, and occasionally
swerving into a well-oiled glissando. Lang invariably followed
him with arpeggios, countermelodies, and enthusiastically
chomped chords. They influenced each other: on show stoppers like "Wild Cat," "Goin' Places," and "The Wild Dog,"
Lang seems to be enthralled by Venuti's challenge, while the
more European numbers, such as "Pretty Trix," the Debussy-
inspired "Doin' Things," and most of the vocals (four of them
sung, incidentally, by Harold Arlen), show Venuti settling comfortably into Lang's less frenetic web.

Under the pseudonym Blind Willie Dunn, Lang was involved in collaborations with black musicians, including King
Oliver and, more rewardingly, Lonnie Johnson, the decade's
other great violinist-turned-guitarist. Yet he never seemed as
spirited with them as he was with Venuti. The Blue Four sessions were white jazz at its best, providing the most distinctive
alternative to the very different kind of chamber music repre-

sented by Louis Armstrong's electrifying Hot Fives and Sevens; listening, for example, to the unhurried phrasing and restful lilt of Jimmy Dorsey's solos on "Little Girl," it isn't difficult to imagine what Lester Young admired in them.

Perhaps the most exciting of the Venuti-Lang dates was the 1931 session for Decca, subsequently reissued on collections spotlighting two of the sidemen, Jack Teagarden and Benny Goodman. They all played superbly. On "Farewell Blues," Venuti comes in on the heels of a Jimmie Noone-inspired Benny Goodman solo. His first half-chorus is a breathless mounting of chords, resolved with a passage of single-note phrases; the second chorus begins with spiraling pattern and modulates to a thin, piping pitch that Venuti vibrates just enough to keep swinging. His attack and tempo-play is luminously displayed on "After You've Gone."

For nearly thirty years, Venuti toured the country in relative obscurity, settling in for long stays at clubs in Vegas, Los Angeles, and Seattle, drinking, gambling himself into debt. In the early '60s, he was signed for a Columbia recording session but another commitment prevented his taking it. A couple of years later, Columbia issued a compilation of his recordings with Lang, called *Stringing the Blues*. But it wasn't until 1967, when Dick Gibson invited him to his celebrated Colorado Jazz Party, that Venuti's genuine reemergence seemed possible. The following year, he triumphed at the Newport Jazz Festival, and Gibson, who takes great pride in his ability to organize bands, got the idea of teaming him with Zoot Sims. Lo and behold, Venuti found his second Eddie Lang in the indomitably swinging tenor saxophonist.

It took about six years before Hank O'Neal's Chiaroscuro label began recording them, but discs were soon proliferating: *Joe and Zoot*, with a version of "I Found a New Baby" so spirited it makes the original sound undernourished, and a "Someday Sweetheart" considerably more inventive than the original; *The Joe Venuti Blue Four*, with a pinnacle of sheer swing in

Venuti and Sims's "My Honey's Lovin' Arms," and exquisite performances of "Remember" and a melancholy elegy called "Blue Too." There were more recordings, with Sims, Marian McPartland, Bucky Pizzarelli, George Barnes, Ross Tompkins—fiery, brooding, ecstatic. The best of these encounters is *Alone at the Palace*, by Venuti and Dave McKenna; he even manages to make "That's a Plenty," the most banal of traditional jazz hobbyhorses, into a violin theme of stature.

In jazz the critical tendency is always to judge a musician by the music he made in his youth, when the innovations were prime and startling. (It has even been said of Louis Armstrong that he ceased to play anything important after the '20s; yet his 1933 "Basin Street Blues" is richer than the 1928, his 1938 "I Can't Give You Anything but Love" is more imaginative than the 1929, his 1955 "Blue Turning Grey over You" is better played and more emotive than the 1930 original, and we could argue all night about the two versions of "Struttin' with Some Barbecue.") A couple of years ago, on a talk show with Joe and Marian McPartland, I noted that he was playing as well now as fifty years ago. Marian corrected me—"Better, he's playing better now." Of course she was right, as I proved to myself that evening; it's all there on the records. It seems to me that Venuti's role in the '70s was as remarkable and valuable as in the '20s because of the constant verve and bravura he brought to jazz, his unrelenting individuality, and the heights to which he inspired several cohorts.

I mentioned at the outset that Venuti was an infamous prankster. Legend has it that he threw a piano out of a seventeenth-story hotel room after making book on what note it would hit; punished a foot-tapping musician by nailing his shoes to the floor; filled a drummer's traps with sand and then shipped them collect; asked thirty-seven bassists to bring their instruments to the corner of Fifty-second Street and Broadway, then drove around the block laughing at the hapless congregation; got Wingy Manone, to whom he once sent a Christmas

present of a single cuff link, drunk, then produced a hacksaw
and divested the trumpeter of his wooden wing; salted and ate
his violin at a Paul Whiteman matinee to protest the leader's
violin solos; and showed his bald spot on a television show
sponsored by Wildroot Cream Oil, announcing, "This is what
Wildroot did for me." Venuti was garrulous and unpredictable
to the end. Nick Brignola, the saxophonist, went to hear him
in a club in Schenectady not too long ago, and Joe was in such
good spirits that he mounted the stage and barked, "Ladies and
gentlemen, I'm gonna do something that I don't usually do.
I'm gonna take a few requests." A woman cried out, "Play
'Feelins.' " " 'Feelins'?" Joe responded. " 'Feelins'! Why, that's
the worst goddam song I ever heard! That's it, no more requests. You had your chance." He played "Sweet Georgia
Brown."

August 1978

The Institutionalization
of Count Basie

Count Basie looked resplendent at Carnegie Hall in the spring of 1977, fully recovered from his heart attack. He carried himself like a well-fed banker, silvered muttonchops framing a radiant smile, as though the enforced year off the road had been rejuvenating. "It sure is good to be back out here again," he said, then sprinkled a handful of Basie notes from the piano as the orchestra snapped into a fervid flag waver. It is a fearsome machine he commands with those spare punctuations, its sections interlocking like huge gears oiled for antiphonal precision, every movement triggered by a pummeling press roll or rim shot. The soloists are essential, but of secondary importance to the monolithic whole.

There was a time, however, when the soloists set the pace for the whole. When Basie first took the band out of Kansas City in 1936, trading regional security for national recognition, he embodied the force of the 9:20 Special itself, hurtling through the expansive American night with a revelation of swing. At a time when big bands in the East were playing increasingly detailed arrangements, Basie's crew, which could *improvise* arrangements out of a common fund of riffs, was scrappy and tough, intimate and exhilarating. The Basie-ites knew that swing could best be furthered by severe streamlining.

Walter Page, who was formerly Basie's boss in the Blue Devils, had switched from tuba to bass in 1926, and soon made a remarkable discovery: a straight-four walk made the rhythm more fluid, while enhancing the freedom of the soloists. Previous rhythm sections were locked into the rigid alternation of tuba on the one and three, and drums on the two and four. Page evened out the beat. Jo Jones, who has credited Page with teaching him drums, but who also had heard such advanced drummers as Alvin Burroughs, Walter Johnson, and A. G. Godley, perfected the "sizzling cymbal," which kept the rhythm flexible and vibrating rather than stiffly knocking at the bass drum. Add Basie's keyboard interjections and perfect tempo settings, and Freddie Green's imperturbable rhythm guitar—musicians call him Quiet Fire—and you have what subsequently became known as the All-American Rhythm Section.

Streamlining was evident in every aspect of the band. Soloists played fewer notes; Basie himself allowed his Fats Waller-tutored left hand to atrophy. Lester Young would gallop on a single repeated note; he would bend and stretch notes with alternate fingerings and use expressive honks and moans. And he played without vibrato. When he coursed in over that seamless rhythm section, emerging from an ensemble riff, as he does on "One O'Clock Jump," dancing and weaving, singing and bellowing, a new tension and sensibility came to jazz. It continues to surprise and mystify.

"One O'Clock Jump," Basie's first hit record but not his best, is a convenient point of departure in discussing the Kansas City riff style. The idea of dividing the dance band into sections that parallel the traditional New Orleans ensemble—replacing the trumpet-trombone-clarinet front line with sections of trumpeters, trombonists, and saxophonists—probably originated in the East with Don Redman and Fletcher Henderson, achieving a special grace in the arrangements of Benny Carter. Some of the specific riff patterns in "One O'Clock Jump" originated with Redman and Fats Waller. Basie, a native of New Jersey until a vaudeville tour left him stranded in the Midwest, was a Waller disciple and undoubtedly understood the effect of riff patterns before he arrived in Kansas City. But as a member of Bennie Moten's orchestra, which also employed the influential southwestern arranger Eddie Durham, Basie saw riff choruses elevated to new stature in such recordings as Moten's "Blue Room." When he took his own band into the Reno Club, playing eight- and twelve-hour nights (a situation in which written arrangements, even had they been abundant, would not have gone far), he mastered the art of establishing riffs on the piano, making them the foundation of the ultimate swing band.

As Dickie Wells, the trombonist, described it, Basie would set up a rhythmic phrase for the trumpets, then a contrasting pattern for the saxophones, and a third for the trombones. In all those hours of playing and jamming, countless phrases were offered, modified, rejected, and perfected. The good ones were remembered and formed a common language. The formulation of head arrangements must have been as exciting for the listeners as for the musicians. (You can hear a head come into being on "Hold the Phone"—on *Sweets, Lips and Lots of Jazz*—recorded in a Harlem after-hours club in 1941.)

Surprisingly, Basie seems to have felt that head arrangements were not substantial enough for the big time. Jo Jones remembers him calling them old hat. (In later years Basie would express the same diffidence about his piano playing; and indeed his long-standing reticence as a soloist is strikingly at odds with Jimmy Rushing's portrait of the young Basie winning cutting contests throughout the Southwest.) When the newly enlarged Basie band—he had only nine pieces at the Reno Club—arrived in Chicago, his doubts were magnified by the cool reception given the imprecise ensembles and give-and-take section work. He had only twelve written arrangements; Fletcher Henderson saved him with a batch from his own stock. Fortunately many of the early recordings were of head arrangements: "One O'Clock Jump," for example, was never written down until Buck Clayton transcribed the record, and some of its elements were recycled into other arrangements, like "Sing for Your Supper" and "Now Will You Be Mine?" The band's mastery of riff ensembles was not yet complete, however, and "Jump"'s out-choruses are not as impressive as those on Moten's 1932 "Blue Room." The full power of the band was soon realized on "Panassie Stomp," "Taxi War Dance," and "Tickle Toe."

It isn't difficult to imagine the impact Basie had on a scene dominated by Henderson's (and Carter's) gentility, Ellington's impressionism, and Lunceford's imperious two-beat. Basie did not have the spit and sparkle or the ensemble fullness of Lunceford, two qualities that Lunceford—who, unlike Basie, was a true midwesterner—probably owed to that other two-beat bandmaster Bennie Moten. But more than anyone else, Basie captured the rhythmic abandon and modernness that were the real significance of swing. What other band would give Lester Young the freedom to begin his solos two measures ahead of time, or allow piano solos to become rhythm-section interludes (something, incidentally, that occurs on Walter Page's rare 1929 "Squabblin"), or encourage two- and four-bar riff dialogues between piano and saxophone, which would later become a bebop cliché known as trading fours? It is to Basie's credit that even when he bartered some of that unorthodox flexibility for greater precision, he retained the drive and relaxation at the core of swing.

Between January 1937 and February 1939, Basie cut fifty-seven sides for Decca records. A number of years ago, Decca released an anthology, *The Best of Count Basie,* with twenty-four selections, five of them featuring vocal choruses. A contemporary audience might conclude that the ratio of instrumentals to vocals was indicative of the band's presentation. But a more recently issued companion volume, *Good Morning Blues,* containing an additional thirty-two sides—all that remains unissued is "Let Me Dream," with a vocal by Earle Warren—sets the record straight. Of the fifty-seven Deccas, ten are piano pieces, twenty-six are vocals, and only twenty-one are big-band instrumentals; of the vocals, two were sung by alto saxophonist Earle Warren, five by Helen Humes, and nineteen by the majestic Oklahoma blues shouter Jimmy Rushing. This valuable collection reminds us that Rushing was far more than just the boy singer; he was the band's most popular asset, and one of its most integral soloists.

The Basie-Rushing relationship stretched back through the bands of Moten and Page to road experiences in the Southwest, when they might challenge a local band on Saturday night and perform in church Sunday morning, Basie accompanying Rushing at the organ. Born in Oklahoma City to a musical family, Rushing seems to have been destined to bring the blues in all its dashing, self-assertive glory to urban prominence. His voice was as rich as dark loam, as round as he was; even as it became encrusted with age, it never lost its inspired lilt. At his best, he could sing ride-out choruses with a brilliance that suggested the steely assurance of a great brass player.

"Good Morning Blues" is characteristic of the way Rushing worked within the band. In Eddie Durham's arrangement, Buck Clayton emerges from a dark, minor-keyed ensemble as if in a dream; Basie follows with a sunny chorus, switching to a major key; Rushing sings three bright, audacious choruses— "Good morning blues, blues how do you do? / Baby, I feel all right but I've come to worry you"—accompanied by Basie's subtle obbligato; the band riffs portentously for a chorus, promenading over the beat. Cryptic, growling, smoke-filled effects heard here were used on other Basie-Rushing records, including "Evil Blues" and "I Left My Baby." But there were also cheery arrangements of pop songs that demonstrated equally well Rushing's power and command of phrasing, like "Exactly

Like You," with his surprising ascending phrase in the first eight bars, and the enchantingly trite "Georgiana," which has an excellent solo by Lester Young.

Helen Humes also sounded glorious in those years, as she does now; perhaps the most effective and unusual example of her singing with Basie is on Cole Porter's "My Heart Belongs to Daddy," where Jimmy Mundy's arrangement and Buck Clayton's sardonic distillation of the melody serve to underscore its cantorial flavor.

The ten piano pieces must have sounded astonishingly succinct when they were first heard. They remain unique, but what a delight it is to note that this is one area where Basie continued to grow. The full maturity of his piano style is to be heard on the 1974 *For the First Time;* "Baby Laurence," for example, shows us how profoundly he has extended Waller, but unlike the early piano sides, which are spare to the point of asceticism, it is delivered with a Waller-like vitality. Of course, Basie is not Waller—nor is he Earl Hines or Art Tatum. He is capable of their subtlety and swing, and even, on a modest scale, some of their ingenuity, but he is best heard in one- and two-chorus solos, as on "Don't You Miss Your Baby?" "One O'Clock Jump," "Doggin' Around," and "Boogie Woogie."

That is not to say that there aren't numerous moments of interest on these ten early piano quartets. There is the chorus of genteel flourishes followed by one of minor seconds on "Red Wagon"; the stride-to-boogie and back of "Oh Red"; the ginger touch and playfulness of "Fare Thee Well"; and the regal poise of "How Long." There are also repetitious turnbacks and an occasionally unimaginative left hand.

By 1942, the tendency toward increasingly sophisticated and complex arrangements, with the accent not on soloists but on contrasting tonal colors, weightier harmonies, and clockwork ensemble punch, was apparent on such pieces as "It's Sand Man" and "Ain't It the Truth." Lester Young is said to have left the band in 1940 because he resented the lengthy rehearsals necessary for the other musicians to learn the written scores; it may be that Young's departure furthered Basie's determination to build a band not dependent on star soloists. When, in the early '60s, he was asked how he went about replacing key sidemen, he said, "Well, you don't try to think about Lester Young or Herschel Evans or Don Byas or anything like that . . . because if you lose them you're through. So, therefore . . . you get yourself more ensemble things." He told the arrangers to "concentrate on the band."

The band that jelled in 1953, after two years in which economics had forced Basie to settle for an octet, was not inspiring, but it was breathtaking. Another reissue, Verve's *Sixteen Men Swinging,* tells the story. One immediately notes two paradoxes. First, as big bands became less popular they became increasingly pop oriented. Basie realized that his orchestra, in order to survive, could no longer be motivated purely by internal necessities, and would have to acknowledge, rather than establish, pop conventions. This was manifested in medium dance-band tempos, melodrama, cuteness, and hit parade tunes. The second paradox is that although Basie was one of the first to foresee the demise of the clarinet (considered too light for modern jazz)—he rarely encouraged Lester Young, who was at least the equal of Goodman or Shaw, to play it—he was also the first to foresee the rise of the flute (a lighter instrument) which became an important contributor to his '50s sound.

Neither of these observations is as pertinent to the Verve material of '53–'54 as it is to the later band material. The rhythm section, with Gus Johnson, was still outstanding, and there were talented soloists in Frank Wess, Frank Foster, Joe Newman, Benny Powell, and Thad Jones. But the stars were the arrangers: Foster, Jones, Ernie Wilkins, and especially Neal Hefti (the first of many Woody Herman arrangers who would write for Basie as well). The soloists were accomplished, not innovative; thus, they were somewhat interchangeable. The charts were cast in what had long been identified as the Basie mold, with layered riffs, screaming brass, swooning reeds. Superficiality encroached, and one's attention was diverted less by the quality of the material than by the band's Holy Roller delivery. The scrappy bunch of individuals was gone, replaced by an iron-bodied machine; train travel had given way to the jet. The most mystifying epiphany in this period of Basie's career must have been his dismissal from Alan Freed's "Camel Rock and Roll Party" in 1956—by which time Joe Williams had given the band a major hit with "Everyday." Freed's explanation was, "Basie is a good friend of mine, and musically he has the greatest band in the country, but it isn't a dance band."

The unmistakable Basie punch rang clear when he returned to Carnegie Hall in April 1977, but there was also a touch of vaudeville. Basie once said, "I like to keep adding things to the book all the time. It inspires the men, I think, to have new arrangements to work out." Yet Jimmy Forrest played the same "Body and Soul" solo he's been playing for two years, and Al Grey played the same "The More I See You" solo he's been using even longer. They are good solo routines, handsomely played, and guaranteed to get a rise out of the audience, but the implication arises that these two men could not do as well improvising on a variety of pieces. (It's difficult to imagine Lester Young playing the same solo even twice.) More problematic is the flashy drummer, Butch Miles, who leaves no turnback unmolested. Like the more talented Sonny Payne before him, he's good show business. The best moments were solos by tenor saxophonist Eric Dixon (this is one of the few Basie bands without a Lester player), altoist Danny Turner, and trumpeter Bobby Mitchell. The sections crackled and popped, but with few surprises.

If even the best of Basie's post-'40s orchestras seem less admirable than the classic Kansas City-rooted band, it is because without the compositional vision of a Morton, Ellington, Mingus, Gil Evans, or George Russell, Basie can't quell our desire for a heroic soloist to stand up and reduce the ensemble to his respectful accompaniment. In jazz, existential bravura still counts for something.

April 1977

Donald Lambert
Strides into View

Maybe it is because most of the people who have written about jazz are white and from the Northeast that so much jazz writing is infatuated with the exoticism of the South. One result is the simplistic up-the-river theory of jazz history, which locates genesis in New Orleans and follows the music up the Mississippi to Chicago, where it leaps first to New York and then to the world. This is the favored theory of writers; musicians have other ideas. Mary Lou Williams of Pittsburgh, for example, once drew a family tree that was reprinted by Jazzmobile, Inc. The bark represents the blues; and the trunk lists, from the bottom up, Suffering, Roots, Spirituals, Ragtime, Kansas City Swing, and Bop. New Orleanians are plentiful among the leaves, but there is no mention of the city itself.

To judge by the writings and interviews, Duke Ellington, Willie the Lion Smith, Eubie Blake, and James P. Johnson aren't smitten with New Orleans either. Their accounts of musical history from the 1890s to the 1920s invariably begin with a litany of strange names, all of easterners: Jesse Pickett, One-Legged Willie Joseph, Jack the Bear, Freddy Bryant, Kid Sneeze, Doc Perry, Gertie Wells, Louis Brown, Lester Dishman, Sticky Mack, Blind Johnny, Jack Wilson, Fats Harris, the Beetle,

Abba Labba, Paul Seminole, and others. They were pianists during that transitional moment when ragtime gave way to the woolier syncopations and antigenteelism of early jazz. The names grow familiar with repetition even while their talents recede into the fog of legend, for unlike the well-documented pioneers of New Orleans, they were not recorded. Even the contributions of the more significant and hugely successful composer-pianists who came of age in the years preceding World War I—Eubie Blake, Lucky Roberts, James P. Johnson—were undervalued. Volumes were written about Jelly Roll Morton, not undeservedly, to be sure, while Johnson's name was omitted entirely from the first attempts at comprehensive jazz histories. Yet, in many respects, Johnson's career echoes Morton's, and he had a more substantial and profound influence on the subsequent jazz styles that evolved in New York.

Morton and Johnson both broke through the constraints of ragtime by infusing their music with swinging rhythms, improvisation, and blues harmonies, but Johnson—like Blake, Roberts, and Fats Waller—also devoted much of his energy to writing Tin Pan Alley songs (successfully) and "serious" extended works (unsuccessfully). Perhaps their achievement in the musical theater distracted attention from their importance in the evolution of jazz. Interestingly, the eastern pianists encountered Morton in 1911 and were unimpressed. Johnson noted that both he and Morton employed cotillion themes for their instrumental works, but shrugged at Morton's capabilities at the keyboard, as does Joe Turner today; Perry Bradford wrote of Morton fading before the Beetle (Stephen Henderson), and even Ellington's noblesse oblige failed him when the subject of Morton came up. Whether the cause was personal friction, snobbery, or unresolved rivalry, there is little evidence to suggest that the New York keyboard elite recognized Morton as a kindred spirit; only Willie the Lion Smith subsequently recorded his compositions.

Yet, if New York refused to recognize Morton's genius, his-

tory has been equally deaf to the musicians on the eastern sea-
board who straddled minstrelsy and ragtime, suggesting their
own synthesis in the process. Even before Johnson, the orthodoxies of Scott Joplin's ragtime were giving way to a freer style
of piano music, as suggested in the work of Eubie Blake, who
was two years older than Morton. The instinct for modernism
is evident in Blake's "Charleston Rag," composed in 1899 (the
same year Joplin's "Maple Leaf Rag" was published), and recorded in 1921 as "Sounds of Africa." Blake uses the familiar
rondo form of ragtime, but he varies rhythmic accents and
turnarounds freely. The A strain places percussive chords against
a walking bass (not unlike the one Ellington used on "It Don't
Mean a Thing"), the B strain is more melodic, and the C strain
introduces a chugging locomotive effect that was picked up by
Johnson ("Jingles," for example) and later apotheosized as a
swing-band cliché—i.e., in the last chorus of Basie's "Tickle
Toe," or, most extravagantly, at the outset of Roy Eldridge's
solo on Gene Krupa's "Let Me Off Uptown." If one doubts the
earthiness of Blake's intentions, one need only listen to the version he recorded for Columbia in 1968, where he shouts "Yes,
lord" at one point and accompanies the third strain by chanting "bum-cha bum-cha." This isn't parlor music.

It was Johnson, though, who signaled a clean break with the
ragtime precursors (he mentioned Blake, Roberts, and Abba
Labba as prime sources), and the implications of his stylistic
leap transcended his immediate circle of influence. Ellington
streamlined his early music through the assimilation of what
came to be known as the stride style; Basie, a Waller disciple
(think of his "Prince of Wails" solo), built the modern rhythm
section on stride principles; Art Tatum, Jess Stacy, and Joe Sullivan employed the idiom, as did Thelonious Monk, and, on
rare occasions ("The Last Time I Saw Paris," "Yesterday"),
even Bud Powell; in recent years we've seen renewed interest in
stride in the hands of archivists and modernistic elaborators

(Jaki Byard, Stanley Cowell, Muhal Richard Abrams, Hilton Ruiz, and others).

The term "stride" simply describes the movement of the pianist's left hand, which plays distant bass notes on the first and third beats of the measure and close chords in the octave below middle C on the second and fourth beats. Stride was at once a social music, heard at parties and for dancing, and a carefully structured listener's music. There was a repertoire of original compositions, of course, but you could also stride pop tunes or classical themes, just as an earlier generation of pianists spoke of ragging various tunes. Stride never won a large audience; it was overlooked in the fad for boogie woogie and all but forgotten during the years of bop. Only Fats Waller achieved real commercial success, but even he rarely recorded unaccompanied solos. Many of the most highly praised stride masters were not recorded in their early years; nor was that neglect rectified in later years. Lucky Roberts (1893–1968), was the inspiration for many pianists and the composer of fourteen revues and numerous classic stride pieces, but, barring the existence of private tapes, his recordings consist of a few 78s, an outrageously commercial LP with a prepared "honky tonk" piano and material like "By the Sea," and half an essential 1958 album (shared with Willie the Lion Smith) on Contemporary. Willie Gant was still playing in New York in 1970, but I've been unable to locate any recordings made by him after 1924. And then there is the case of Donald Lambert.

He does not appear in the *Encyclopedia of Jazz* or most of the histories, but he is always mentioned in discussions of the stride giants. According to Ed Kirkeby, Fats Waller's biographer and manager, "Donald was one of James P.'s favorites, and could cut anybody on a good night." Eubie Blake also admired him, and told of a concert in the '40s when he shared the stage with Lambert and the Lion, and Lambert "wiped us both off the stage." The same thing happened when they were reunited at Newport in 1960. Zutty Singleton told Dan Morgenstern, who wrote the only article on Lambert I've been able to find (*Jazz Journal*, January 1960), that Art Tatum himself once declined to follow Lambert at a Bundles for Britain benefit. When the expatriate pianist Joe Turner appeared in New York in 1976, he recounted competitions between Tatum, Johnson, Waller, himself, and the others, and cautioned me not to forget "the Lamb, he was one of the greatest."

But how was one to assess a musician whose recordings consisted of four perfunctory jazzing-the-classics sides, made in 1941, and a long-unavailable album of piano-drums duets recorded shortly before his death? Recently, two albums of Lambert solos, a windfall, both culled from private tapes made in the years 1959–62, have appeared on specialist labels: Pumpkin's *Harlem Stride Classics* and IAJRC's *Meet the Lamb*. They have more than specialist appeal.

Little is known about Lambert, except that he was born in Princeton in 1904 and died in Newark in 1962, and was a private, uncompromising, musically illiterate, and fiercely competitive left-handed pianist with short fingers. He worked New York in the late '20s but spent most of his life playing small bars in Jersey. Rudi Blesh has described him (in *They All Played Ragtime*) as not intertested in popular acclaim, and Morgenstern tells of an evening when he was supposed to open at Café Society but spent the night entertaining friends in a local bar. He did not stint, however, in the presence of other pianists, and was known to be a terror at cutting sessions. In his witty, informative notes to the Pumpkin set, Dick Wellstood relates a story about the time Lambert traveled to Harlem to challenge Tatum, who was conceded to be the number-one man. As Wellstood tells it, "He found Tatum and Marlowe Morris (considered second only to Tatum) sitting in the back room of some bar. Lambert flung himself at the piano, crying, 'I've come for you, Tatum!' and things of that nature, and launched into some blistering stride. Tatum heard him out. When it was all over and Lambert stood up, defiant, Tatum said quietly, 'Take him, Marlowe.' "

I hear nothing in these records to support the not so infrequent claims that Lambert was Tatum's match in improvisation or execution, but his exhilaration in the throes of stride is affecting, and there is nothing by Johnson, Waller, the Lion, Roberts, Turner, or anyone else quite like it.

James P. was Lambert's model; on these albums he plays four Johnson instrumental pieces, one of his pop songs, and two pieces associated with him, as well as instrumental numbers and songs by Roberts, Blake, and the Lion. His transformation of pop songs into the language of stride, the right hand splashing sumptuously against the vigorous left, are exemplary, but the classic compositions from the stride repertoire go further in defining the music's ambitions and range.

Johnson's "Keep Off the Grass" is splendidly performed by Lambert. The primary strain is lean, tough, and aggressive, with a knowing recklessness common to much Afro-American dance music. Lambert underscores its power, accelerating at the end and then stopping on the dime of the first beat of the last measure. If his performance seems too boisterous for actual dancing, it's a perfect example of what Ornette Coleman calls dancing in your head. The Lamb romps unerringly through "Harlem Strut," and makes the not quite fairly titled "Daintiness Rag" an anthology of favorite themes from Johnson and Roberts. "Old Fashioned Love" was one of Johnson's two hits from the 1923 show *Running Wild* (the other was "Charleston"), and is a rare example of a song that enjoyed currency both in jazz and country (Bob Wills, later Merle Haggard) circles. Johnson recorded it with a combo (excellent solo by J. C. Higginbotham) and later with a drummer; and Joe Turner, who played it on a Freddy Jenkins date, turned his solo on a grandiose reference to Louis Armstrong's "West End Blues" cadenza. No one, however, has invested the melody with the brightness and swing Lambert summons forth. The piano is rotting and the high notes ache for mercy, but Lambert makes the cursed instrument sing, and his two choruses, with modest embellishment and tempo-play and insistent accents on the third beat, soar. On the best of the Johnson-related selections, Edgar Sampson's "If Dreams Come True," Lambert's interpretation owes nothing to Johnson's; he begins with a chorus of moody, dissonant chords and follows with one in which the right hand tap-dances the theme against some of the best walking bass you'll ever hear, another in full-bodied stride, and a fourth fueled with exuberance.

"Carolina Shout" is a disappointment. More than any other piece, this 1914 composition represents the burgeoning of the new school. Its B strain has a pleasantly rural goofiness, and the C strain introduced the ring shout into Harlem piano; Ellington, Waller, and Turner were among those who cut their cuticles on it by slowing down the roll on their pianolas. Johnson's 1921 recording was a thing of energetic beauty, but I prefer the 1938 *Spirituals to Swing* version, where he really shouts that third strain. Lambert's performance is relatively workmanlike; his left hand avoids the rhythmic alterations patented by Johnson, and his right misses some of the sweeter harmonic turns. On the other hand, he is stupendous on the Lion's "Hold Your Temper" and on Lucky Roberts's "Pork and Beans," a contemporary of "Carolina Shout." The introduction on the Roberts is fanciful, and he introduces the bass pattern as though he were winding up an old car before stepping on the gas. The third strain has the effect of a release, harmonically, and by ending the piece with it, he concludes on a mountaintop, pulling into an arpeggiated skid rather than a coda.

I don't mean to ignore his splendiferous reworkings of pop songs, which usually begin with a straight chorus, followed by a stride tattoo. His show stoppers include "Rose of the Rio

Grande," "The Trolley Song," "I'm Just Wild About Harry," "The Lady's in Love with You," "It's All Right with Me," and a madly cascading "Russian Lullabye," with references to "Volga Boatmen" and "Lover Come Back to Me." This is music to get drunk on. Listen to the vertiginous symmetry of his "When Your Lover Has Gone"; he plays sixteen bars rubato, with deflated chords, and then strides into the sunlight for a second chorus (the pivot point is a lovely ascending arpeggio in bar six), rushes the tempo for an additional half-chorus, and then brakes into a restful, rubato close. During a simultaneous medley, he plays "Tea for Two" with the left hand, and unrelated melodies—"April Showers," "Because of You"—with the right.

There is a superb example of Lambert's avuncular jazzing-the-classics style, which works especially well because the piece is itself a ragtime classic: "Russian Rag" is credited to Rachmaninoff, but only the first three notes of his "Prelude in C-Sharp Minor" are borrowed as a springboard for a performance that is the emotional obverse of the ponderous original. Lambert is credited with two compositions—"Don's Mother's Song," a naïve romantic fragment, and "I Love You Madly," which is really "Sonny Boy" via Fats Waller's "Clothes Line Rag." At least they are handsomely played.

In terms of improvisational freedom and technique, stride is limited and narrowly conceived, yet its emotional message is one of liberation and heady irreverence. Several stride men—from Blake to Monk—have described the music as freedom itself, and one often feels, while listening to Lambert move from a sober exposition of melody into a propulsive stride, that he is marking his freedom with every lateral movement of his left hand. His rhythms resemble nothing so much as the relentless churning of a locomotive, and the endings often wind down like air escaping from the engine's brake. Stride embodies the freedom of personal bravura—hence the fierce competition between its exponents—and its key paradox is that the musician is never more a mechanism than when he is caught in the spirit of stride's rhythmic intoxication. Of course, the trick is to be a well-oiled machine without being mechanical. Lambert's music is gloriously human.

March 1978

Professor Longhair Woogies

If Professor Longhair were given to pronouncements, he might find himself echoing Jelly Roll Morton's famed dictum: "If you can't manage to put tinges of Spanish in your tunes, you will never be able to get the right seasoning, I call it, for jazz." The Spanish tinge has a tango inflection in Morton's music and a rhumba beat in Longhair's, yet the way it changes a song's color (in Morton's phrase) "from red to blue" is an important link between the consecutive New Orleans traditions of jazz and rhythm and blues. Both musicians favor polyrhythms and tenacious bass ostinatos, and Longhair has absorbed Morton's theory of riffs ("No jazz piano player can really play good jazz unless they try to give an imitation of a band, that is, by providing a basis of riffs") and breaks ("Even if a tune hasn't got a break in it, it's always necessary to arrange some kind of a spot to make a break").

Longhair's three-day stopover at the Village Gate in May 1979 (it was part of his first northeastern tour) gave me the chance to finally see a remarkable sixty-one-year-old bluesman whose international reputation has increased in inverse proportion to his international availability, whether on records or in concert. And it provoked questions about his lineage. He is often spoken of as the foundation for New Orleans rock and roll; as the mentor of Fats Domino, Huey Smith, Allen Toussaint, and Mac Rebennack; and as a tragically neglected pioneer pianist. But where does his music come from, how innovative and influential has it proven to be, and why have we heard so little from him? In trying to ferret the professor (born Henry Roeland Byrd) from beneath the hype, Morton seemed a good place to begin the search for a pedigree.

The Latin element is essential to the musics of Morton and Longhair. The Spanish tinge was widespread in nineteenth-century America, and its presence in black music certainly precedes Morton's keening rhythms (for example, Joplin's "Solace—A Mexican Serenade" and Pickett's "The Dream"), but his beginnings as a barrelhouse pianist, fusing the niceties of ragtime with the blues, punching staunch trombone figures with his left hand, are a basis for measuring subsequent generations of New Orleans barrelhouse men. There are some biographical similarities. Like Longhair, Morton started out on guitar (his teacher was Spanish) and drums before progressing to the keyboard. Both served apprenticeships on the second line—following the parade bands and absorbing the jaunty two-beat rhythm that underscores almost every style of the city's vernacular music—and with the city's itinerant, competitive party pianists. Morton was mesmerized by the plangent bass patterns of one Mamie Desdume, who was missing two fingers on her left hand and could play (so Morton claimed) only one blues. His ability to superimpose cross-rhythms against a repetitive bass walk, ring dissonant overtones in the treble, alternate backbeat accents with downbeat emphases, and construct a blues from a vocabulary of tremolos, displaced accents, and fast chording ("Fat Meat and Greens" is an effectively simple example) is echoed, on a far more primitive level, in the work of Longhair, Fats Domino, and other postwar blues ticklers.

Yet ultimately the differences between Morton and Longhair are more considerable, and the latter's primitivism is the key issue. He has none of Morton's genius for melody, orchestration, or improvisation. His improvisational gifts are exceedingly minor, in fact, and if a Martian were to judge their work, it might very well conclude that Longhair came first, providing the groundwork for Morton's more ambitious achievements. And yet Longhair's style was partly shaped by the national pianistic rage of the 1930s, boogie-woogie. If Morton dazzles with compositional complexity, Longhair engages the spirit with forthright expression. Morton inherited the sixteen-bar strains of ragtime, and colored them with the blues and the habanera; Longhair inherited the twelve- and eight-bar boogie-woogie blues, and arranged it around a fervent rhumba rhythm. In both cases, the peculiarly buoyant parade rhythms of New Orleans adumbrated the result.

In a lengthy *Living Blues* interview in 1975, Longhair says his main influences were Stormy Weather, Rock Sullivan, and Isadore Tuts Washington—all unrecorded honky-tonk pros of the 1930s. They're only names to us, but a listen to the boogie-woogie masters who did record demonstrates that idiom's unmistakable impact on Longhair and his tribe. It's a kind of untutored piano playing that achieved its apotheosis in the Midwest, although originating in the Southwest at the turn of the century. W. C. Handy heard boogie-woogie as a boy in Memphis, and Morton remembered it from his early days in Storyville; its first semimythological figure, boogie's Buddy Bolden if you will, was a man called Stavin' Chain, who played in a railway construction camp in Texas in 1904, and later reappeared as a metaphor for sexual prowess in Morton's "Winin' Boy." The style's most salient characteristics are an eight-beats-to-the-bar bass walk in the left hand, burly cross-rhythms in the right, and a volubility that reflects its functional origin as dance music. Boogie-woogie flourished in all the industrial camps where provisional honky-tonks and gin mills were built to accommodate workers, and an analogy with the function of disco records is not far-fetched: with few exceptions, notably some Meade Lux Lewis compositions, a boogie-woogie performance has no beginning or end, just a succession of blues choruses that keep the dance beat going as long as the pianist can hold out. Its practitioners were largely self-taught and semiprofessional; the language was limited. But each of its great interpreters found a unique voice within its strictures, often expressed in a single lick or break or chording routine that would be quickly absorbed by the others.

Longhair is essentially a boogie-woogie pianist, bringing a particular accent and style to blues piano. Even the distinctively Latinized Longhair pieces like "Mardi Gras in New Orleans" and "Tipitina" reflect the tradition of Afro-Cuban rhythms in boogie-woogie. In his 1940 essay "Three Boogie Woogie Blues Pianists," William Russell wrote of Jimmy Yancey that his "music is the closest approximation to African dance music which has been heard in North America for over half a century. . . . The very close resemblance of many passages in Yancey's solos, both in sonority and rhythm, to the highly developed music produced by a group of African drums of definite pitch is obvious." He went on to locate the "Afro-Cuban rhumba" rhythm in the second chorus of Yancey's "State Street Special." Yancey, too, was an unrecorded mentor for years, admired by all the b-w specialists in Chicago, including Meade Lux Lewis, Albert Ammons, and Pinetop Smith. His music embodies b-w at its most thrilling, as vivacious polyrhythms are propped together with impressive two-handed coordination, and moving, as the blues are made pungent with subtle glissandos and dissonances. In the *Living Blues* interview, Tad Jones suggests that Longhair's playing "is a marvel of blues keyboardists all over the world, superimposing very fast triplets on a syncopated 8/8 rhumba beat." But there is nothing new about that. Yancey does it in "State Street Special" and Meade Lux Lewis does it in the third chorus of what is probably the best known of all b-w recordings, "Honky Tonk Train." Moreover, it is one of the simpler cross-rhythms in Lewis's performance. Even the rapid descending chords of Longhair's breaks are anticipated in the seventh chorus of Yancey's "Yancey's Stomp."

And there is another similarity between Longhair and b-w, this one something of an eccentricity. Writing about Cripple Clarence Lofton, Russell refers to his "peculiar phrase and period lengths." Consider a handful of Longhair's recordings and see how peculiar chorus structure can get. The first chorus of "Tell Me Pretty Baby" is ten and a half measures, because Longhair gives the second measure twelve beats and omits measures five and six of what proves to be a twelve-bar blues; the last chorus of his "Mardi Gras in New Orleans" is thirteen measures because he doubles the tenth-measure break. "Ball the Wall," from 1953, is a twelve-bar blues performance in which the first chorus is fourteen bars, the penultimate one ten, and the solo piano seventh is thirteen. This chorus merits some scrutiny: the first three measures are a quotation from "Organ Grinder Swing," with a stop-time accent on the downbeat; the fourth and fifth measures lead predictably into the subdominant; but the seventh, ninth, and eleventh measures are all repeats of the previous measures (six, eight, and ten)—one is surprised to realize that the chorus is *only* thirteen bars. "Ball the Wall" also showcases a Longhair specialty that is indisputably his: four fast triplets in the fourth measure, moving from the tonic through the third and fifth of the chord to the octave. He does this all the time, and the rhythmic effect is enchanting.

Boogie-woogie at its best requires fantastic digital control (during the height of the b-w fad, Jose Iturbi tried his hands at it with dim results), but it is basically an illiterate musician's music. I suspect that one reason it did not catch on among the New Orleans Creoles of Morton's day was the high standard of musical literacy—as Alan Lomax wrote, "Almost any Creole old-timer can recall his childhood musical instruction—given in the strictest style of the French Academy." By the late '30s, the standards in New Orleans had changed. The Creoles, who had played a major role in the development of jazz, were sup-

planted by blacks who then left the city; a successful New Orleans revival was spearheaded in 1939 with the rediscovery of
Bunk Johnson, but jazz in New Orleans had ceased to evolve.
It was Longhair's generation of blues-driven barrelhouse men
who revitalized the Afro-Cuban polyrhythms and drove them
home with a vitality that took on increasing significance during
the war, as jazz became too complicated to move the dancers.

Longhair's eminence in New Orleans stems from his prowess
as a pianist in an environment closer to the railway and mining
camps of the '20s, where function was inseparable from art,
than to the Café Society apex of boogie-woogie, where virtuosic
flair was its own reward. His style is rough but irresistible; the
power and constancy with which he plays those left-hand patterns suggest pistons instead of fingers, and his right hand
shows equal muscularity in working split-second tremolos. A
sashaying two-beat is always operating, regardless of meter, and
Longhair really makes his overtones echo and bleed. Yet it was
Fats Domino who sold a million copies of "The Fat Man" in
1949, and Domino who made the transition to rock and roll. I
don't think Longhair's relative obscurity can be explained entirely by his maidenly refusal to travel, nor am I entirely satisfied with the obvious explanation that Domino is a better singer.

In this regard, a comparison of Domino's 1952 cover of
Longhair's "Mardi Gras in New Orleans" with the 1949 original is revealing. Longhair plays an oddball ten-measure introduction with whistling, sings two vocal choruses (making the
tenth measure of every chorus a break), permits a sloppy instrumental passage in which the saxophonist plays in half-time
while the bassist goes into a brisk walk that he has to abandon
after a measure, sings another chorus, and concludes with two
whistling choruses. Domino's commercial savvy (or that of his
music director, Dave Bartholomew) is in evidence from the first
notes of his version—an exciting twelve-measure introduction
beginning with four solo piano measures and a heavy backbeat.
He follows with five choruses, whistling the first and last and

singing the three in the middle. The instrumental chorus is gone and the rhythmic support tidier. When Longhair recorded the song in 1975 (*Live on the Queen Mary*), he adopted Domino's introduction.

Of course, "Mardi Gras" wasn't much of a hit for Domino either—his real breakthrough came with a succession of blues that had hook melodies and releases, and pop songs. Domino is great because he could make the blues palatable to the masses with few compromises. He retained Longhair's walking bass, but finessed the cross-rhythms into uniform triplets, and though he can be as cavalier as Longhair about the distribution of beats, his results are invariably smoother. Longhair is of an older generation; he is a bluesman, and the blues have rarely captured the American public unless gussied up with hooks, gimmicks, and obvious dance rhythms. Even Huey Smith, who adapted Longhair's rhumba rhythm for "Barbara" and "Rockin' Pneumonia," achieved his brief success with novelty rockers.

What makes Longhair special is a rhythmic eccentricity and variety that aren't likely to endear him to the multitude but are bound to please anyone with an affection for the blues. In "Walk Your Blues Away," he uses the archetypal walking bass with a strong accent on the first, third, and fifth beats; "Hey Little Girl" has a stronger mambo rhythm, accenting the first and fourth beats and even omitting the third beat during the piano solo; "Willie May" (and its very fast instrumental counterpart, "Boogie Woogie") uses an eight-to-the-bar ostinato stretched over two 4/4 measures; the triplets and the heavy backbeat on "She Walks Right In" prefigure the recordings Ray Charles made for Atlantic in the mid-'50s. For that matter, Longhair's rhumba rhythms prefigure the Spanish tinge on several Atlantic hits by Ruth Brown, the Coasters, the Drifters, and others. Then there is the question of his singing, which for some reason is grossly underrated by many of his admirers. Its hollow middle-register plaintiveness, deviating into a croak on the bottom notes and cracking into falsetto in the uppers, is quite versatile. He gives Hank Snow's "I'm Moving On" a countrified gambol that is refreshingly original; even where his blues melisma is conventional, as on "Cry to Me," the spareness of his phrasing—the ability, exemplified by Domino, to achieve maximum individuality with minimum effort—is utterly convincing. And he phrases his vocals freely without altering the rock-bottom rhythms he plays on piano ("Hey Now Baby" is a good example).

At the Gate, Longhair's excellence as a bandleader was particularly apparent because his five accompanists preceded him with a forty-five-minute set of their own, divagating between Grover Washington's middlebrow funk and more successfully realized Coltrane swing. When Longhair sat down at the keyboard, all the parts came together. He opened with an instrumental blues in which the first four bars of every chorus were solo piano, and the last eight a horn riff beginning on the third beat of the measure. The set was perfectly coordinated with originals, standards, and boogie-woogie standbys—it seems that Longhair has spent forty years picking and choosing his ultimate patchwork. The spirit was infectious, and those one-measure piano breaks had the effect of Roman candles.

There aren't many Jimmy Yancey records, and since all but a couple of tracks are out of print, I assume nobody cares. I don't suppose many people care that there is a paucity of representative Longhair either, but something should be done about it just the same. Not because he fathered rock and roll, but because he is a blues musician with a small claim that is entirely his. The Professor has turned out to be the liveliest repository of the New Orleans tradition. However much he may have been a progenitor, he is undoubtedly of a dying breed.*

June 1979

* Professor Longhair died in New Orleans on January 30, 1980. He was sixty-one.

The Charlie Parker Reissue Parade

There were at least three Charlie Parkers: the structuralist, who ordered his solos with lucid purpose; the would-be midbrow, who pursued pop conventions with alternating respect and contempt; and the self-reveler, who jogged on razor blades for exercise. The structuralist generally confined himself to the studios, where he could perfect his statement or substitute one more daring. The generally high quality of the material Parker was willing to discard—the alternate takes—suggests how rarefied was the level at which he operated. Still, the master takes were not chosen arbitrarily, and a dilettantish approach to the collating of his recordings can lead to disaster, as witness Warner Bros.' entry into the Charlie Parker business.

The tasteful, gray album jacket modestly proclaims *The Very Best of Bird* in small, lower-case print, and, for once, the hyperbole might have been justified. Warners leased the sides Parker cut for Ross Russell's Dial Records in 1946–47; long unavailable on an American label, they *are* the very best of Bird (although not all of the very best), and one of the most celebrated series of recordings ever made. At the time it was compiled, Warners' involvement with Parker was not exclusively musical—the company was also preparing a film biography with

Richard Pryor, a project that was subsequently shelved. Yet the three "presenters" of this two-record reissue insist it was motivated entirely by love for Parker's music. The package, notwithstanding an enclosed booklet with reproductions of six paintings inspired by said music, does not testify to that love.

As a bandleader, Parker recorded for three labels: Savoy (1945–48), Dial (1946–47), and Verve (1946–54). The six Dial sessions form a particularly rewarding sequence, tracing his progress from a tragic stay in Los Angeles to a triumphant, relatively healthy reaffirmation in New York. Here are his scintillating ballads ("Embraceable You," "Bird of Paradise"), stunningly reasonable pyrotechnics ("Night in Tunisia," "Crazeology"), elegant blues ("Relaxin' at Camarillo," "Cool Blues"), expressions of an utterly relaxed yet imperious command of form and content ("Ornithology," "Yardbird Suite"), and surprises such as the nearly cubistic design of "Klact-oveeseds-tene" or the heart-rending lyricism in "Lover Man." The Dials were more varied than the Savoys in choice of material and instrumentation. Among the guest soloists were Lucky Thompson and Wardell Gray (representing, respectively, the lineages of Coleman Hawkins and Lester Young), and Erroll Garner and J. J. Johnson.

Dial recorded thirty-three titles in all, not counting the numerous alternate takes issued under different names, and the Warners set could have accommodated the master takes the way Bob Porter anthologized the Savoys for Arista, and Bob Hurwitz the Verves for Polydor. Instead, only twenty-six selections, plus the alternate "Night in Tunisia" solo known as "Famous Alto Break," are included. Of the missing titles, "The Gypsy," "This Is Always," and "Dark Shadows" are understandably absent, but not "Crazeology," "Lover Man," "Bongo Beep," and "Quasimodo." Far more serious than these omissions, however, is a general ineptness in choosing performances. No fewer than seven titles, among them some of Parker's most admired recordings, are represented by inferior alternate takes. The album jacket doesn't tell you this, for the probable reason that the presenters—Bob Krasnow, Stewart Levine, and Raymond Lofaro—don't know it. Here are the botched items followed by the take used and, in parentheses, the master take: "Out of Nowhere" take B (A); "Moose the Mooche" take 1 (2); "Ornithology" take 3 (4); "Stupendous" take B (A); "Bongo Bop" take B (A); "Klact-oveeseds-tene" take B (A); "Scrapple from the Apple" take B (C).

In order to find out which cuts were the master takes, the three jazz lovers might have spent ten minutes consulting a discography or a few hours listening to the records, or they might have called Ross Russell, who produced the sessions and wrote liner notes for this reissue. Evidence that Russell himself did not listen to the Warners' pressings can be found in the notes, where he is describing his favorite Parker recording, "Klact-oveeseds-tene": "It's a hair-raising trip. There is a weird unison theme supported by urgent polyrhythmic percussive figures. The saxophone enters—a mad machine gunner spraying short bursts of notes at random and in all directions, a series of fragments of sound." A vivid description, but not of the more orthodox performance that wound up in this collection. And why use the discarded take of "Moose," a pale reflection of the finished work, with its chaotic intro and busy piano, or of "Scrapple," when the original was distinguished by an eloquent tempo and one of Duke Jordan's loveliest introductions?

Parker is one of the few improvisers whose alternate takes we do want to hear, for they show us how he developed a solo and how extensive was his improvising. In a few cases, the alternates are as rewarding as the masters—I prefer, for example, the faster second take of "Cool Blues." But some of the choices here are inexcusable. "Ornithology" is a revealing example of the manner in which Parker resolved the tensions between Tin Pan Alley phrasing and that of modern jazz. The theme was crafted by Little Benny Harris from a lick Parker played on Jay McShann's "The Jumping Blues," so, in effect it is a blues phrase extended into pop-song form (using the chords of "How High the Moon") against which Parker welds new blues phrases of surpassing lyricism. Listening to it in tandem with the alternate take (also known as "Bird Lore"), one is amazed that the earlier version, with its swing triplets, sour intonation, and discursive structure, could have been so ingeniously refined into the finished masterpiece. *The Very Best of Bird* gives us only the warm-up.

According to a liner comment, "This compilation has been edited from the six-album limited edition on Warner Bros. Records." Actually, Warners bought the rights to the excellent six-volume *Charlie Parker on Dial* series issued by English Spotlite in the early '70s. Warners didn't even bother to edit for minor corrections—they simply repackaged them in a cloth-covered box, for which the paintings mentioned above were commissioned, in a limited edition of 4000 copies worldwide (1200 were slated for the U.S.). In other words, thanks to Krasnow and company, the whole of Parker's music is once again generally unavailable: the handsomely produced box was never distributed to retail stores. It's a corporate prestige symbol.

Having said all that, I should note again that the two-record set is the only collection of Parker Dials in general circulation. If you can't find the imported Spotlites, you'll want it for what it does offer. Only one cut is without value—"Max Making Wax," recorded at the ' Lover Man" session at which Parker suffered a breakdown. I've been listening to some of these sides for as long as I've been listening to jazz, and I can never hear them without marveling anew at Parker's equanimity, imagination, and depth of emotional resource. There are other joys as well: drummer Max Roach's aggressively bristling accompaniment, and the famed introductions by pianists Duke Jordan and Dodo Marmorosa. Miles Davis was in his stodgy, apprentice period, but he played quite well on the March 28, 1946, session, as did Lucky Thompson. Wardell Gray's conception wasn't entirely formed by early 1947, and he played his best solos on different performances from Parker (for example, he's more commanding on an earlier take of "Camarillo").

I'll discuss one performance at length because of an interesting discovery I made the other day. "Embraceable You" has a single chorus by Parker that is supremely beautiful and wondrously played. Like "Bird of Paradise" (which is based on "All the Things You Are"), it hardly touches base with the song that ostensibly inspired it, and Parker might well have given it his own title. We know from an earlier recording called "Meandering" and several subsequent versions of "Embraceable You" that Parker was especially comfortable with this chord progression, but the other performances have nothing to match the six-note motif—neither paraphrase nor counterpoint—with which he develops the Dial solo. He states it almost offhandedly the first time, repeats it four times, intensifying and extending it so that the improvisation seems motivated exclusively by melodic, temporal, and emotional considerations, as though the harmonic bounds were incidental. It is one of the slowest performances in jazz (less than $J = 65$), yet it is laced with thirty-second notes. As a result, when he develops the six-note motif into a two-measure phrase (measures six and seven), imposing a triplet over an already lightning-fast melody, he runs out of breath. But never again. For the rest of the solo, his phrasing is so authoritative and relaxed and singing that when he winds down with a legato two-measure configuration (measures 27 and 28), only the listener is left breathless.

The accepted wisdom about this solo is that Parker invented that opening motif, but he probably didn't. The third volume of Bluebird's *The Complete Artie Shaw* includes the song that was most likely Parker's source. It's called "A Table in the Corner," by Sam Coslow, who is better known for "My Old Flame" and "Cocktails for Two." In Shaw's 1939 recording, the song is an undistinguished vehicle for Helen Forrest. It was also recorded by Jimmy Dorsey, Jack Teagarden, and Larry Clinton around the same time, but has languished in justified obscurity ever since. Parker adapted the opening phrase and the first modulation. Obviously, this in no way detracts from the originality of Parker's solo; quite the contrary. In addition to providing further evidence of his syncretic memory and insight into the workings of his mind, it shows how the trite, forgotten ditty of one songwriter and the durable harmonic pattern of another could be transformed by Parker's genius into a work of narcotizing power and transcendent mood.

As noted, the problems that beset the Dials were avoided in the Savoy and Verve reissues. Parker completists can obtain *The Complete Savoy Studio Session* in a five-record box, or a two-volume anthology of the master takes (*Bird/the Savoy Recordings*), with the alternates forthcoming on supplementary albums. Parker always used a quintet format on Savoy, and more than half the material was based on the blues or "I Got Rhythm"; with few exceptions—the eight-bar arabesques on "Koko," the contrapuntal themes on "Chasin' the Bird" and "Ah-Leu-Cha"—the structural designs were unchanging. And yet there is little repetition, no lassitude, nothing predictable. Like all great improvisations, Parker's flights unfold with an internal, storytelling logic, removed from the specific exigencies of chord changes. The distinct qualities of "Constellation," "Chasin' the Bird," and "Ah-Leu-Cha" transcend the sameness of their harmonies. And there is no greater or more varied series of blues recordings than "Parker's Mood," "Now's the Time," "Blue Bird," "Perhaps," "Cheryl," and the cheerful "Barbados." The galloping extravaganzas—"Koko," "Klaunstance," and "Bird Gets the Worm"—remain unequaled as examples of emotionally vital, virtuosic inventions that take their structure but not their character from the harmonic contours of pop songs.

The May 1947 session is interesting for the turnabout suggested in the playing of Parker and Miles Davis, whose session it was. Davis's compositions have none of the straightforward attack of Parker's lines, and for once, the trumpeter, whose burry eighth notes so frequently dispelled the magic of Parker's slicing offensives, is self-assured and commanding, while Parker, encumbered with a tenor sax, is relatively uneasy and workmanlike.

For its first collection of alternates, Savoy has come up with the disingenuous euphemism *Encores*. In most instances, it is obvious why these takes were rejected. Yet if some are simply inferior ("Donna Lee," "Chasin' the Bird"), others compensate with clues to Parker's working habits. The first take of "Thriving on a Riff" (also known as "Anthropology") begins with the head, has no piano solo, and finds Parker using quotation instead of the slash and sweep of the master take. On "Buzzy," he begins his second chorus with the slurs he would subsequently use to kick off the master take. The alternate solo on "Half Nelson" is not played nearly as well as the original, but it contains riskier ideas. The session led by Miles Davis is more interesting for Davis's originals than for the solos—"Sippin' at Bells," in which the contours of the blues are turned inside out, probably marks the real birth of the cool. But Parker's eight bars on "Milestones" show that his idolization of Lester Young did not arrest his appreciation of Coleman Hawkins, and his "Little Willie Leaps" chorus is better organized, if ultimately less successful, than the original. On "Bluebird," (a bluesman's blues, as compared with the ingeniously effete "Sippin' "), Parker's solo is as intriguing as, if less emotive than, the one on the master; the first chorus is engineered on a motif, while the second begins with a phrase reminiscent of Benny Carter.

Within two years of the Savoys, Parker was recording for Norman Granz and fulfilling his own desire to work with a string section. Unlike Dizzy Gillespie, who saw strings as a way of introducing advanced musical elements from Europe into his work, Parker, like Armstrong before him, embraced their all-American banality. They provided plenty of contrast, but not enough tension, and the results are mostly tepid. There were exceptions, most notably Parker's flawlessly exciting performance on "Just Friends," included on *The Verve Years 1948–50*, along with such small-band gems as "Passport," "Bloomdido," "Melancholy Baby," and "The Bird." The only alternate take included is "Leap Frog," from Parker's reunion with Gillespie and Thelonious Monk, and the two versions are dramatically different. Another interesting Parker-with-strings piece is "Easy to Love," with a Jimmy Mundy arrangement that Parker often performed in concert. When he double-times his way off a launching pad of hack cellists, he is a match igniting. Compare it with the more characteristic Joe Lippman arrangement of the same song, where Parker is somnambulant. Both versions, as well as "Au Privave" and "She Rote" (with Davis again), a sprightly session with a Latin rhythm section, and a generally excellent quintet date with Red Rodney, are on *The Verve Years 1950–51*. The final volume of Verve masters, *The Verve Years 1952–54*, is made up mostly of tiresome strings collaborations, a vocal choir arranged by Gil Evans to no great avail, wooden readings of Cole Porter songs, and another Latin session; it also contains three of Parker's classics—"Confirmation" (perhaps his finest composition), "Now's the Time" (a penetrating update), and an electrifying sprint called "Kim." But what of the alternates, Verve?

The self-reveling Parker is brought searingly back to life on a newly discovered private tape made in Chicago in 1950. *Charlie Parker at the Pershing Ballroom*, on Zim, unveils the visionary Bird, the Bird maligned·for inflicting jazz with chaos and bad tone. Parker was one of the first to recognize that jazz timbre would have to be reconsidered, just as he was prescient in feeling the pinch of harmonic shackles. It took Ornette Coleman to make the radical break by forging a pitch that sounded like a scale of quarter-tones, but Parker anticipated Coleman, and his frustrations are chillingly felt in his first five choruses of "Anthropology," "Hot House," and especially his second solo on "Get Happy," where the exhilaration is sustained through the hypnotic balance of long and short, fluid and stuttering phrases. The details, the smatterings of violence, and the explosive releases are admirable, but they are subsumed in the total effect as intellect and unrestrained passion boldly enhance each other. This is true also of the granite-faced ballad performances, "I Can't Get Started" and "Out of Nowhere." Sadly, the solos by Parker's pick-up band, allegedly consisting of the three Freeman brothers, were not recorded, though a dreadful Billy Eckstine imitator was. But Parker is all you want here—he is a beautiful and terrible Daedalus, flying straight for the sun's eye.

1976–78

There's No One Like Sonny Rollins

Sonny Rollins's long-time admirers have come to feel possessive about him. When in 1974 he released *Horn Culture,* a seeming capitulation to commercial interests, the critical fraternity tugged fretfully at his cuff like the schoolboy who pleaded with Shoeless Joe Jackson after the fixed World Series of 1919 to say it wasn't so. Rollins meant to reassure when we spoke one wintry afternoon, huddling against the cold on the floor of the music shed on his nine-acre estate in Germantown, New York: "You have to be a Sonny Rollins believer," he said, "and I won't let you down. People may view what I'm doing as a temporary change, but I don't think it's a significant one. I'm not thinking about anything except reaching a point in my music where I can be happy with what I'm doing."

So far as changes go, Rollins's new departure wasn't particularly radical, for if he succumbed to the backbeat and coloration of rock, he sealed off no doors to the past. Unlike Miles Davis, who veered precipitously from his past to steer down one binding musical avenue, Rollins kept all his options open. "The music I'm trying to create is beyond the idiom," he continued. "I like to hear people say, 'Man, you didn't do what you were doing Monday,' or 'Man, I never heard you play like that before.' Asking me if I'm happy with a new record is like asking me if I'm happy with the way I played last night. One day it will be different and you can look back in retrospect. Asking me to look back now is hard. Remember what Satchel Paige said."

Rollins has never stood still long enough for anything to gain on him, and his sound, which took on a husky, scratchy quality in the '70s, commensurate with his electrified rhythm section, has changed almost as many times as his record-label affiliations. He is the youngest and one of the last of the seminal jazz tenor saxophonists. There are presumably several gifted tenorists in formative stages, but none can presently demand time at Rollins's podium. He started on alto after hearing Louis Jordan and the Tympani Five at an Elks Club on 134th Street, then encountered the patriarch of the tenor, Coleman Hawkins, and learned "how to be a proud man playing a big horn." Bud Powell, whom Rollins considers the ultimate musician, was a neighborhood influence, as was Thelonious Monk: "I was trying to finish high school at the same time as rehearsing and playing all night—whenever I was *able* to play. Thelonious had a young band and he gave me a chance. Monk was a magician. The musicians would look at his music and say, 'Oh no, this is impossible, how can I make that jump from here to there, it can't be done, hey man, what is this?' And by the time we'd leave that night, everyone would be playing it and it would be beautiful.

"I wasn't like the guy who started out, played for years and years, found a style, and then somebody heard him and got him a record date and everybody liked him. That's not my story. My story is that from the time I was a teenager, I was on records with great musicians. I've put a lot of things on records as I've progressed, but I'm not looking for any kind of satisfaction from my past records. I'm trying to get at it now, tomorrow night, the next record, the concert at Carnegie. I'm interested in my music lasting while I'm alive. I'm not writing for the future."

In 1955, Rollins recorded a stirring album called *Worktime,* with two extraordinary performances—"There's No Business Like Show Business" and "There Are Such Things"—that took jazz a step beyond the shadow of Charlie Parker, demonstrating an unprecedented ability to sustain lengthy improvisations with authority, coherence, and wit. In jazz, twenty-five is a tender age for that degree of maturity to assert itself. A year later, when he recorded "Blue Seven," "Ezzthetic," and several other remarkable solo inventions, he was proclaimed the master of thematic improvisation in a boldly perceptive essay by Gunther Schuller. Yet by the decade's end, when Ornette Coleman, Cecil Taylor, and John Coltrane were spearheading new directions for jazz, Rollins took his second of three sabbaticals, leaving the music scene for two years of study and contemplation.

Since returning from his last sabbatical, in 1972, Rollins has been searching obsessively for the proper context. His is the dilemma of needing to be modern without abrogating past accomplishments. He's experimented with modes, free jazz, unaccompanied tenor solos, soprano sax, lyricon, overdubbing, electric accoutrements, shuffle rhythms, blowing into an unattached mouthpiece, a rainbow of tones, and a diversity of song structures. The long-time admirers wonder why an instrumentalist of such power and fecundity should beggar after unproved trends when all he needs is a rhythm section and the stock repertoire. But an improvisor has to stretch his limits all the time if he isn't going to buy a nightly rut of requested favorites. And whatever the results, Rollins's enjoyment of funky saxophone is genuine—thirty-five years ago he was mesmerized by Louis Jordan, and today he's rediscovering Jr. Walker. The dybbuk that pushes him to the edge won't let him look back in complacent satisfaction. "Don't ever shrink from the belief that you have to prove yourself every minute, because you do, and probably it's a healthy thing," he said. "When you sound good, it gives you the encouragement to go on, that's what it's all about. Everytime you get there, you're encouraged to go farther. That's one of the natural things you can only get from yourself."

As the '70s took shape, however, there appeared to be not one Sonny Rollins but two. The dynamic pathfinder of the concerts and nightclubs justified all the talk of pushing beyond the past, the edge, the self, the idiom, and left audiences palsied with pleasure and awe. A stony doppelganger deposited strangely timorous echoes of the real thing in a series of unfailingly disappointing (though often interesting) records. You don't have to follow live jazz for very long to know that records are misleading, though subsequent generations tend to interpret them as the final truth for purposes of evaluation. Rollins believers who knew only the records were particularly hard-put to keep the faith and assumed a creative decline. *The Cutting Edge* (1974) found him raging against a cluttered rhythm section in a live performance compromised by one in a string of flashy guest stars (Rufus Harley) and undistinguished material; the album's salvation was a lovely reading of Edward MacDowell's "To a Wild Rose" that sounds better every year—as time vitiates the memory of versions that were far superior but unrecorded.

Nucleus (1975), despite its pop façade, was more intriguing. It displayed several approaches to pitch, and five Rollins originals that altered the usual blues and 32-measure-AABA forms. "Lucille" is an eight-bar fragment; "Are You Ready" is AABA, but forty measures long; "Azalea," a more conservative piece with a conspicuously avant tenor chorus, has a twelve-bar release. Even the sole ballad, the Debussy-derived "My Reverie," is thirty-six bars. The rhythm section is seven members strong, and on several selections the simple riffs and stagnating rhythms straitjacket the saxophonist. The discomfort of his solo on "Gwaligo" or "Are You Ready?" suggests that he knows damn well he's too big for this simplistic stuff, but can't transcend it.

Only the thematically conceived improvisation on "Cosmet" and the slightly less well-ordered "Azalea" really work. "My Reverie" compares interestingly with his 1956 version—it is achingly slow. In '56, he played two and half choruses with lush vibrato and amiable swing; it was an unspectacular but inventive, dignified performance. Twenty years later, he divided each of three choruses in two, alternating his own episodes with the other soloists. He sang the melody with conviction, but failed to build on it, settling merely for a gruff sweetness.

The Way I Feel (1976) was a desperate attempt to enter the soulsax sweepstakes, and Rollins couldn't even disguise his own boredom. By contrast, *Easy Living* (1977) was an album with many splendid moments, though taken as a whole it seemed rather begrudging when compared with the prolific concerts he gave that year. The jubilation is captured, but the solos sound more jolted than drawn. "Isn't She Lovely" was nearly a hit for him, thanks to contagious repetitions, a clever George Duke introduction, an ascending riff on the tail of every chorus, Tony Williams's lucid backbeat, and Rollins's lustrous tone. "Easy Living" is one of his strangest ballad performances on record— gritty, perverse, gut wrenching, and thoroughly antithetical to the qualities usually associated with the song. A minute-long duet by Rollins and Tony Williams on "Down the Line" made you wish they would go on much longer, just as you wished Rollins and his label, Milestone, would better document the exhilaration unleashed at his concerts.

Exhilaration promised to be the very point of *Don't Stop the Carnival* (1978), the most graphically disappointing Rollins album because the highs and lows are so extreme. The juxtaposition of a magnificent "Autumn Nocturne" and a soporific "Camel" proved that he had never played better, or worse. He corraled two guests for this double-disc live recording—drummer Tony Williams, who played well except for an obtrusive busyness on the title selection, and trumpeter Donald Byrd, whose meek sound and concept demonstrated the wisdom of

Katherine Anne Porter's caveat: "If you misuse your talent, it will leave you." Still, two masterpieces—"Autumn Nocturne" and "Silver City"—were cause for celebration. The former exemplified the new Rollins in its lucid excitement, elaborate wit, discursive logic (no thematic improvisation here), and willful sense of fun. For the first time since the 1972 *Next Album,* his maniacal creativity, multiple pitch variations, and breathtaking tempo-play were captured on an American record. The unaccompanied segment tempered the theme with references to "To a Wild Rose," "Home Sweet Home," and other ditties, and when he swaggered out of rubato and the rhythm section came in you couldn't help cheering. The delirious multiphonics of "Silver City" showed that Rollins was still the foremost virtuoso on his instrument.

For most of 1978, Rollins toured with an all-star package (McCoy Tyner, Ron Carter, and the unbilled Al Foster), a situation that distracted him from the good band he'd just formed. By the time the Milestone Jazzstars reached the end of the tour, the three leaders achieved a fascinating peaceful coexistence, but the album, *In Concert,* was recorded early and was marred by an indifferent sound mix and relatively uninspired performances. Rollins was delighted to return to his own group, and his every euphoric appearance reestablished him as the most commanding of improvisers and a showman of almost irresistible demeanor.

Nearing the half-century mark, Rollins finally blossomed into an entertainer in the best sense of the word. This was not entirely unexpected: his flair for performing rites—whether manifested in a Mohawk haircut or a wending-through-the-audience ritual—and his personal magnetism, crazily enhanced by foghorn voice and mooncalf facial expressions, have long constituted a distinctive stage presence. But it was eccentric and distant, like Thelonious Monk dancing in circles or Miles Davis preening morosely. Now he offered a new kind of relationship with his audience, springing directly from the generous impulses of his music and furthered by intelligible announcements and thank-yous (idiosyncratic enough to maintain distance, genuine enough to promote friendship), costume (T-shirt, suspenders, and floppy hat), and physical manipulation of the saxophone (waved vertically like an axe, swayed horizontally like a dancing partner, held aloft like a trumpet). His stage manner was the perfect correlative to his music, a choreography of musical authority. Audiences responded enthusiastically not only to petition encores but to reward each of his most ecstatic solos. An engagement at New York's Bottom Line was typical.

The creative level was so constant that the individual pieces were all but subordinated by an overriding songfulness and energy. He opened with a two-bar cadenza, interrupted himself to introduce the musicians, and then dove right back into the furnace. He was in a playing mood, also a thoughtful mood, a composer's mood. He improvised formal designs beyond the ones he'd rehearsed, and his every decision—whether to play a cadenza, change instruments, accompany another soloist, trade fours, interpolate quotations, whatever—was riveting for its unpremeditated intentionality. Rollins actually listens to the musicians he hires for his bands, and this makes spur-of-the-moment dialectics, puns, and fluent transitions an ongoing reality. The pieces weren't merely played, they were shaped.

Two performances of "In a Sentimental Mood" produced two points of view. One was introduced with a Garneresque chorus by pianist Mark Soskin and concluded with a straight reading of the theme by Rollins on lyricon (he made it sound like a shofar—strange that this bastard of technology should enable him to get down to the pastoral). The other performance opened with a sax cadenza that rolled and twisted into the theme, where his incredibly knotty phrasing picked the chords clean and packed each measure with a rush hour's quota of notes. After the piano solo, he picked up the lyricon, but this time he put it aside after sixteen bars, bounded back with his

tenor in the middle of the release, and promenaded another cadenza in which low-flying honks accelerated into childlike nineteenth-century references, achieving a final transformation as
Chopin's Funeral March.

Rollins consistently toyed with quotations. Some were random felicities, as when his "Easy Living" cadenza passed through
a forest of his own compositions, standards, military anthems,
and parlor songs. There was an acerbic reference to "Dixie"
during "Harlem Boys." Yet the most interesting use of quotations went beyond humor and acerbity to extend the development of an idea. During "And Then My Love I Found You,"
he quoted the primary phrase of "Moten's Swing" and then repeated it with just enough changes in rhythmic definition and
melody to make it work not as a passing riff but as an integral
motivic phrase that furthered the narrative structure of the
solo. The melodious theme was newly composed and a good
candidate for lyrics. The new piece I liked best, though, was a
calypso ("Little Lu") that managed alternately to suggest the
Mexican Hat Dance and "Inamorata," and catapulted Rollins
and Al Foster into orbits just short of hallucination.

His structural sixth sense was nowhere more apparent than
on two blues. He began "Strode Rode" with the last four measures of the theme, extending them in a fiery, freely lyrical cadenza. Only when the rhythm section entered did he play the
staccato notes that start the piece; the four-bar tag phrase
served as an *idée fixe* throughout the following solo. On the
minor blues "Keep Hold of Yourself," which he dedicated to
Coltrane, he taunted his accompanists into solos with provocative nudging phrases, and made all his re-entrances on the last
two measures of the chorus—a ploy evoking memories of Louis
Armstrong's "Hotter Than That."

I thought of Armstrong several times during the Rollins concerts of recent years, chiefly, I suppose, because for me no other
living musician operates on Armstrong's pinnacle. More specifically, I'm reminded of the flamboyant virtuoso Armstrong

became in the '30s, when he seemed to settle comfortably into the tunes and rhythms of the swing era and yet transformed them with the sheer stubborn might of his incomparable sound and a nearly arrogant economy. Armstrong turned transient melodies into steely artifices as timeless and calculated as the playthings in Yeats's Byzantium. Rollins visits those heights, and like Armstrong, lessens the terror inherent in such unrelieved glory with an utter naturalness of expression; he gives the illusion of playing what he's hearing. His music is human and stylish and warm and intense and lucid and funny and fecund and, finally, ecstatic and deeply moving. It has often been charged that Rollins failed to inaugurate a new direction for jazz, as though this were the ultimate measure of achievement in the idiom; yet the impact of his music has permeated the work of countless musicians, and not just saxophonists, from the neo-boppers to the avant-gardists. His followers do not swim in a single school, they are everywhere. At a time when jazz was conspicuously leaderless, the most significant contribution he could make was a set of standards for creativity, discipline, and seriousness. In concert, he did that, emerging as a champion when there was a dearth of champions.

But why were there no Rollins records, or only parts of records ("Autumn Nocturne" and "Silver City"), to hold up beside his concert performances? The album with which he closed the decade, *Don't Ask,* had episodes to recommend it but little more. It had nothing remotely as captivating as his live renditions of "In a Sentimental Mood" or "Easy Living," or of "Harlem Boys" and "Don't Ask." These last two are on the album (Milestone even edited a four-minute take of "Harlem Boys" for airplay), but they sound like warm-ups. At the Bottom Line, he played "Harlem Boys" impetuously, working through a riff section to a final statement that stopped on a dime. The recorded version is stodgy and ends, as does "Disco Monk," with an unconvincing fadeout. Rollins's balladic solo

on "Disco Monk" is okay, and so are his performances of the
title piece and "And Then My Love," though they are rather
perfunctory: of the six choruses he plays on the latter, only two
depart from the theme with any real determination. There is
a gem, however, in "My Ideal," a neglected ballad once associated with Coleman Hawkins. Rollins plays it as a duet with
guitarist Larry Coryell, yet another guest whose work recalls the
taunt of a tutor to one of King Arthur's knights: "It was well
enough done, but it reeked of technique."

The crazy thing is that every type of jazz demographics suggests that Rollins would sell more records to a coalition of
long-time admirers and devoted younger followers than to the
dilettantes to whom his compromised albums presumably pan-
der. The Soskin–Foster–Jerome Harris rhythm section he put
together in 1979 was his best band since the mid-'60s. There
were no guitars or cluttering percussion, and the lean, driving
swing of his cohorts charged Rollins's music. The jazz audience, not consisting entirely of fools, knows the difference between the real Rollins and the doppelganger. It knows he
doesn't need a "special guest" to share the burden. And Rollins cannot be unmindful of the response he generates, that sincere and knowing and awe-stricken love. I hope he gets his hit;
if that will relieve him and his producer, Orrin Keepnews, of
the pressure to make every album something a little fancier and
a lot less meaningful than what he radiates so effortlessly in
concert.

No one can say what the future will hold for Sonny Rollins,
except that there will be surprises, new syntheses, and an abun-
dance of remarkable music. There's no one else like him. He is
a far more honest and communicative saxophonist than ever
before, and the unpredictability his odyssey affords the music
lover is perhaps unique at this stage in jazz history. Notwithstanding all those masterpieces from the '50s and '60s, there is
still every reason to believe that his best work lies in the future.

"I have no other interests," he says, and one can only wonder if there are any limitations for a man so committed, so resourceful. At fifty, Rollins should have the world at his feet, and if the live Rollins and the recorded Rollins come together again, he might.

1976–80

Float Like Jelly Roll
Sting Like the Blues

In July 1975, David Murray organized a loft concert that introduced a new generation of Californian musicians to New York—Arthur Blythe, Stanley Crouch, Ray Anderson, and Mark Dresser were present, while James Newton, Butch Morris, and Bobby Bradford were represented through their compositions. "These are some of the players who will keep the music honest," I wrote at the time, and the intervening years have found most of them unleashing caustic, probing alternatives to the compromises of fusion. Blythe, at thirty-five, was the oldest of the performers, the one with the most immediate ties to the orthodoxies of swing and blues. In contrast to Murray, who tempered the rich timbral language of Albert Ayler with his own pensive concerns, Blythe was meticulous with his tone and with every note and phrase. The fat sobriety of his sound seemed less beholden to his forebears in the new music than to the pithy sixteen-bar storytellers of a much earlier day.

As we got to know Blythe's music better, its exactitude of expression proved as refreshing as his technical command of the alto saxophone. This was true of both the intonational and structural aspects of his improvisations, and the detail with which he organized a composition or an entire concert. At one performance, he played two half-hour sets with Olu Dara in which thematic variations were pellucidly linked to brisk, catchy, and original riffs; at another, he introduced the unusual, clean instrumentation of alto, tuba, and conga; at others, he employed the fragmented chording of guitarist James Blood Ulmer or a fiery, bop-oriented rhythm section that he called In the Tradition. He was also becoming a familiar sideman with, among others, Chico Hamilton, Gil Evans, and more recently, Lester Bowie and Jack DeJohnette. Here was an artist able to subordinate his considerable technique to the problems of musical organization; a saxophonist who, despite the presence of recognizable influences, had his own sound and style; a man in his late thirties who was all but unknown to the jazz-going public. The swooning of some writers in New York is more easily understood than the total neglect he experienced in his native state. For me, he is one of the four or five most stimulating jazz musicians to come to the jazz fore in the past decade.

His work has now been documented on three representative albums—*The Grip* (India Navigation) and *Bush Baby* (Adelphi), both recorded in 1977, and *Lenox Avenue Breakdown* (Columbia), recorded in 1978. The fact that the Columbia disc represents that label's most adventuresome jazz signing since Ornette Coleman was dispatched in 1972, and will doubtless garner more attention than the other two combined, lends it particular interest. If Columbia can tap Blythe's potential audience, the album could be the wedge with which other loft veterans break through to larger audiences. But it would be cruel irony if Blythe were undermined by his own label's unchecked enthusiasm. A Columbia ad appearing in *Down Beat* referred to him as "perhaps the most innovative musician ever to put alto sax to his lips." With support like that, Blythe won't need detractors.

Each album is skillfully made and significantly different from the others; textures range from unaccompanied alto on "My

Son Ra" to the sumptuously arranged septet piece "Odessa." The music is generally accessible, as far as these jaded ears can tell—surely the themes, variations, and arrangements are rigorously defined, and if the rhythms aren't always as forcibly stated as on *Lenox Avenue Breakdown,* they are relatively straightforward. Blythe is a modernist, of course. His preference for dissonance is deepseated, and the unmistakable influence of John Coltrane hovers over his improvisations. Yet the historical figures I'm most reminded of are Benny Carter (in Blythe's soloing) and Jelly Roll Morton (in his composing). I wasn't surprised to learn that Blythe had never encountered Carter's music in California, since distinctive tones aren't inherited, but are largely a matter of personality and environment. Blythe's apprenticeship in rhythm-and-blues bands with electric guitars helps explain the largeness and volume of his sound, but his rectitude and sly elegance, both of which suggest Carter, are more likely a reflection of character. If influences could be neatly charted, an obvious case could be made for Cannonball Adderley as a link between the two; but it isn't stylistic continuity I mean to suggest as much as an affinity of temperament. For whatever reason, plum tones are back. Similarly, Blythe shares with Jelly Roll Morton a near-puritanical rigor in structuring his music, a flair for contrasts in melody, texture, and tempo, ornateness and a penchant for march rhythms, and especially a floating buoyancy in his ensembles. Again, it's not a question of direct influence but of grasping dormant elements in a tradition and bringing them back to life.

Little has been written about Blythe, and in an attempt to find out how he got to where he is, I asked him and Stanley Crouch about the years in California. Arthur was born in Los Angeles in 1940, and raised in San Diego in a house filled with the sounds of recorded music. His mother favored the blues and particularly the flamboyant-sounding alto saxophonists Johnny Hodges, Tab Smith, and Earl Bostic. Blythe was equally enchanted with trombone glissandos. He started playing at

nine, and at fifteen was working in a rhythm-and-blues band
formed in imitation of Bill Haley. He thought of rhythm and
blues as black music, and jazz as white—the reason being simply
that the jazz musicians touted by the local media (like Bob
Cooper and Paul Desmond) were white. It was the experience
of hearing Thelonious Monk that turned him around, and soon
afterward he discovered Adderley and Coltrane. He began
studying in earnest with a tenor saxophonist named Daniel
Jackson and with Jimmie Lunceford's lead altoist of the mid-
'40s, Kirtland Bradford, who advised him, "Don't study a particular style, your style will develop from everything you hear."
After moving to L.A. in the late '50s, he spent several years practicing, then finally hooked up with Horace Tapscott's Underground Musicians Artists Association (UGMAA) in 1963. He
was associated with Tapscott's orchestra for the next ten years,
and made his recording debut on Tapscott's *The Giant Is
Awakening.*

It was during the early years with Tapscott that Blythe
earned his nickname, Black Arthur, and first encountered
Crouch. Blythe had read an essay on Scott Joplin and James
Reese Europe that filled him with pride about the achievement
of black musicians, and was excitedly filibustering on the subject one night. A colleague laughed, "You're so black you can't
help yourself, so we better start calling you Black Arthur." The
sobriquet stuck, with what for Arthur was a disheartening result—whites interpreted it not as an indication of pride but of
fearsome militancy. This was the mid-'60s, and both he and
Crouch insist that any emphasis on blackness was a sure way
of losing work. When I told him he was alphabetized in Feather
and Gitler's *Encyclopedia of Jazz in the Seventies* under "black,"
he laughed in disbelief. He met Crouch in 1966, while playing
a concert with Tapscott opposite a quartet made up of Crouch
on drums, Walter Lowe on trumpet, Erroll Henderson on bass,
and Raymond King on piano. Blythe subsequently became a
member of the group, which was a cooperative led by whoever

hustled the gig. It was for this band that he wrote "Bitter Suite," which combined a fast section employing the highest register with a ballad that resembled "Autumn in New York." After they played a concert opposite the Bobby Bradford–John Carter quartet, Bradford joined them; by the early '70s, David Murray and Mark Dresser were regulars.

According to Crouch, Blythe's style was already mature by 1966, and his technique widely acclaimed by other musicians. Coltrane was the musician Blythe found most absorbing, though he was also fascinated by the structural concepts of the avant-gardists recording on ESP-Disc; Crouch suggests that his inclination toward riff figures was partly inspired by the rhythmic patterns McCoy Tyner and Jimmy Garrison created in the Coltrane quartet. To Arthur, Coltrane was the "spiritual leader" who brought "cleanliness, respect, and pride back to the music after a period of degradation with heroin." He says of Coltrane, "We were vulnerable to him," but he was also listening to Adderley, Hodges, and Parker, if not as closely: "They set the language up. I don't omit certain traditional nuances from my playing, but I have to play them in my own way." Most of the music his band played was free, stylistically and economically— "We were the rebels," he says, and there was little work outside of colleges, and no press. He resigned himself to working harder on the saxophone—practicing circular breathing by blowing on a candle flame, and investigating multiphonics. And he began working with younger players, including Azar Lawrence. In 1968, he visited New York, but was so intimidated he hotfooted it back to L.A., where he stayed until 1974, when Azar asked him to play on his first album, *Bridge into the New Age*. Then it was back to New York and a $150-a-week job as security man for a Broadway porno parlor to raise the money to bring his wife and three kids east. He played around town with Charles Tyler, Ted Daniels, and others, but it was Chico Hamilton who enabled him to give up day jobs. The gig with Hamilton lasted three years and produced three unsatisfactory records—Blythe says the first session was best, but that it was destroyed by overdubs and the excision of solos. At a Sunday afternoon concert at the Tin Palace, Gil Evans heard him play and offered him several tours with his big band; his solo on Evans's arrangement of Charlie Parker's "Cheryl" was a standout.

Blythe associates consonance with lightness, sympathy, and fantasy, and dissonance with a "darker reality, a deeper, more spiritual inner being." If I prefer Blythe's music to a lot of the avant-gardism that is satisfied to induce trances and exploit virtuosic techniques, it's because I love the high-stepping optimism at the core of the swing tradition; Blythe demonstrates both fealty to and innovation within that tradition. Jazz, blues, and balladry intersect in his work, and while his increasingly catholic listening may lead him from Waller to Schoenberg, his work is never impoverished by chic effect. He is candid about his influences, singling out Eric Kloss, the blind, prodigal saxophonist from Pittsburgh, in whose work Blythe finds a useful blend of African and European elements. And certainly, a Kloss riff like "One, Two, Free" bears comparison with the kinds of riffs Blythe favors, as does Kloss's manner of bulleting through the lower register or the dynamic range he uses in a solo like "Outward Wisdom," on the album *Consciousness*. Certain stylistic mannerisms, melodies and rhythms are part of the language, Blythe says, and, by example, notes that he was unaware that his primary phrase on the spontaneous "Off the Top" was a borrowing from Ornette Coleman. Ultimately, his music transcends its sundry influences with its own ring of authenticity. Its deliberateness takes different forms.

Of his three albums, *The Grip* covers the most ground. Riffs are clearly his preferred means of achieving order. A performance like "Lower Mile" is too tightly reined to the thematic material, but the improvisation is full of melodic confidence, and a unique kind of tension is created by his will toward poise. After the theme, he offers a handsome, stately phrase, pauses, and then elaborates—fastidiously but with an ever growing urgency in the cry of his sound. The contrapuntal "As of Yet" is a hypnotic construct of vamp, polyphony, homophony, and a ballad strongly indebted to "Spring Is Here." The precision of the theme is complemented by the sporting excitement of his solo and the splendid puffing of the sextet, evoking a New Orleans parade band once removed. The title piece also employs counterpoint, as a stiff-legged theme gives way to a "free" improvisation that, for all its headiness, is continuously impressive in its tonal manipulation, organization, and feeling. The flexibility of tubist Bob Stewart, who even-handedly switches from accompaniment to counterpoint, is an immeasurable boon. "Sunrise Service," a duet with cellist Abdul Wadud, reminds me of late Coltrane ("Offering," for example), and is notable for sustaining a mood through a tempo change and a theme/improvisation/theme format. At the outset of the ad lib section, Blythe's tone lightens, and the piece goes into time; thereafter he reverts to his harder sound for accent and contrast. His vibrato trembles so broadly toward the end that an iota less control would render it bathetic. But the control is there, and so is the resourcefulness of Wadud's responses, and the piece holds together.

Bush Baby, with the relatively skeletal alto, tuba, conga trio, resulted from an impromptu session; the single takes used for the album testify to the closeness of Blythe and Stewart and Ahkmed Abdullah, whose work on conga is fittingly self-effacing. The best piece is "For Fats," a sixteen-bar blues with an eight-bar addendum. It was composed on the piano, with a vamp and triplets meant to convey Fats Waller's stride (though they more closely approximate something from Morton), but he subsequently added bop harmonies in deference to Fats Navarro, and ultimately came to regard it as a dedication to every Fats, including himself. The three-way phrasing is plush and

fluid, the climaxes and retards seamlessly achieved; Blythe
chews over his short locutions and promenades the long ones.
Almost as affecting is "Mamie Lee," written for his wife, and
basically a blues that fluctuates in duration. It's stated in alto-
tuba unison; then Blythe breaks away and Stewart pursues with
accuracy and wit. Some of the tubist's sustained notes suggest an
arco bass, and near the end he plays two-note chords, as horn
players are wont to do these days. "Off the Top" employs the
key figure from Ornette Coleman's "The Blessing" in a tour de
force that unravels with unexpected logic for a spontaneous invention. In his notes to *The Grip,* Blythe wrote, "The tuba
was, after all, the original bass instrument in the New Orleans
band, and was later replaced by the bass violin when the music
moved indoors." It's not inappropriate to infer that Blythe has
taken the music outdoors again, for he has achieved not only
the ebullient stride of a march band but a crafty blend of
dance rhythms. At the same time, the tuba gives his ensemble a
gentle naturalness of expression entirely different from that
possible with a bass. A tubist cannot play a constant four beats
to the measure or maintain constancy in breathing, and Blythe
allows the changes in breath patterns, the natural pauses in
Stewart's phrasing, to shape their performances as dialogues.

With *Lenox Avenue Breakdown,* a bass is added, and because
it is usually assigned unchanging ostinato figures the tuba is
relegated chiefly to textural contributions. The ensemble is
tightened, the backbeats insistently pronounced, but the fluid-
ity of an interacting ensemble diminished. The result is a different kind of record, with lavish tonal colors and a thickly
layered bottom. Blythe's outstanding solo is on "Sliding
Through"; the theme and Cecil McBee's bass solo are in 7/4,
but Blythe's elaboration is in four. He begins with a nobly stat-
uesque, self-sufficient phrase, as on "Lower Nile" (his initial
figures always reward particular attention), and develops it

with an increasing intensity that finally rivals the explosive-
ness of "The Grip." The ensemble here and on the title selection is fortified by overdubbing of the alto and flute parts,
and Jack DeJohnette, whose splashing cymbals are integral
throughout, makes rhythmic waves that Blythe negotiates like
a crusty mariner. "Down San Diego Way" is an exotic, jostling
Latin stew, with Guillermo Franco's percussion spicing an 8/4
bass/tuba vamp. Alto and flute play the first part of the theme
out of phase, uniting for the primary riff, and Blythe's improvisation is keynoted by an audacious pirouette—a phrase he re-
prises for his second solo on the piece. He primes every note
for maximum dance-beat emphasis, while sustaining graceful
swoops and curves and a variety of blue shadings. James Newton's flute solo is right in character. The "Lenox Avenue Breakdown" riff, one of Blythe's best, is generally eight and a half
bars, but while the solos are vigorous—Blythe jauntily hints at
borrowed riffs like "Now's the Time" and Stanley Turrentine's
"Sugar"—the constancy of the bass ostinato weighs on the whole
performance. This, not so incidentally, is the only one of the
four pieces that does not end in a fade. The fadeout on "San
Diego" is too abrupt, and the one on "Sliding Through" comes
just as Newton seems about to play a fine solo—only the one on
"Odessa," which also has the only solo by James Ulmer, serves
as a convincing close.

Lenox Avenue is lusty, *Bush Baby* intellectual, *The Grip*
both. That each is different while obviously the product of a
single intelligence is an index of Blythe's approach and
range. The one aspect of his music not represented is balladry, and he is considering devoting an album to songs by
Ellington, Strayhorn, Monk, and Coltrane. I don't want to
add to a critical backlash by making undue claims—the records
are eloquent evidence and will find their own place in the
world. His is not a revolutionary music by any means, and he
is not a new Bird or a new anyone else. But his voice is real

and vital and distinctive, and it transmits the passion of music with spirit and gracefulness in a language suitable to the times. Black Arthur means not having to search for your roots anymore because they are there at your fingertips.

May 1979

*Composers
and Movements*

Treemonisha *from on High Breaks Loose*

> Hear Aunt Hagar's children harmonizing,
> Hear that sweet melody,
> It's like a choir from on high broke loose.

Aunt Hagar, who jumped up at Old Deacon Splivins and shouted "Why all this razzing about jazzing?" in the W. C. Handy blues that bears her name, defended her brood's jazzo-patin' with an earthiness appropriate to the blues. She didn't know her more refined cousin, Treemonisha, who many years before, in 1866, the first year of Reconstruction, was discovered in her infancy beneath a Sacred Tree in a black community near Texarkana. The couple who adopted her saw to it that she was educated, despite personal sacrifices, and thus equipped her to lead her people from superstition into a state of grace, also delineated by music—a spine-tingling, high-stepping "real slow drag." Two such strong women would have had much to say to each other, but even as Hagar guided her blues people around the world, Treemonisha's resilient nineteenth-century fantasy waited sixty years to be transfigured from a forgotten manuscript.

Scott Joplin died for her, sacrificing his life and work in the hope of seeing his opera brought to life. He had started out in life in circumstances similar to his heroine's, but then the fantasy went awry. The genius from Texarkana, Texas, whose musical education was procured by his mother's working as a domestic, who became an itinerant pianist when still a teenager, who endured bordello gigs to compose the first million-selling song—"Maple Leaf Rag"—in the history of popular music, becoming, thereby, not only the King of Ragtime but the daddy of Tin Pan Alley, ended up an obsessed Ahab on the carcass of a grand opera that no one wanted even to acknowledge. *Treemonisha* was a cautionary fable for blacks, but it was also an assault on the white ownership of America's fine arts. If ragtime, a blend of "weird and intoxicating" syncopations with European formalism, could bring black music into the homes of middle America, then perhaps his opera would establish Joplin as the palace-crashing leader of his people. He might have withstood criticism, but he did not plan on silence. So the opera became a tar baby mocking his talent and presumptuousness. He stuck one limb into it, and then another. But there was no brier patch and no Brer Fox to outwit. Brer Fox was over at the Follies listening to "Alexander's Ragtime Band."

In 1976, Scott Joplin won a Pulitzer prize, and according to the account in the New York *Times,* the prize was largely for *Treemonisha,* described as his greatest work. One hesitates to throw a wrench at such a pleasantly ironic, self-congratulatory, but deserving award, except that poor Scott, who died in 1917, is being used as a lever against more considerable black achievement. He has been found worthy because he has been discovered by the conservatory, because his music does not require improvisation, and because he wrote an opera to prove his seriousness. *Treemonisha* was Joplin's longest, most ambitious work, but by no means his best. It is brilliant but flawed, and the relation it bears to his imperishable short pieces is not unlike that of Pound's *Cantos* to "Hugh Selwyn Mauberley." Moreover, Joplin's accomplishment is a slice of pie when compared with the extraordinarily comprehensive vision of Ellington. Perhaps in another half-century, Ellington will be the recipient. In 1965, however, when the judges for the music prize voted to present Duke Ellington with a special award for a life's achievement, the full Pulitzer committee—much like the '30s New Orleans radio announcer, who said, "I can't announce a nigger," when Louis Armstrong was waiting in the wings—couldn't allow that prize to be awarded.

In any case, be grateful that *Treemonisha* is now with us permanently, thanks to a German company, Deutsche Grammophon, which has just issued a luscious recording of the Houston Grand Opera production. (It is attractively packaged with a booklet including essays by and about Vera Lawrence, who, with Rudi Blesh, spearheaded the Joplin revival.) There has been a good deal of patronization and embarrassed condescension toward Joplin's opera, though few are immune to its charm. One thing black artists have never sought is cheek-pinching condolence from white critics, and I have yet to speak to a black who is as bothered by *Treemonisha's* mammyisms as whites are. The libretto is not only better than that of *The Magic Flute,* it's simply not as bad as it's been reputed to be. The least one expects from a libretto is a series of syllables on which to hang the music; the most one is likely to get are words that work *with* the music. There are sections of *Treemonisha* that do not work, but there are more frequent passages where the sentiment of the song is glove-matched by the music. That Joplin wrote both words and music attests to the seriousness he attached to the fable. The tendency to dismiss the content of the opera as doggerel was not abated by the staging seen in New York, for the 1975 premiere.

Frank Corsaro conceived the production as though taking his cue from Rudi Blesh's description of *Treemonisha* as "the legend of a Negro Eden." The Negro neighborhood was made a kindergarten of innocent children. This kind of reduction was very much in keeping with a tradition in American opera. *Porgy and Bess* and *Four Saints in Three Acts,* which is about

Spaniards, both employed all-black casts to convey childlike
dignity. It is as though white audiences can bear to reflect on
America's lost innocence only when the morality dramas are
enacted by the colored folk. But Joplin's opera is less about innocence than about education, a subject that concerned him no
less than it did Booker T. Washington, and Treemonisha's
learning is postulated as a path beyond the superstition-enforced
innocence of her people. This is no Eden. It is a community
surrounded by strange animals, magical rituals, and black-
hearted villainy. Joplin described·the evildoers as "three very
old men," making clear their ties to slave days. Corsaro presented them as three slick Sportin' Lifes. The pacifism Treemonisha espouses is no more innocent than Christ's, Gandhi's, or
Martin Luther King's, and Joplin would probably have characterized it as wisdom. Certainly, Treemonisha is a moral figure
of stature, and her "real slow drag" a sweeping statement of
fearless optimism. The innocence in *Treemonisha* stems from
the artist's occasional failings, not the nature of the fable itself.
Treemonisha, the recording makes clear, can withstand an
adult interpretation.

Perhaps the blacking-up aspect of the libretto—the Joel
Chandler Harris dialect—represents what Joplin imagined to
be a compromise with the establishment, but it is more likely
an honest attempt to depict an uneducated, rural community.
The principal problems in language result from Joplin's mania
for rhyming, and clumsiness in this area is frequently reflected
by clumsiness in the music. It is not difficult, however, to gloss
over those moments in a work that grips the heart and raises
the spirit, from the four-measure "happiness" motif of the over-
ture through three invigorating dances, two majestic arias, and
some of the most stirring choral singing in American music.

Although it is not a ragtime opera, *Treemonisha* is suffused
with exotic syncopations swaying over diminished sevenths, and
Gunther Schuller's conducting of his own inspired and authentic arrangements brings out the most dashing and dramatic

qualities of the score. From the opening song by Remus, the raggy turn-of-the-century idiom is pronounced, though too much of the first act is taken with establishing Treemonisha's origin, in a monotonous aria sung by her mother. It is soon followed by a wonderfully effective sermon by the Parson Alltalk, with reeling congregational response; this passage is used to set off Simon's advocacy sermon on superstition in the second act. Joplin treats his villains with a humanity that undermines any bitterness one might expect from a messianic composer. The threnodic "Tis true, tis true" is the hapless lament of a frightened people, palsied before Simon, and contrasts movingly with the response of Alltalk's followers: "Oh yes, ah feel lak I've been redeemed." This is Joplin's art at its most illuminating.

Simon may sing too sweetly as he prepares to throw Treemonisha into the hornets' nest, but his vulnerability is quickly revealed as he becomes victimized by his own superstition. Remus, disguised as a scarecrow, rescues Treemonisha and races off with her, singing the not quite ungainly couplet "Come let us leave these woods at once/Because I hear some very strange grunts." The final three sections of Act Two make for a stunning conclusion—it begins with the workers resting in the field, singing barbershop harmony with banjo accompaniment, picks up steam in a brief transitional interlude, and erupts into the pulse-quickening syncopated choral singing of "Aunt Dinah Has Blowed de Horn."

The instrumental prelude to the third act is followed by an expert contrapuntal song expressing the despair of Treemonisha's mother and the staunch but cold comfort of her father. But after Treemonisha arrives safely home, spirited in by the "happiness" strain, the opera winds down unexpectedly into its weakest section. The heroine's "You will do evil for evil" is hopelessly banal, and the long triple-meter aria by Remus, elaborating on the idea of goodness ("Remember . . . the creator is watching you") cannot compare with other Joplin waltzes of the period, such as "Bethena." Then, just as unexpectedly, the work goes into full throttle. Ned, expressing community sentiment, sings "When Villains Ramble," the opera's finest song, and from its first line there is now a momentum that is no less exhilarating for being restrained and cautiously developed. The chorus is at its most powerful in begging Treemonisha to lead the community, and when she accepts, she inaugurates the new day with the prancing, strolling schottische "A Real Slow Drag." She sings, "Move along, don't stop/Don't stop dancing," and you wish they never would. That is the power Scott Joplin's tar baby had but couldn't reveal sixty years ago. "It's like a choir from on high broke loose."

May 1976

Doin' What Comes Naturally

Irving Berlin, this country's unofficial but incontestable song-writer laureate, turned ninety in May 1978, and characteristically refused all interviews and public appearances: "Age," he was quoted as saying, "is no mark of credit unless you do something constructive with it. For a guy who keeps having birthdays it becomes damn boring." Berlin's reclusiveness helps define his legend. Like Ellington, he has been miserly in nurturing the portrait by which posterity will know him, and because we'd rather succumb to a vicarious realization of the American Dream than take seriously our native geniuses, we know very little. The first Berlin biography was written by Alexander Woollcott in 1925, the third and most recent by Michael Freedland in 1974. From these, numerous articles, and book chapters, we get a life sketched in clichés, colored by breezy anecdotes and lively, curmudgeonly quotations, which, since they are rarely credited as to source and date, encircle the subject like canon law.

The bare bones of the story rattle with all the phrases once beloved of backstage musicals and grade-school teachers—melting pot, rags to riches, hard work and dedication, Mr. Show Business, entertaining the troops, God bless America. Israel Baline was one of eight children born to a Russian rabbi and cantor near the Siberian border in 1888. When their home was destroyed in a Cossack pogrom, the family emigrated to New York's Lower East Side, where the prodigal son dropped out of school after two years to sell papers and ran away from home at fourteen to lead a blind street singer. Harry von Tilzer, the music publisher, soon hired him to sit in the audience at Tony Pastor's Music Hall at Union Square and reprise, as though spontaneously inspired, the big number in the shows. His first chance as a songwriter came two years later while he was working in a Chinatown saloon run by a white man called Nigger Mike Salter. When the pianist at a neighboring bar wrote a local hit, "My Muriuccia Take a Steamboat," Salter enviously prevailed upon his two singing waiters to do the same. "Marie from Sunny Italy," the first of many Berlin dialect songs, was the result, but its chief importance lay in a printer's error on the sheet music crediting the lyric to I. Berlin; while successfully auditioning for a Tin Pan Alley staff composing job in 1908, he completed the Americanization of his name.

Berlin's first seminal songs came in 1911 with "Alexander's Ragtime Band" and 1912 with "When I Lost You." The former was so overwhelming a hit that Berlin was dubbed the king of ragtime, a misconception that lingers to this day. Fifty years ago, the first writings on jazz by Gilbert Seldes and Henry O. Osgood accorded Berlin a high place in the annals of jazz; in an otherwise useful survey of his career, Paul Baratta writes in the May 1978 issue of *Songwriter*, "As the man who took ragtime when it was little more than a mannerism of the pianists in the rathskellers and bordellos and made it into a custom of the country, there must, of course, be a chapter on Irving Berlin in any history of jazz, for jazz is ragtime gone daffy." The foolishness of that sentence is multilayered, and yet Baratta himself quotes from Jerome Kern's famous letter to Woollcott: ". . . I certainly object to the absurd implication that Irving Berlin is an explorer, discoverer, or pioneer in what is childishly called ragtime. . . . Irving Berlin has no place in American music. He *is* American music; but it will be by his verse and his lovely melodies that he will live, and not in his diabolically clever trick accents." There is nothing diabolical about "Alexander's Ragtime Band" (the clever accents would come later with "Everybody Step" and "Puttin' On the Ritz"), but then Berlin once told Max Morath, "You know, I never did find out what ragtime was."

Still, as Seldes noted, "Alexander's Ragtime Band" was a "crystallization" of the new spirit in American song. The invitation of the opening line of the chorus—"Come on and hear"—mesmerized several countries, serving as an oblique conduit for the rhythmic excitement of black music, even though it is very nearly devoid of rhythmic interest. Indeed, its only syncopations are in the verse, where eleven out of sixteen measures begin with a rest—a device used by Joplin in the first three strains of "Maple Leaf Rag" and later adapted by Gershwin for his ballad "The Man I Love." The ABAC-structured chorus has nothing to do with ragtime (unlike the "counter" melody of "Play a Simple Melody," which does capture ragtime's rhythmic lilt), but its interpolated song fragments—a bugle call in measures 11–12, "Swanee River" in measures 27–28—tend to give it symbolic value as a transition from both the march and minstrel traditions. Harmonically, it is twice congruent with the blues—in the use of the minor third, and in the key change (C to F) from verse to chorus, the standard blues progression of a fourth. In his invaluable *American Popular Song*, Alec Wilder suggests that this is the earliest instance of two keys in a pop tune.

Berlin followed it with other rhythm songs, including "Everybody's Doing It" and "That Society Bear," but his most significant achievement of the following year was inspired by the death of his first wife, weeks after their wedding. "When I Lost You" shows the influence of his idol, George M. Cohan (measures 5 and 6 are borrowed from "45 Minutes to Broadway," until the flatted ninth replaces Cohan's F-natural), and is not one of his most distinctive ballads or waltzes. It is, however, the first ballad by the composer of "All Alone," "What'll I Do," "Always," "How About Me," "How Deep Is the Ocean?" "Remember," and "They Say It's Wonderful," among dozens of others. Moreover, it is well crafted—Berlin's songs rarely waste a note—and though sentimental, not mawkish.

Berlin is the most successful songwriter who ever lived, and probably the most prolific. His 1500 published songs are estimated to be half those he actually wrote, and their diversity and, in so many instances, ubiquity tend to push the songwriter even further into the shadows. For Berlin had the unique gift of writing songs that seemed to belong in the public domain— pace Irving Berlin Music Corporation and ASCAP—even before the ink was dry. What is wholly personal in Berlin is not his style, as Wilder admiringly demonstrates, but his honest eclecticism, lucidity, and wry wit—his faith in song. Berlin is a committed populist. "The mob is always right," he has said: "A good song embodies the feelings of the mob and a songwriter is not much more than a mirror which reflects those feelings." When apprised of a songwriter who said his songs must please him first, Berlin laughed and told Max Wilk, "*I* write a song to please the *public*—and if the public doesn't like it in New Haven, I change it!"

In the late '30s and '40s, an army of unionizing folksingers led by Woody Guthrie set themselves in opposition to the June/moon Tin Pan Alley hacks, insisting that their songs were of the people, that they could both activate and pacify. It's impossible to think of a songster with a more resolute belief in community and song than Berlin, or one with a longer list of epochal songs to his credit. Yet Berlin's political conservatism combined with the astounding popularity of his songs diverts contemporary audiences from a proper evaluation of his achievement. Berlin is not quite the primitive or weathervane he makes himself out to be. His work has set standards for balladry, novelties, rhythm numbers, and theatrical songs. More than most of his colleagues, he consistently avoids the standard AABA form (in part, because he came to maturity before that form was firmly codified); his melodies and harmonies are often challenging. Yet his songs reveal an instinctiveness for the anthem, the theme, the jingly melody that gnaws at the listener, suggesting for all its craftsmanship an irreducible level of musical expression. How is it that a Russian-born Jew should write the best-known patriotic song since "The Star Spangled Banner," the most popular Christmas song since "Silent Night," the only universally known Easter song?

"God Bless America" was composed in 1918 (two years after Woodrow Wilson proclaimed Francis Scott Key's verse the national anthem), for Berlin's army show, *Yip Yip Yaphank*, but he withdrew it for fear of painting the patriotic lily. It stayed in his file cabinet for twenty years, until Kate Smith requested a flag waver. The ABCD-structured chorus is more martial than inspirational, and it's interesting that the verse, with its more pronounced major-minor circuitry, is rarely sung. "White Christmas" violates the standard Christmas-song theme in focusing on nostalgia rather than celebration—it's about idealized Christmases of the past, which is why it had such a profound effect during the Second World War. "Easter Parade" started out as "Smile and Show Your Dimple"—Berlin was smart enough to throw out the lyric and save the tune for a rainy day. There are other themes: "There's No Business Like Show Business" is so emblematic of the theatrical mythos that one is surprised to realize it is only a little over thirty years old; "A Pretty Girl Is Like a Melody," commissioned by Florenz Ziegfeld to introduce his chorus line, was immediately adopted as the standard beauty pageant theme; "Oh How I Hate To Get Up in the Morning" was the serviceman's lament through two world wars. Then there were the songs designed so acutely for a particular performer that each ensured the other's success—Al Jolson, Eddie Cantor, Ethel Waters, Harry Richman, Fred Astaire, Bing Crosby, and Ethel Merman were particularly indebted to him.

The key to Berlin's universality may lie in the Lower East Side of his boyhood, where the theatrical profession was dominated by minorities and provided an escape from melting-pot poverty. The changeover from minstrelsy to vaudeville did not end the accent on racial and national caricatures, and ambitious young songpluggers like Berlin quickly mastered the dialect songs of the day, employing Yiddish, Italian, German, and Irish motifs. The most challenging sensibility, the one that best captured the new American vitality, was to be found in black music, a recognition intuited by most of the major Jewish performers of the day. The symbiotic relationship that developed between black jazz musicians and Jewish songwriters in the '30s has been widely noted, and it seems certain that the give-and-take stretches back to the turn of the century. Note the similarities between cantorial singing and the blues tradition—the ubiquitous minor third, vocal wailing, spare harmonies, improvisation—and you begin to understand why Gershwin, Arlen, and Berlin (each of their fathers was a cantor), as well as Kern, Rodgers, Weill, and Johnny Green, provided so much of the standard material for jazz improvisation. Most of them haunted Harlem theaters, admiring the snap of Eubie Blake's rhythms, the homey resilience of James P. Johnson's melodies. In *World of Our Fathers,* Irving Howe explains the affinity of Jewish performers for blackface as an instance of immigrant outsiders adopting the mask of the native outsiders—"with one woe speaking through the voice of another. . . . Blacking their faces seems to have enabled the Jewish performers to reach a spontaneity and assertiveness in the declaration of their Jewish selves." (Half a century later the adaptation of black-music mannerisms provided a similar liberation of the self for white southerners, most notably Elvis Presley.)

For all his alleged ties with ragtime and jazz, however, Berlin is less frequently interpreted by jazz musicians than are many of his peers. No single Berlin song has endured as a jazz standard on the order of Kern's "All the Things You Are," Green's "Body and Soul," or Gershwin's "Lady Be Good." Through jazz, I developed much more awareness of the other songwriters mentioned, along with Youmans, Porter, Waller, McHugh, Schwartz, Carmichael, even Romberg, than of Berlin. Yet I knew Berlin's name first, because of the rock-and-roll records I bought in the late '50s. If the blue effects in Gershwin and Arlen lent themselves to swing, the openhearted melodies and built-in pep of Berlin's early work were as irresistible to the rhythm-and-blues-influenced pop of the '50s as they were to four preceding decades of pop: Sammy Turner did "Always," the Isley Brothers "How Deep Is the Ocean," Fats Domino "Easter Parade," Lloyd Price and Freddy Cannon "Blue Skies," the Ravens "Always," "Marie," and "White Christmas," and Ray Charles, who was my bridge from rock and roll to jazz, "Marie" and "Alexander's Ragtime Band."

As there are numerous distinguished performances of Berlin by jazz singers and instrumentalists, the question arises why his songs aren't played more frequently. Several possibilities come to mind: since the '30s, jazz musicians have too often settled into a 32-bar AABA safety clutch, while Berlin's best songs show greater playfulness in structure; Berlin's rhythm songs are infectious, but they don't swing and often can't be swung; some of his best ballads are waltzes, and it is standard procedure for jazz musicians to reconceptualize waltzes in duple time, which can be a bother; some of the songs once popular with jazz musicians—"Blue Skies," "Marie"—have become clichés; Berlin consciously wrote songs for emoters and "the mob," not extrapolators. The most interesting jazz adaptations of Berlin have toyed with rather than negated the architecture of his songs, for example, Sonny Rollins's inspired romp on "There's No Business Like Show Business," a twenty-four-bar verse with a forty-eight-bar refrain. Rollins begins with the refrain, following with a fifty-six-bar chorus that combines the verse (stretched over thirty-two rather than twenty-four bars) with the last twenty-four bars of the refrain; his third and fourth choruses are likewise forty-eight and fifty-six bars long. In Teddy Wilson's recording, "This Year's Kisses" sounds as though it had been written for Billie Holiday and Lester Young, who wring insuperable loveliness from its sparsely noted twenty-eight bars. Mary Lou Williams's arrangement of "Blue Skies," called "Trumpet No End," was a great favorite of Duke Ellington's, allowing the brass section to complement the headiness of the B part with bloodcurdling high notes. Coleman Hawkins's "Say It Isn't So" was one of his finest ballad performances, making dramatic, almost modal use of the song's half-stepping cadences and repeated notes. Thelonious Monk's ingratiating solo interpretation of "(Just One Way To Say) I Love You" stayed relatively faithful to the release, but through rhythmic displacement and melodic alterations radically restructured the A theme. Ray Charles took obvious pleasure in "Alexander's Ragtime Band," characteristically extending it with a gospel call-and-response insertion and a Dixieland coda; Jaki Byard suggested both affection and parodistic bemusement in his version, plunking verse and chorus with dogged innocence, filling in the spaces with staccato chords and primitive syncopations. For me, the definitive "Russian Lullabye" is the rocker Jimmy Rushing made of it, but John Coltrane's greased-lightning version of both that song and "Soft Lights and Sweet Music" are remarkable not least because his velocity never decimates the songs' luminous chords. Coltrane, collaborating with Johnny Hartman, was restrained and movingly lyrical on "They Say It's Wonderful." After hearing Roy Eldridge's assuredly swinging "The Song Is Ended," it's difficult to imagine its ever having had life as a ballad. Then there are Ethel Waters's "Waiting at the End of the Road" and "Supper Time," Fats Waller's "Mandy," Lee Wiley's "Some Sunny Day," Sarah

Vaughan's "Cheek to Cheek," Ella Fitzgerald's and Louis Armstrong's "I'm Putting All My Eggs in One Basket," Betty Carter's "Remember," and the versions of "Isn't It a Lovely Day" by Art Tatum and Billie Holiday.

In recent months there have been four record anthologies drawing attention to Berlin. Monmouth-Evergreen's two-record *Say It with Music—The Years 1921–33* is condensed from a three-volume set issued on Berlin's eightieth birthday. Although good musicians are present, most of the thirty-four songs are done completely straight by an undistinguished choir. Ten Berlin songs are superbly rendered by Fred Astaire and members of Jazz at the Philharmonic on *The Astaire Story*, a DRG-Archive reissue of 1952 recordings. Astaire's "Puttin' On the Ritz" is a rare example of Berlin having to update the original lyric, which patronized Harlem swells. *The Vintage Irving Berlin* is a fine collection of fifteen songs, but, as part of the New World Records anthology, can be found only in libraries.

Happily, the best collection is an imaginatively edited four-record box available to one and all from the Book-of-the-Month Club, called *There's No Business Like Show Business—The Magical Songs of Irving Berlin*. There are unfortunate and inevitable omissions, but the forty-eight cuts are drawn from the realms of jazz, pop, and theater (rock and roll is excluded). There are delightful performances by the Boswell Sisters, the Andrews Sisters, Tony Bennett, Lee Wiley, Maxine Sullivan, Crosby, Armstrong and the Mills Brothers, Astaire, Holiday, and jazz bands led by Red Norvo, Red Nichols (Benny Goodman is the uncredited soloist on "Nobody Knows"), and Chick Bullock. Harry Richman's "Puttin' On the Ritz" (the good, uncredited trumpet solo is by one Fuzz Menge), Cantor's "Mandy," and Ethel Waters's "Heat Wave" are definitive, as is the Ethel Merman–Ray Middleton duet on "Anything You Can Do"; Judy Holliday's "How About Me" is surprisingly effective, and Jolson's hilarious "I've Got My Captain Working For Me,"

from 1919, is a perfect application of theatrical flair to a glee-
fully vengeful army song.

I've neglected large areas of Berlin's accomplishment—his innovative double-melody duets ("Play a Simple Melody," "Just
in Love"); his contributions to film and theater (*Top Hat* and
Annie Get Your Gun are pinnacles in their respective me-
diums); his army shows and songs, which never betray a touch
of jingoism; his general intelligence as a writer of verse; not to
mention songs as sundry as "Lazy," "Supper Time," "Let's Face
the Music and Dance," "I've Got My Love to Keep Me Warm,"
"Say It with Music," and "I Love a Piano." And I haven't mentioned Berlin's business savvy, which, in Tin Pan Alley lore, is
admired almost as much as his music. As soon as he started
making money, Berlin scrambled to buy up the copyrights on
all his early songs. As composer, lyricist, publisher, and producer, he owns his work as few artists do, something he makes
clear at every turn. He has given up all royalties from "God
Bless America" (they go to the Boy Scouts) and a few other
songs, but he will not permit writers to print excerpts of his
songs, and his intolerance for tampering led to a landmark Supreme Court decision when he futilely sued *Mad* for parodying
a lyric. He is said to be worth more than $100,000,000—"White
Christmas" alone earns an annual royalty upward of $60,000. I
should add that he knows no music theory, can play the piano
in only one key (F sharp—his upright has a lever that transposes
keys), and that many of his songs were composed by dictation.
With all that money and adulation and untutored genius, it is
still unfashionable to talk about Berlin's art in academic circles,
where art is what pop isn't. Yet as the times that produced Berlin's best songs recede from memory, the songs themselves continue to linger with their own transcendent charm. Berlin has
fixed it so that he will fade into a knot of impressive anecdotes,
but his songs show every sign of being imperishable.

January 1979

Ellingtonia

1. At the Pulpit

The photograph of Duke Ellington on the cover of the album from his third sacred concert, *The Majesty of God* (RCA), is uncommonly appropriate. Standing before a microphone with his hands clasped before him, he has an unself-conscious, boyish smile on his face. His eyes are closed, whether in deference to the spotlight or a prayer isn't clear. He appears to be basking in the artificial light, and the choirboy attitude is enforced by the ruffled bow under his chin, the collar of a blue satin jacket dappled with white or silver specks. His hair, carefully groomed in front, trails anarchistically over his shoulders. The picture denies the illness ravaging his tired frame. Six months later he was dead, and there can be little doubt that he attached great significance to the last edition of what he considered his most important work, the sacred concerts.

The third sacred concert is revealing, moving, and on occasion inspired. Performed at Westminster Abbey after hasty rehearsals, it is illuminating not least for showing how Ellington coped with the insoluble problem of having outlived his band. Of the major Ellington interpreters, only Harry Carney and Russell Procope were present. Cootie Williams did not make the trip, and Paul Gonsalves, who did, was taken ill at the last minute; his solos were given to Harold Ashby, the last of the· saxophonists called upon to retain the Ben Webster sound in the Ellington palette. The fine Swedish singer Alice Babs was recruited, however, and the maestro predictably focused the new work on her, Carney, and the piano. The orchestra, a shadow of its predecessors, was relegated to the background. Most of the music acquits itself admirably on its own terms.

The three sacred concerts differ in several ways, so an arc in the composer's attitude can be traced from the energetic, proudly secular *Concert of Sacred Music* (RCA), created in 1965, to the more ambitious and strenuously verbal *Second Sacred Concert* (Fantasy), in 1968, to the quietly effective last work. "These concerts are not the traditional mass jazzed up," Ellington worte. His familiar dictum "Every man prays in his own language and there is no language that God does not understand" reminds the listener that he did not attempt to apply his genius to an established idiom, but rather to bring his own music intact to the church. The difference between playing for people, whether at the Cotton Club or Westminster Abbey, and creating for the greater glory of God, was not lost on him. When Fr. Norman O'Connor commissioned a jazz mass (apparently never completed), Ellington pondered the conflict: "One may be accustomed to speaking to people, but suddenly to attempt to speak, sing, and play directly to God—that puts one in an entirely new and different position." He prayed on his own musical terms, and celebrated the talents of his collaborators accordingly; "All the members of the band played in character," he said of the first sacred concert. He did not abandon the Cotton Club; he brought the Cotton Club revue to the pulpit.

Although the sacred concerts (hereafter SC1, SC2, and SC3) are preserved on records, it's necessary to note a quality of the music lost on disc—its aural affinity for the cavernous architecture of great churches. I did not attend any of Ellington's church services, but I recall how impressive even recorded excerpts sounded echoing through St. John the Divine at Ellington's funeral. Considering the ingenuity with which he surmounted the limitations of recording studios in the late '20s (which is why Ellington records sound so vivid compared with contemporary sides by Fletcher Henderson), it seems likely that he conceived his instrumental and vocal orchestrations in terms of the church acoustics he knew so well.

SC1 was a patchwork of the new and the old. Of the new pieces, the most important was "In the Beginning God," which occupies a third of the album. Throughout the concerts, Ellington used difficult modulations and intervals, culminating in the larynx-twisting "T.G.T.T." (SC2) and "Is God a Three-Letter Word for Love" (SC3), one of his last songs. This characteristic is evident in the first six notes of "In the Beginning God," corresponding to the first six words in the Bible, and nobly stated by the baritone sax of Harry Carney, who also introduced SC2. When I first heard the Brock Peters vocal, I thought it mundane; I've come to admire its generosity and lack of pretension. Ellington was ambitious, but rarely pretentious, and those works for which he wrote narratives and recitatives suffer more from sugar-coated cleverness than undue extravagance. The verities Ellington held most dear are commonplaces—love, omnipotence, glory, freedom—and he honored them simply and directly. "In the Beginning God" becomes a series of climaxes: Cat Anderson playing his high notes, Louis Bellson dazzling on drums, the choir reciting the books of the New Testament over Paul Gonsalves's cumulus clouds of tenor sax. Another new piece, a rocking, offhanded new setting for "The Lord's Prayer," sung by Esther Marrow, is undistinguished.

A couple of selections were recycled from Ellington's 1963 production *My People,* but the best of the older music originated in the '40s. "New World a-Coming" was composed for one of his postwar Carnegie Hall concerts, and in the late '60s, he rearranged it as a piano concerto for the Cincinnati Symphony. On SC1, it is a superbly played piano solo, its jaunty spirit and tricky bass figures colored by sensitive minor-key melancholy (much of the sacred concerts is in the minor key). Of equal significance is the revamped "Come Sunday," outfitted with a new introduction, definitively performed, and thoughtfully revised from the original version in *Black, Brown and Beige*. Jimmy Hamilton's clarinet beeps reminders of the Ray Nance pizzicato-violin introduction, and there is now an interlude for Cootie Williams's trumpet and sensuous reed writing before Johnny Hodges's miraculous chorus. "David Danced Before the Lord," with tap master Bunny Briggs, brings the record to an exciting conclusion; it was originally performed in *My People,* but the music is "Come Sunday" played fast.

A change of heart overtook the composer for SC2, which consists exclusively of new music. Not content with his musical message, he added long recitatives of varying success, full of outright proselytizing. Some of the choral sections are reminiscent of school pageants, and I suspect he may have had in mind just such an application. This was one of the last times the classic Ellington band of the '60s would record, and his obsession with the project is reflected in his producing and financing the tapes himself, and then selling them to Fantasy records. Some of the melodies are dim—"Something About Believing" could have been turned out by any number of Broadway tunesmiths—and Toney Watkins's gospel shouting is a good deal less invigorating than intended.

Yet there is great Ellington here. "Praise God," a wondrous vehicle for Carney, is reprised in a thunderous finale, "Praise God and Dance," with shining performances by Alice Babs and Gonsalves. "The Shepherd" is a slow blues for Cootie Williams, with stop-time passages and shifting orchestral accompaniment. Several selections have an airy, ecumenical quality. The uneven "It's Freedom" boasts a jubilant passage based on a Willie the Lion Smith lick, and an evocative song crafted from just the word "freedom." Babs is stunning in her duets with Hodges and Procope.

The winning vocalist is at the heart of SC3, where the purity of her a capella work on "Every Man Prays in His Own Language" displays an emotional serenity one associates with the singing of children. The memorable "Is God a Three-Letter Word" brings to fruition several melodic suggestions in SC2, notably "Heaven" and "Almighty Heaven." Ellington conjures a new and poignant unaccompanied piano setting for "The Lord's Prayer," and, on "Every Man," allows for a solo by Art Baron, on the recorder—its natural, diaphanous sound echoing with quiet awe in this hushed presentation. The scrupulously crafted "The Majesty of God" is the conclusion and highlight of the concert. Ellington's spirited piano sets the stage—a reference to "Things Ain't What They Used To Be" wafts by—and the variations are lovingly spun by Carney and Babs until the full orchestra plots the resolution.

I am told that significant portions of SC3 were edited from the record, including the final section of "The Majesty of God." Clearly there was tampering with "Every Man," since the music fades up on the third syllable of the title. There are more serious problems: Toney Watkins's feature is his most palatable on record, but his recitation in the middle of "Three-Letter Word" is disconcerting to say the least; there is a trite advertisement for the United Nations, called "The Brotherhood"; and Ellington is zealous in his declaration of faith—he has Watkins sing, "If you don't believe in God / Then brother you don't exist." Considering the evident problems with space, the inclusion of a ninety-second speech by the chairman of the UN association is puzzling and annoying; the deathless message could have been printed on the liner.

Hastily, let me repeat that these complaints should not deter anyone from hearing Ellington's final testament. Despite great adversity, he was even in these last months a perceptive and unflinching artist. Indeed, the best moments of *The Majesty of God* suggest that his art was still peaking.

2. *In Search of* Black, Brown and Beige

Duke Ellington's "tone parallel to the history of the American Negro," *Black, Brown and Beige,* is probably less heard than any musical work of comparable reputation. Its fame, both critical and popular, has steadily increased in inverse proportion to its frequency of performance. The cautious Martin Williams has described it as "undoubtedly" the greatest of Ellington's extended works; even New York's Governor Carey singled it out for mention in declaring April 29, 1976, Duke Ellington Day. Yet the composer never recorded *BB&B* in its entirety. Stung by the generally negative response that greeted its 1943 premiere, he chose instead to dole out portions over the next thirty years, usually to favorable reviews. In this patient manner—I presume intentionality—he cultivated a demand for the complete opus. At his second Carnegie Hall concert, eleven months after the one that debuted *BB&B,* he offered only two excerpts, explaining to the audience, "We thought it would be better to wait until the story was a little more familiar before we did the whole thing again."

Perhaps he was rebuking us. Ellington would revisit sections of *BB&B* for the rest of his career, but he recorded no more than a brief condensation of the original piece, plus subsequent elaborations on a few of its themes. For the rest, there is a cloudy tape of the original performance, which, though widely circulated among collectors, was kept from public consumption until the late '70s, and a lacunary score from which only Ellington could have reconstructed the complete work.

Now there are indications that this ambitious, seminal music will find a new audience: Monmouth-Evergreen released a 1972 performance conducted by the English bandleader Alan Cohen, who with Brian Priestly assembled a complete arrangement from the tape and the score, with only fifteen measures "surmised"; Dick Hyman conducted Cohen's transcription, with some alterations, at the 1976 Newport Jazz Festival at Carnegie

Hall; several months later, Maurice Peress brought the Kansas City Philharmonic to Carnegie and conducted his own symphonic amplification—made at Ellington's request—of something he disingenuously calls *Black, Brown and Beige Suite,* but which is in fact only the first episode, "Black"; and Prestige has issued the original tape on *The Duke Ellington Carnegie Hall Concerts—January 1943.* None but the last was entirely satisfactory, though all demonstrated the music's enduring virtues.

Ellington had been promising a long concert piece on Afro-American history for several years when the unveiling was scheduled for January 23, 1943. He was riding high on the wave of his greatest artistic successes (both the miniatures of 1939–42, and the theatrical extravaganza *Jump for Joy*), and reeling from losses in the band's ranks—Jimmy Blanton, Cootie Williams, Barney Bigard, and Ivie Anderson. Wartime sentimentality contributed to an easing of tension between representatives of lofty art and pop culture, and Ellington, who was creating internationally acclaimed art in what was natively considered a folk milieu, was the ideal symbol for what turned out to be the false promise of oneness in American music. As it happened, the January concert was both a benefit for Russian War Relief and the anniversary of Ellington's twentieth year as a bandleader in New York. He was presented that evening with a plaque signed by thirty-two prominent members of the musical world, among them Leopold Stokowski, Walter Damrosch, William Grant Still, Earl Hines, Arthur Rodzinski, Roy Harris, Count Basie, Fritz Reiner, Kurt Weill, Paul Robeson, Aaron Copland, Benny Goodman, Jerome Kern, and Marian Anderson. He had prepared a bountiful program appropriate to the event.

BB&B was placed right before intermission. Ellington has said it ran fifty-seven minutes, but he may have been including the spoken introductions. His biographer, Barry Ulanov, clocked it at forty-five, which is more consistent with the tape.

The hall was sold out—as was the repeat performance at Boston's Symphony Hall the following night—and Ellington must have been acutely aware that the magnitude of what he was attempting—a concert work by a "jazz" musician—might obscure the actual accomplishment. This was a time when everyone pretended to know what jazz was except the people who created it.

Older jazz critics, of the Rudi Blesh–Rex Harris ilk, considered *BB&B* empty—they expected Ellington to stick with hot jazz *circa* 1927. The classical critics, excepting long-time Ellington admirer Irving Kolodin, were dubious about its structure, agreeing with the usually astute Marxist classical/jazz critic Sidney Finkelstein, who lauded the parts but not the sum. Others attacked Ellington for being pretentious, a charge that in this context was unfathomable but predictable. In any case, after recording excerpts in 1944, about eighteen minutes' worth, Ellington abandoned *BB&B* until the late '50s. On the other hand, the concert was successful enough to ensure his annual return to Carnegie Hall with a new work throughout the decade.

BB&B is frequently characterized as a suite, a string of unrelated miniatures, but it is no such thing. The "Black" segment alone is a twenty-one-minute tone poem comprised of two central themes, "Work Song" and "Come Sunday," which develop and intertwine, emerging simultaneously in the final section of "Black," called "Light," and are then reprised in the "Beige" finale. There are also two ingeniously crafted subordinate themes—a heavily rhythmic ensemble counterpoint to the seven-note "Work Song" phrase, and a keening introduction to Johnny Hodges's celebrated exposition of "Sunday," plucked and bowed by Ray Nance on violin. "Black" is overlong, however; trombonist Joe Nanton fails to justify the generous space allotted him; and some of the transitional segues are amateurish and transparent.

"Brown," the most episodic section, is the most nearly perfect. Acknowledging "the black contribution in blood," it is compassionate, witty, patriotic, and acidic. It includes the raucous "West Indian Dance"; the immensely effective "Emancipation Celebration," where the jubilance of the young free blacks—expressed by Rex Stewart—is set in relief by the fearful commiseration of the older folks, represented in mournful duets; and "The Blues," a recitation sung by Betty Roche, which, naturally, is not a blues. This last part, dealing with the blues as a state of despondency rather than the cyclical form with which Ellington frequently dispelled blue feelings, is curiously un-Ellingtonian. In fact, the passage indicates Ellington's interest, beginning in the mid-30s, in composers and orchestrators tangential to his own tradition, including Gershwin, Delius, and Debussy. The line "sighing . . . crying . . ." is rooted in Gershwin's "They Pass By Singing," which fragment Gershwin may have speared from Debussy's *Nuages*. Ellington's eclecticism was the conscious manifestation of his best instincts, though, and "The Blues" is more effective than one might have expected.

A more ironic eclecticism is reflected in the "Sugar Hill" section of "Beige," which depicts Harlem's crème de la crème (the piece is also known as "Creamy Brown"). The suitably nostalgic "Sugar Hill Penthouse" builds to a voicing of clarinet above the saxophones—the trademark sound of Glenn Miller. It may be, as Gunther Schuller has pointed out, that Ellington himself invented that sound with the 1938 "Lost in Meditation," but in 1943 the technique was a signpost of white dance music, and therefore appropriate to a concluding passage wherein the assimilated Negro has gone from black to brown to beige. It is followed by the reprise of Hodges playing "Come Sunday," Ellington's magnificent spiritual. "Beige" is a continuing movement, but again the seams show. If his technique was not yet fully up to his conceptualization, his antennae were sharp as ever. At the conclusion, "Sunday" is taken at a dance-band tempo, in prophecy of "David Danced," his '60s feature for tap dancer Bunny Briggs. Percussive motives, patriotic airs, and a

constant, shifting antiphony give the work added cohesion, but
the most important unifying factor is the programmatic content. Much of Ellington's finest music was conceived with programmatic specificity; *BB&B* anticipates the masterly thematic
suites (*Such Sweet Thunder, Far East Suite*), the extended impressionistic orchestrations (*The Tattooed Bride, Ad Lib on
Nippon*), the near-perfect rhapsody *Harlem,* and even the pioneering television revue *A Drum Is a Woman.*

In 1958, Ellington collaborated with Mahalia Jackson for the
Columbia album *Black, Brown and Beige.* It consists of five extended movements based on "Work Song" and "Come Sunday,"
plus a spontaneous setting for the twenty-third Psalm. Ellington's lyric for "Come Sunday," introduced here, was the best he
ever wrote. But why was this excellent session so misleadingly
titled? Had he decided that these themes were all that were
worth preserving from the original? If so, he soon changed his
mind. Five years later, he reorchestrated "Come Sunday," adding the "David Danced" variation, "Light" (retitled "Montage"), and "The Blues" for the revue *My People,* presented at
the Century of Negro Progress Exposition in Chicago. "Come
Sunday" was interpreted three times in the 1965 *Concert of Sacred Music.* On the posthumously issued *The Intimate Ellington* (Pablo), there is a languorous performance of "Sugar Hill
Penthouse" (retitled "Symphonette") recorded in 1971, and indicative of Ellington's abiding pride in the materials of *BB&B.*
Yet the complete "tone parallel" remained unrecorded at his
death.

The problems in trying to re-create *BB&B* as a part of the
living repertoire are many. The Alan Cohen version has fine
section playing, but the rhythms are sluggish and the solos undistinguished—"Come Sunday" is played on soprano sax with
cornball grace notes that Hodges would have found intolerable.
The truism that Ellington wrote for specific individuals hardly
needs repeating, but in light of the Maurice Peress performance, a concomitant truism, that the instrumental techniques

of those individuals must be absorbed, does. Hodges was the master of glissando; precision and stunning tonal control were at the heart of his style. The altoist with the Kansas City Philharmonic was intent on beating Hodges gliss for gliss, with vulgar results. A melody as beautifully crafted as "Come Sunday" is not dependent on the talents of Hodges or Ray Nance, but they imbued Ellington's composition with their own musical personalities; in attempting to imitate them, the Peress musicians achieved only an unwitting parody—mannered saxophone playing with a fulsome vibrato.

When the Philharmonic shouted the "Work Song" theme, the excitement of the music was real and irresistible, but ineptness in replicating Ellington's stylistic trademarks—especially on the part of the brass players—made it seem more of a period piece than it is. The trumpets played with a deadening concision of sound; the plunger-muted soloists were at best workmanlike, and occasionally ugly. In a plunger solo, every note must be shaded with deliberation or the result is mere coyness. Jazz does not need to be legitimized; it needs to be trusted. Presumably a conservatory-trained virtuoso willing to embrace this music and study the instrumental stylings could achieve something like authenticity. Without that commitment, you can have Ellington's melodies but not Ellington's music. Of course, the rhythmic problems were even more considerable.

BB&B—and not just "Black"—is a rich, buxom work. Its stirring, affirmative self-confidence, proliferation of melodies and rhythms, and command of moods can only benefit Symphony Hall; subscribers bored with the romantics and weary of the avant garde should find it intriguingly new, yet accessible. But until a conductor with as intransigent a vision as Ellington's is commissioned to prepare *Black, Brown and Beige* for performance, it will have to be done in the Ellington manner. So far, no one from the jazz or symphonic worlds has measured up.

1975–77

Three or Four
Shades of Mingus

Charles Mingus died January 5, 1979, of a heart attack, in Cuernavaca, Mexico, where he was undergoing treatment for amytropic lateral sclerosis. Though confined to a wheelchair for most of the preceding year, he had been busy composing and recording—two ambitious orchestra works, "Something Like a Bird" and "Three Worlds of Drums," were recorded under his supervision, and there was an unfinished collaboration with Joni Mitchell. In a career that spanned nearly forty years (he dated "The Chill of Death" to 1939, when he was seventeen), Mingus was a bassist, pianist, composer, arranger, bandleader, record producer, festival organizer, and autobiographer, and he achieved something of lasting importance in every area. His large and bewildering legacy defies too quick an evaluation.

If Mingus didn't actually introduce fear and trembling into jazz, he was its most persistently apocalyptic voice. He could communicate joy as generously as any practitioner of what is generally considered a joyous music, but he often asked us to run the gauntlet with him before emerging triumphantly on the mountaintop. The records affirm the diversity and courage of his music, its relentless honesty and prophetic impact, its masterpieces; and they show that no composer-bandleader-instrumentalist since Ellington encompassed more of jazz's accomplishment and promise. Mingus *was* the black-music experience in the United States—in its hybridization, its questing after form, its improvisation, competitiveness, impertinence, outrage, intellectualization, joy, emotionalism, bitterness, comedy, parody, and frustration.

He was one of the handful of jazz composers who developed the small ensemble, contributed durable works to its repertoire, and enlarged its potential. His presence was a beacon on any bandstand. Bass walks edged with iron prodded and halted, chastened and praised the members of his Jazz Workshop, and if his instrumental comments alone were insufficient, he would shout encouragement or criticism, on occasion firing and hiring a musician in the same set. Yet only a moment later he would look as impassive as Heifetz, his imposing figure hulking around the bass, listening, listening. And always those leathery fingers were in control.

The power and expressive tone of Mingus's bass was always immediately recognizable. In the early '60s, he made the bass talk ("What Love," "Epitaph"), but those were merely extreme examples of a style that always suggested something of the human voice. His solo introduction to "Haitian Fight Song" was potent and pleading, and even the vamp with which it concludes, rising and lowering in dynamics, suggested a new tonal virtuosity, as did the invincible ostinato on "Prayer for Passive Resistance." Mingus avoided the purity of sound passed from Jimmy Blanton to Ray Brown, preferring to make each note reverberate as though the string had snapped against the wood. In this sense, there was a link between his peerless technique and the expressive slap-style bassists of Pops Foster's generation. Sometimes he enjoyed reviving Foster's style with affectionate parodies, and when he made the change from a two-beat to his own driving 4/4, as he does on "Jelly Roll," the point was always the continuity of tradition and never modernistic putdown. Although his influence on contemporary bassists is widely acknowledged by jazz and classical players, Mingus frequently insisted that he was unable to develop fully as an instrumentalist because of the time devoted to composing for and training the various editions of the Jazz Workshop. Yet there are numerous bass solos of rare magnificence in his recorded work, for example, the five-chorus improvisation with which he climaxed Jimmy Owens's "Lo-Slo Bluze" at the 1972 Newport Jazz Festival—New York (released on the defunct Cobblestone label as *Newport in New York '72/Vols. 1 and 2*). It's a fantasy for bass, and a microcosmic interweaving of several aspects of his compositional style—authentic rural blues licks, bebop, the Ellington influence (the third chorus is built on "Rocks in My Bed"), metrical ploys (double-timing and half-timing) handled with an emotional wallop that recalls Louis Armstrong's "Muggles," chromaticism, and swing-era walking (fast and slow).

Mingus revered Duke Ellington, with whom he shared the knack for composing vivid musical portraits of musicians, friends, and places—they were, in fact, the most autobiographical of composers—and the determination not to be limited by fads and categories. Only Mingus rivaled Ellington's compositional variety in the jazz tradition, and in the area of longer works he was in some respects more successful. Ellington's reputation is in no way dependent on his extended compositions (I except the suites), as rewarding as they are, but Mingus's concert music—"Half-Mast Inhibition" (1946), *Black Saint and Sinner Lady* (1963), "Meditations on Integration" (1965), "The Shoes of the Fisherman's Wife Are Some Jive Ass Slippers" (1965), "Music for 'Todo Modo'" (1976)—is essential to any evaluation of his work. Moreover, Mingus pioneered extended compositions for small ensembles, replacing the string-of-solos method with elaborate, architectonic structures in such remarkable performances as "Pithecanthropus Erectus" (1956), "Los Mariachis" and "Ysabel's Table Dance" (1957), "Folk Forms"

(1960), "So Long Eric" (1965), "Sue's Changes" (1975), and numerous others.

"Pithecanthropus Erectus" established Mingus's place in the jazz vanguard, signaling his rejection of clinical experimentalism in favor of the blues tradition itself. The thematic material is striking—a mysterious, modal melody propelled by a throbbing bass walk, climaxing with a three-beat rest, and resuming, with a sudden shift in dynamics, as a thirty-two-bar extension played with steadily increasing polyphony. Its most startling feature in 1956 was not the modality or the break or the uncommon structure, but the intensity that resulted from employing the extreme registers of the saxophone. Like the same album's "A Foggy Day," which also employs cacophony, "Pithecanthropus" was conceived programmatically (it concerns the evolution and destruction of the first man), which may explain why the saxophone blasts and squeals sound a bit studied.

Mingus also shared with Ellington an ability to train musicians in the exigencies of his music, compelling them to avoid clichés, and ultimately drawing from them their finest work. The question of autonomy in the Jazz Workshop is a difficult one. It is often noted that Mingus not only encouraged but insisted on originality—his exhortation to "stop copying Bird" was familiar to musicians and audiences alike at one time—but some Workshop graduates complained of chafing at Mingus's autocracy. Shafi Hadi has said that he didn't feel free to express himself, and Ted Curson remembers Mingus ordering Eric Dolphy not to play the bass clarinet. (That Dolphy played it anyway was interpreted as evidence of Mingus's particular respect for him.) At least one broken jaw and one sprained ankle have been attributed to musical disagreements. Still, the evidence adds up in Mingus's favor—many journeyman musicians, including Jerome Richardson, Richard Williams, Dick Hafer, J. R. Montrose, Wade Legge, Bobby Jones, Charles McPherson, Lonnie Hillyer, and Michael Brecker, achieved their best playing with him. The reputation of trumpeter Clarence Shaw is dependent solely on his three albums with Mingus; equally impressive is the consistently high quality of Shafi Hadi's performances on several Mingus sessions. Then there are the Workshop graduates who became major personalities themselves—Dolphy, Jackie McLean, Rahsaan Roland Kirk, Ted Curson, Jimmy Knepper, Booker Ervin, Roland Hanna, and Jaki Byard. The most loyal Mingus disciple was Dannie Richmond, a onetime rock-and-roll tenor saxophonist who at Mingus's suggestion switched to drums for *The Clown,* and became the heartbeat of his music, sensitized to its every nuance much as Sonny Greer's intuitive approach to the drums was annealed to Ellington's music.

In the late '50s, Mingus loomed over jazz, personifying the period's modernism and confessionalism. "I am about me" was the theme of his numerous public statements. With so much emotion so freely conveyed, he was soon characterized as angry and unpredictable, and even his humorous works were interpreted with wrinkled brow, both the scathing caricature of "Fables of Faubus" and the dadaistic slapstick of "Passions of a Man." Mingus was angry and proud, but he knew how to gauge his own abilities and didn't take New York like a hurricane until he was ready—there had been a long apprenticeship with Louis Armstrong, Dinah Washington, Lionel Hampton (who recorded Mingus's first influential composition, "Mingus Fingers," in 1947), Red Norvo, and others. He recorded and composed throughout the '40s and early '50s, working briefly with his two idols, Ellington and Parker, experimenting with cool jazz and what would later be termed third-stream directions, before everything fell into place with the first Jazz Workshop sessions. His combativeness against the exploitation of black musicians also began long before he had a national reputation, when he formed Debut records, the first of several unsuccessful attempts to operate independently of the recording industry.

He was always good with words, and by 1959 was known to

berate noisy audiences with brutal contempt and chilling wit. Diane Dorr-Dorynek once transcribed a diatribe at the Five Spot: "I listen to your millions of conversations, sometimes pulling them all up and putting them together and writing a symphony. But you never hear that symphony—that I might dedicate to the mother who brought along a neighbor and talked three sets and two intermissions about the old man across the hall making it with Mrs. Jones's son in the apartment below where the schoolteacher lives with Cadillac Bill. And how she's thinking of taking up teaching if Mary gets any more minks like that white one she just gave her sister Sal, who's in and out on weekdays and leaves town on weekends with her Rolls-Royce full of pretty teachers. And how it's difficult to keep the facts of life from her daughter Chi-Chi. . . ." Recitations were employed in his music—there were collaborations with Lonnie Elder and Jean Shepherd—and rumors about a 1000-page autobiography called *Beneath the Underdog* were current when I began listening to him in 1963. Provocative excerpts appeared, but they didn't show up in the 365-page book that eventually appeared under that title in 1971. Mingus decided against a strict autobiographical approach or an exposé of the music business, producing instead a fearsome *Bildungsroman* that depicts his initiation into sex, music, therapy, depression, and love, in a singular style, mostly dialogue, partly dialectic, sometimes parody. The evocations of Ellington and Fats Navarro have been widely admired, but there are equally accomplished passages about his father, other musicians, and women (the sixteenth chapter portrays one relationship in the style of the breakfast sequence in *Citizan Kane*). Edited by Nell King, it is harrowing and revealing, obfuscating and boastful. What happened to the rest of the manuscript?

The book's publication signaled Mingus's return to music after a mystifying hiatus of five years, when he was said to be semiretired. The comeback was formally marked by a triumphant concert at Philharmonic Hall early in 1972, with a twenty-piece orchestra and several guest soloists (Gene Ammons was most prominently featured). The music, eventually released on the album *Charles Mingus and Friends in Concert,* included rousing performances of two nearly forgotten pieces from the early '50s, "Jump Monk" and "E.S.P.," and his euphoric Methodist hymn, "Ecclusiastics." "Mingus Blues," a dialogue with Ammons, demonstrated his profound respect for the elemental power of church music and the classic blues form, as did "E's Flat, Àh's Flat Too," a blues jam with a standout contribution by flutist James Moody. The high point was a new work, "Little Royal Suite," written for Roy Eldridge and played by eighteen-year-old Jon Faddis, whose reputation was made that night. It is characteristically varied in design, as serialism and Jelly Roll Morton meet on a stage of billowing ostinato figures and throbbing dissonances.

More impressive still was the release that year of *Let My Children Hear Music,* his first studio-recorded orchestral record since the 1960 *Pre-Bird Mingus,* and his densest and most exhausting album. The weakest selection, "The Chill of Death," is a naïve period piece from his confused teens, when he fell under the sway of Strauss's *Death and Transfiguration* and Yoga, and attempted to will himself to death. A spoken parable describes death as a woman and hell as Mingus's fate; its inclusion served to emphasize his eclectic, "pre-Bird" interests, and to illuminate his development as a composer. In the album's masterpiece, "The Shoes of the Fisherman's Wife," the early concerns—courage, fear, hesitation, acceptance—find a purely musical correlative. It's tempting to interpret its three major themes impressionistically, but then Mingus operated at an emotional, often rapturous level. It was in part the vividness of his romantic imagination (he rejected techniques that weren't "spiritual") that made the longer works credible and absorbing. Recurring stylistic episodes—improvised dialectics by two or more horns, modal ethnicity, Ellingtonian Sugar Hill sophistication, Parker's extravagant virtuosity—were used as building blocks in Mingusian fantasies, where the lingering shadow of childhood was as alive as the intimacy of death.

The *Three or Four Shades of Blues* album (1977) represented an attempt to broaden his appeal by using electric guitars and young white musicians associated with pop-jazz fusions. The results were amiable and relaxed, particularly the title work, a witty casserole of acknoweldged influences. Yet when Mingus first heard the tapes, he was contemptuous and sent a scathing telegram to his producer, accusing the label of making him look ridiculous. When the record outsold all his others, he changed his mind. But if Mingus controlled those collaborations while he was alive, they've gotten out of hand since his death. A memorial concert at which his songs were played by a fusion band, and larger works by an orchestra laden with fusion-oriented soloists, vitiated the music's spunk and verve. The Joni Mitchell project, as she completed it, was tepid, unswinging, and sentimental. Only a small ensemble called Mingus Dynasty, consisting of Jazz Workshop graduates, demonstrated how vital a role Mingus's music could still play in the jazz repertoire, but it too founders in the absence of Mingus's leadership.

Mingus is misinterpreted by those who take his example as license for facile eclecticism. He believed and rejoiced in the priorities of swing and the blues; he extended the emotional and technical scope of jazz within its essential idiomatic constraints. The *Pre-Bird Mingus* album was designed to show that Mingus was precocious, ambitious, and modern before he encountered Charlie Parker, but he was a pre-Bird musician in a more profound sense: in his love of pure emotion as exemplified in the blues, the church, and the polyphony of New Orleans; in his willingness to embrace the full panoply of jazz styles; in his absorption of the colors, styles, subtleties, and charms of Ellington and Tatum. He brought all of that into the modern era with individuality and a startling magnanimity of expression. He could swing as hard as any musician ever had (the last chorus of the remake of "Better Get Hit in Yo Soul" or "Hora Decubitis," for example), he wrote distinguished ballads ("Old Portrait," "Good-bye Pork Pie Hat," "I X Love," "Carolyn Keikki Mingus"), and he continuously drew on tradition, assimilating European techniques as well as those of black music, rejecting only cant, slavishness, sentimentality, and dishonesty. And for all his orneriness, he was astonishingly consistent in performance. No one enjoyed his music more than he, and even during the worst of evenings there was always one moment when the gaunt, dissatisfied-face gave way to dimpled grin and flashing eyes as the spirit of his music soared, took hold, and warmed everyone present.

1978–79

Ornette Coleman, Continued

In the fall of 1959, Ornette Coleman brought a quartet comprising Don Cherry, Charlie Haden, and Billy Higgins from Los Angeles to New York's Five Spot. The furor that ensued is well documented. Within a few months, Ed Blackwell replaced Higgins, and within three and a half years, Coleman, having played Einstein to Charlie Parker's Newton, retired for two years, never fully to resume a constant regimen of performing and recording. His every subsequent return signaled another attempt at innovation—unorthodox stylings on violin and trumpet in 1965, his nine-year-old son as drummer in 1966, chamber music and Dewey Redman in 1967, *Skies of America* in 1972, and Prime Time in 1976. These later incarnations spurred new controversies, while the achievements of Coleman's original quartets were thoroughly absorbed into jazz.

1. *Magnum Opus*

Skies of America (Columbia), the finest symphonic writing to come out of jazz, was recorded in London in nine hours, following two rehearsals. Coleman's craftsmanship and the confidence with which he steered eighty-five musicians through the difficult work earned him a standing ovation from the London Symphony. It has been performed only once since then, with the Symphony of the New World, at the 1973 Newport Jazz Festival—New York, and Coleman's inability to have it performed more frequently frustrated his attempt to realize a compositional theory he calls harmelodic modulation.

Harmelodic playing would allow each member of the orchestra to improvise range at will—that is, use any octave while playing the same notes in the same harmonic relationship. The idea is to vary the music with each performance, and toward that end Coleman would permit any instrument or combination of instruments to be substituted in the improvised sections. Furthermore, the work can be started anywhere and the parts placed in any sequence. He had previously employed his theory in writings for string quartet and woodwind sextet, and would subsequently make it the basis of his electric band, Prime Time. For the recorded version of *Skies of America,* Coleman notated the entire composition, including the important tympani part, and played all the improvisations himself; David Measham conducted.

Coleman, in the theoretical apparatus outlined in his own liner notes, says that the texture of his orchestral writing results from "the total collective blending of the transposed and nontransposed instruments using the same intervals." He also says that "there are eight themes and a harmelodic movement for each theme," although there are twenty-one titled sections, ranging in duration from "The New Anthem" (thirty-one seconds) to "Love Life" (four minutes thirty-four seconds). His formulations give the impression of a more complicated and radical music than the ear actually hears—the work is readily approachable and can be enjoyed without the footnotes.

The skies of Coleman's America are often sullen and overcast, with storms sluggishly brewing above earthly rumblings, but they are illuminated by the robust glare of his alto saxophone, and by the heady thrust of bright melodies swarming through the massed strings. He has assembled a compositional montage including so typical a Coleman melody as "Holiday for Heroes" on the one hand, and the Coplandish "Sunday in America" on the other; Stravinsky and Mingus are other discernible influences, but every part is imbued with Coleman's individuality, and though the textures are thick, the music is never unwieldy. There are logy moments, compounded by a muddiness in the orchestration, but generally the passages of great sadness and loveliness and passion were lucidly conceived and straightforwardly played.

The first theme—built on two long descending tones followed by two long ascending ones—serves as a recurring motif. Additional melodic snatches reappear in different contexts, lending unity to the sundry themes. Side one concludes with an enchanting theme, "The Artist in America," which introduces Coleman's declamatory alto coursing over the strings in a mood of jubilation. It's a particularly lively entrance. Coleman reappears in "Foreigner in a Free Land," and plays throughout the second side. His phrasing extends to the limits of his breathing and conveys a vertiginous sense of ingenuity and surprise; especially noteworthy is his unaccompanied solo on "The Men Who Live in the White House." *Skies of America* offers numerous pleasures to Coleman's admirers, but it is a major achievement by any standard and mandatory listening for those interested in contemporary music.

2. Dancing the Blues

Ornette Coleman calls his first recording since 1972 *Dancing in Your Head* (Horizon), but he might also have called it *Dancing on Your Feet*, or, had he a taste for Blake, *Songs of Innocence and Experience*. It consists of two lengthy variations on "Theme from a Symphony," recorded in 1975, and a 1973 encounter with the Master Musicians of Joujouka, Morocco. It is so cantankerously alive you can't listen to it without moving around.

As testimony to his powers as an improvisor, it is a radiant companion to *Skies of America,* and proof that the blues can no longer be defined purely in terms of traditional structures.

"Theme from a Symphony" is "The Good Life" from *Skies of America,* here elongated by repetition from a quasi-blues to a delirious chant, and improved by a funkier final cadence. An introduction by guitar establishes a rhythm-and-blues framework, but Coleman is the only soloist. Supported by an exceptionally sturdy rhythm section (two guitars, bass, and drums), he streams over the backbeat with strength, certitude, and imagination. In fact, if these two long solos were transcribed, you could probably catalogue a concordance of Coleman's musical vocabulary from them. Without referring to the theme, he offers one fresh lick after another, almost any one of which would sit nicely in the most primitive of blues settings.

Unexpectedly, they bring to mind Charlie Christian, who in such extended improvisations as "Swing to Bop" prefigured Coleman's rhythmic momentum, burnished tone, and a procedural style that meshed a limitless fund of riffs with longer, lyrical phrases. Because he used song forms, Christian tended to alternate riff and melody, as did Lester Young, according to the cyclical structure of the song. Coleman eschews A themes and releases and even bar lines, but like Christian, he crafts his solos with attention to infectious riffs, of which he is also a prolific master, and more melodic figures. The constant yet tempestuous rhythms will encourage some to dance; others will be alienated by the unvarying intensity. Coleman's sound—that natural, gut-wrenching cry of his horn—demands attention.

Coleman organized the performance according to his harmelodic concept, in which instruments are not transposed to a concert key, and he probably wrote the two phrases that bassist Rudy MacDaniel alternates behind the theme and periodically during Coleman's solo. The bass makes the only references to the theme, apparently in premeditated collusion with drummer Shannon Jackson: on a couple of occasions, we hear choked cymbals followed by MacDaniel's theme reprisal. But even without that reminder, you never stop hearing the theme in your mind's ear, because of the unflagging rhythmic pulse and Coleman's ability to sustain the jubilance of his theme throughout the improvisation. Coleman is the singingest of instrumentalists—I'd love to hear him (and Sonny Rollins, too) record with a reggae band.

We get a different kind of pollination in "Midnight Sunrise" with the Joujouka musicians, a mesmeric encounter in which Coleman blends unexpectedly well with the Moroccan horns over an oddly affecting rhythmic pattern. In his notes, Coleman writes of resolving "Western and Eastern musical forms," and this he accomplishes much as Ellington did, by remaining true to himself, to his personal voice, while admitting the influence of other cultures. There is not an iota of pastiche in his music; he brings out the blues in everyone he works with (even the London Symphony). Everyone triumphs accordingly—and in unison, to use one of Coleman's favorite phrases.

Body Meta (Artists House), recorded at the same sessions that produced "Theme from a Symphony," is another chapter in Coleman's restive struggle to stay ahead of his audience. It's not the sustained firecracker that the earlier release was, but the variety of settings—five very different pieces—provide greater insight into the workings of Prime Time, his electrified quintet. If Coleman had recorded the material acoustically, or even with an electric band working along the lines of his celebrated quartets and trios, they would be received as examples of a classic style. But Coleman persists in forging ahead, harmonically and rhythmically (the melodies linger on). Coleman's original approach to harmony was revolutionary because he did away with superimposed chord progressions, yet the serendipitous harmonies that resulted were basically consonant, since the musicians were attempting to complement each other's key changes. With Prime Time, Coleman is attacking harmonic rules from another angle, by deliberately placing different keys in opposition to

each other. A wall-of-sound illusion is thus effected, as the contrasting keys make every instrument seem equal, and the sonic
space created by these clashing harmonies makes it possible for
the listener to sing or play along in any key and sound right.
You have to learn to listen to Coleman's music all over again—
his solos haven't changed appreciably, but a new and bizarre
environment has to be traversed to hear them. The rhythmic
evolution is subtler; a backbeat is implied, yet the rhythms remain unimpeded by bar lines or, for the most part, fixed
patterns.

Perhaps the most revealing place to begin is "European
Echoes," since Coleman's 1965 recording of that waltz was a
particular triumph. The new version is so radically altered it
could have passed with another title. The first version (on *At
the Golden Circle, Vol. 1*) had an A theme with three notes per
measure and an accent on every second beat, and a longer B
theme with two notes per measure on the first two beats. In the
new version, the A theme is twice as long with the accent on
the first beat (it's the difference between *da DEE da da DEE da*
and *DEE da da da DEE da da;* to accentuate the nursery-song effect in the later version, he syncopates initial measures as *DEE
da-da da-da*), and the B part is completely revised as a brief an-
archic figure that breaks with the waltz meter. This performance is unusual both because the harmonies are fairly consonant during the theme recitations (they broaden like parting
icebergs during Coleman's improvisation), and because Coleman's solo is rather tenuous, lacking the compelling lucidity of
his solo fourteen years before. "Voice Poetry" and "Home
Grown" are excellent Coleman performances. The first begins
with an interlude by the two guitars, bass, and drums on Bo
Diddly's signature rhythm figure; Coleman enters wailing the
blues with long, crying tones, and proceeds with short, fragmented melodies that bustle and build with characteristic invention. "Home Grown" is a surreal hoedown, a swinging
refraction of rhythm and blues with giddy colors from the dis-

cretely voiced instruments. Coleman's solo ends with a sequence of sustained pitches and frenzied, circular licks that wind seamlessly into the theme. "Macho Woman" is a lusty blues, and "Fou Amour," a dirge almost fatally cluttered by the accompaniment, which is supportive everywhere else.

3. Something Old, Something New

Old and New Dreams, a quartet consisting of Don Cherry, Charlie Haden, Eddie Blackwell, and Dewey Redman, was organized in 1978 to celebrate the achievements of the original Ornette Coleman quartets. Originally reunited for a recording session by Italy's Black Saint label, the musicians successfully toured the United States in the spring of 1979, including two sold-out performances at the Public Theater in New York. The sheer accessibility of the performances—the adoring audience whooped with recognition at the themes and endless improvisational conceits—almost made me forget that this happy music had once represented the climactic blow in what George Russell had termed the "war on chords." In perfecting the Coleman method of unfixed key centers and rhythms, where pitch was a matter of personal expression, where tried-and-true licks would no longer get you through a solo, these musicians helped alter every aspect of jazz.

Cherry's solos displayed a poignant tone, alternately broad and chipped, and were wrested from a cornet instead of his usual pocket trumpet. They were built with short, melodic fragments and vibratoless vocalisms, and were intensely rhythmic, as was the whole band. On the boppish "Dewey's Tune," he punched his discrete figures with febrile concentration against the relentless surf of Blackwell and Haden, augmenting his lyricism with pensive delivery. Melodic invention is rare in jazz, as it is in all musics, and Cherry's ability to combine four or five notes in songful tunes that weld into sustained improvisations is the hallmark of his achievement. His penchant for parabolas of unaccented eighth notes provides effective contrast. At the end of a Coleman blues, Cherry brought the tempo to a halt to play Albert Ayler's "Ghosts" as a reflective ballad; on two other pieces, he played rocking piano figures in unison with Haden's bass to establish another kind of rural funk. And yet for all the diversity and authority of Cherry's playing, the horns occupied a reticent, even introverted role in comparison to the rhythm players, whose dancing challenge never subsided. Redman actually seemed uneasy for much of the performance. Redman is earthier than Cherry on the Black Saint session, but his warming blues riffs were infrequently asserted, and only rarely did his personal, Mobleyesque sound take charge; he actually sounded unfamiliar with Coleman's "Lonely Woman." His most convincing solo was played on musette.

Haden and Blackwell were marvels, separately and together, and there was nothing more rewarding about this remarkable ensemble than the way the center of rhythmic action passed from one to the other. The bassist's approach to time is unique; he alternates ferocious walks with relaxed ostinatos, spare note patterns, and the longest phrases I've heard short of circular-breathing hornmen. The result is a kind of swinging rubato. Haden's tone is positively burnished, and when he is possessed by rhapsody, as on "Lonely Woman" or "Chairman Mao," he can make your skin tingle. His every solo was a highlight, studded with hammering-on techniques, below-the-bridge plucking, and double stops for color. He is constantly attentive, and no one since Mingus has made the bass sing with more emotional impact. In many ways, Blackwell is his twin, and he actually translated some of Haden's ideas to the drums in split-second relays. He is the group's primordial soul, always swinging, though his rhythms fall into patterns that demolish bar demarcation. These patterns can be melodious—for example, the montage of snares, toms, cymbals, and rim shots that served as a vamp for "Chairman Mao"—and smoldering, as on one of

Cherry's piano pieces, where the cross rhythms sounded like a tribal drum choir.

Much has happened during the past twenty years to the four musicians whose Old and New Dreams remain so winning and inspiriting—particularly an increased concern with musical internationalism. The changes, the maturity, the mutual admiration could only enhance and refine the concept behind Ornette Coleman's original "change of the century." Unlike Columbia's V.S.O.P. and Milestone's Jazzstars, this was a real reunion, not a one-shot publicity coup. I hope they reunite long enough to make more recordings and give everyone smart enough to want to hear them the chance. Going a mile farther, imagine *Free Jazz, Part II*—a collusion of Old and New Dreams with Prime Time.

4. Jazz-Funk After Prime Time

It was Albert Ayler's conviction that the new jazz of the 1960s could be a people's music, its rustic ardor consummated in rather than tempered by the vivacious rhythms that had always nourished black music. But Ayler's nervous synthesis was swayed by a flower power compromise, and his own power blanched accordingly. With Ornette Coleman's *Dancing in Your Head*, free improvisation, modal ostinatos, and the high decibels and coloration of rock found a genuinely indivisible form; his marathon solos proved that free expression could actually expand within the discipline of funk. A quartet organized early in 1979 by Coleman's disciple James Blood Ulmer and sampled at the Public Theater took that merger a bold step further.

Ronald Shannon Jackson, a charismatic drummer whose presence in the bands of Coleman, Cecil Taylor, and Ulmer amounted to a one-man crusade for expansive, two-beat percussion, was the music's vital center. He used an overgrip in both hands and pealed melodically over the traps, effecting a fast, pinched champing on the high-hat, heroic echoes from the toms, bell accents on a tiny cymbal, and constant bass-drum rumbling. In tandem with the bassist, Amin Ali, who generally alternated riffs and drone chords with a fiery eight-beat walk, Jackson's rhythms were decisive but not constricting.

The most arresting virtue of Ulmer's guitar playing is that it doesn't sound like anyone else's. He doesn't play long, fluid phrases with triplets tumbling over minor thirds, in the manner of jazz guitarists, nor does he inch chromatically upward with the facile melodrama of rock guitarists; he uses a wah-wah pedal all the time but never for a wah-wah sound. His sound is choked and vocalized, embellished with generous hand vibrato, and his solos follow a procedure reminiscent of Coleman—a series of units made of short, agitated riffs that build to a sustained phrase or an exclamatory wail. The intensity of his playing has a lot to do with the understatement and originality of his ideas (he is never glib) and the relaxed independence with which those splintered phrases float over the rhythm. Yet David Murray and not Ulmer was the most exultant soloist. In this band, he put aside his usual nod time to play on or ahead of the beat, barreling vortically through the registers of the tenor sax, and his density was the perfect, aggressive foil for Ulmer's ellipses.

For all its vitality, the quartet was not yet a complete success. The written material was generally interesting, but its range was modest, and Ulmer seemed indecisive about just how willing he was to have his music ruled by a metronome. I'm reluctant to suggest that those selections where the rhythms were most free meandered, since it was evident from the startling precision of the themes and transitions that the musicians knew exactly what they were doing. But if a band can rock it should rock without apology, and the unity of purpose that can make a singular concept soar beyond workshop intentions was only intermittently present.

The themes were superbly played in and out of phase, and

the deft unison of guitar and tenor luminously bright. One piece, a second cousin to Coleman's "Cross Breeding," made use of asymmetrical pauses, and another grew layer on layer from an unaccompanied Ulmer solo that revealed his affinity for old-time blues guitarists, as he hammered a primitive echoic matrix of single notes and chords. At the apex of the band's best crescendos, a kind of centrifugal force was generated, and as I concentrated on the feverishly massed voicings rather than the soloist-plus-rhythm combinations, the center stayed as calm as a hurricane's eye. A question remained: how many people will endorse a people's music that insists on anarchy as part of the democratic way?

1972–79

The AACM in New York

When Muhal Richard Abrams, the cofounder and first president of Chicago's Association for the Advancement of Creative Music (AACM), moved to New York in the summer of 1976, he was assured of finding a modicum of work in the musician-owned lofts that proliferated at the time. As an alternative to the nightclubs and bars where jazz is usually heard, the lofts attracted an adventurous coterie, and Abrams's reputation was such that his arrival seemed a crest on the wave of recently relocated musicians from Chicago, St. Louis, and California. The impact of these players on the local music scene was great, as was New York's impact on them. As Abrams noted, "New York will accelerate anything that comes here."

The significance of so many obscure but accomplished musicians working under rotating leadership, usually but not exclusively in loft venues, was widely recognized, but misconceptions arose. There was, to dispense with the most common of them, neither a loft nor an AACM style of jazz. Loft jazz is any jazz played in a loft; "AACM music," in Abrams's words, "is all the people in the AACM." Loft concertizing encouraged kaleidoscopic ensemble combinations and a willingness to experiment, but the helter-skelter race for bookings discouraged steadily working groups, and many musicians were disinclined to master one another's scores.

In fact, a distinguishing characteristic of the new movement was that it wasn't a movement at all, at least not one with significant stylistic parameters. A few rules obtained at concerts produced under the auspices of the AACM—e.g., all participants had to be members, all music had to be original—but even they were designed to encourage originality and independence. The new wave was ecumenical, capable of absorbing all sorts of creative musicians; unlike previous new waves, however, it was bolstered by a social and political support system. It balanced the tradition's past and present, and its ideal representative was both virtuoso and classicist.

Free jazz was well into its third decade when the AACM revitalized New York jazz; as an evolving substyle, the avant-garde had already outlived swing and bop and cool, having been variously called the New Music, the New Jazz, and the New Thing. I prefer Ornette Coleman's phrase "free jazz," with its suggestion of boundless tolerance and the absence of pandemic assumptions about form and rules of play. American music was in a state of crisis in the mid-'50s, when the agitation was first felt: pop had grown feeble and decadent, and jazz forgot the breath of its history long enough to allow the rigors of bop to become a vice. There were notable attempts even before 1950 to keep innovation alive (consider the work of Thelonious Monk, Miles Davis, Lennie Tristano, George Russell, and Charles Mingus), but standards had become inflexible, as evidenced by the shameful repudiation of Monk during his most creative years. Recognition came to Monk, though, as it did not to such lesser but valued craftsmen as Herbie Nichols and Jaki Byard.

The presence of an accomplished advance guard was undeniable by the late '50s, and Ornette Coleman, Cecil Taylor, and John Coltrane emerged as its leaders. Yet the diversity of their approaches to a newly charted freedom, as opposed to the relatively tight-knit Parker-Gillespie school, failed to indicate how widespread was the frustration among young musicians. Only with the spate of new-music recordings in the mid-'60s, frequently accompanied by militant haranguing, did a generation of players who felt tyrannized by chord changes find the confidence to search for something else. Ironically, the hegemony enjoyed by rock, and the resultant refusal of major record companies to document the ongoing developments in jazz, contributed to the renaissance in pure improvisational music: Stripped of access to star-making machinery, musicians were increasingly willing to shoot for the moon. Nonetheless, there was the problem of survival.

Several musicians started their own record labels in the early '50s, and in 1960, Charles Mingus and Max Roach formed the Jazz Artists' Guild in an attempt to assume control over all aspects of their careers. In 1964, Bill Dixon organized a four-day festival in New York, called the October Revolution in Jazz, from which grew the Jazz Composers' Guild, and Horace Tapscott created the Underground Musician's Association in Watts in Los Angeles. For various reasons—conflicting egos, racial tension—they all failed. By 1970, some of New York's best-known musicians felt desperate enough to make assaults on the media. Under the banner of the Jazz and People's Movement (which included Rahsaan Roland Kirk, Cecil Taylor, Lee Morgan, Archie Shepp, Andrew Cyrille, Freddie Hubbard, and Roy Haynes), they disrupted several television talk shows. The result was a single appearance on the Ed Sullivan show by an all-star band, to which a curious response was printed in the letters column of *Down Beat:*

"I respect the musicians who appeared on that show," the letter concluded, "but you can count me as one who knows they didn't do shit but make some small amount of bread for a very few. Of CBS, I ask: was that the token show—our only choice?"

It was signed "Leroy Jenkins AACM violinist." Jenkins was

hardly known outside of Chicago at the time, nor was the AACM, despite painstaking chronicling by local writers and the release of a few remarkable records. The average *Down Beat* reader could understand Jenkins's anger, but not the source of his aloofness. Musicians, however, had known about the AACM for years; in the wake of so many unsuccessful cooperatives, its principles were adopted by artists' groups in other cities, including St. Louis (Black Artists' Group), Detroit (Strata), and New York (Collective Black Artists).

The AACM grew out of a band Abrams founded in the early '60s. The Experimental Band, as it was called, had no particular identity, depending on the resources of its diverse arrangers and musicians, among them Eddie Harris, Donald Garrett, and Victor Sproles. Abrams was the oldest, with playing experience dating back to the late '40s, but the authority he carried stemmed from personal qualities suggested in an oft-quoted statement by Joseph Jarman: "Until I had the first meeting with Richard Abrams, I was like all the rest of the 'hip' ghetto niggers; I was cool, I took dope, I smoked pot, etc. . . . In having the chance to work in the Experimental Band with Richard and the other musicians there, I found something with meaning/reason for doing. . . ." Roscoe Mitchell credited the Experimental Band with freeing him from the strictures of prevailing styles.

Abrams—an amiable man who looks like an Egyptian carving: high shoulders, prominent cheek bones, a long chinbeard, and a mustache that thins to a pencil line—described the Experimental Band as doing "innocent things, like the AACM, but in a larger setting." Three members—Steve McCall, Phil Cohran, and Jodie Christianson—met with him to map out a tentative format for a more comprehensive organization. In 1965, a meeting was called for all the musicians in the city interested in promoting their own music and "setting up a showcase to bring to the public music that otherwise could not be heard through commercial channels." The AACM emerged with about 100 members and a few basic rules, like the one about performing original works: "We were not in the business of showcasing standards." Abrams considers the infatuation jazz musicians had for Tin Pan Alley in the '30s and '40s a diversion, insisting that before jazz became popular the musicians played their own music—"So we were just hooking up with the real tradition. Besides, there was so much talent, so much originality, and we thought it should be encouraged."

A year after the initial meeting that gave birth to the AACM, producer Chuck Nessa convinced Delmark Records, a Chicago label with a large blues catalogue, to let him record some of the AACM musicians. *Sound,* by the Roscoe Mitchell Sextet, remains one of the decade's seminal albums. It provided an introduction for most jazz enthusiasts to six imaginative and refreshing instrumentalists: trumpeter Lester Bowie, trombonist-cellist Lester Lashley (now involved in studio work), tenor saxophonist Maurice McIntyre (also known as Kalaparusha), percussionist Alvin Fielder (now running a pharmacy in Mississippi), and the extraordinary Wilbur Ware–inspired bassist Malachi Favors, who was largely responsible for the introduction of "little instruments." (Abrams: "They had to do with our thoughts regarding African instruments.") Little instruments, some of them homemade, include harmonicas, kalimbas, bells, recorders, sirens, kotos, whistles, temple blocks, and log drums. Their presence was ubiquitous in the music of the Art Ensemble of Chicago (which grew out of Roscoe Mitchell's Art Ensemble, which grew out of the AACM, which grew out of the Experimental Band). The paradoxical use of relatively inexpressive instruments to flesh out almost obsessively expressive works was matched by a paradoxical use of minimalist melodies to construct extended canvases.

The three selections of *Sound* were archetypal. The two themes constituting "Ornette" admiringly evoked Coleman at a time when most of the jazz world was under the blanketing spell of Coltrane. Roscoe Mitchell's liveliness, his bulleting phrases and great bursts of sound, were well displayed. The side-long "Sound" combined tableaux that have since become familiar components in the music of the Art Ensemble: Debussyan piping-in-a-glen, welcome-to-the-inner-sanctum creaking, infantlike whimpering contrasted with belling dynamics. In place of a succession of solos, "Sound" employed abrupt juxtapositions. Colors changed even more rapidly on "Little Suite," as a harmonica blues, with recorder, bass, and scrapper midrash, gave way to a precipitous march, a lyrical theme, saxophone harmonics, a recorder-bass duet, shouts, and kissing sounds. In his notes, J. B. Figi described "Little Suite" as "a patchwork quilt of staggered statements," and like a quilt its shape was mutable.

During the next two years, Nessa started his own label and released two immensely satisfying albums. *Numbers 1 & 2,* with a Mitchell cover painting that returned Picasso's *Three Musicians* to their African source of inspiration, was Lester Bowie's first album. On "Number 1," the three participants played little instruments, and although there was no drummer the density achieved was startling; Joseph Jarman—"the AACM's theater man," according to Abrams—was added on "Number 2," and the results were notable for the ensemble invention and the precision of each man. *Congliptious,* by the Roscoe Mitchell Art Ensemble, manipulated a plethora of jazz instrumental techniques to an unprecedented degree. These musicians were as responsive to the delta blues and Chuck Berry as to Ellington and Miles Davis, and within the course of one piece, Bowie might play parade trumpet with saccharine vibrato, long, low melody tones out of Miles Davis, Rex Stewart growls, and staccato firecrackers that were pure Bowie. His outstanding unaccompanied trumpet solo, "Jazz Death?" begins with a brassy harumph followed by a corny trill, which Bowie interrupts in the person of Dave Flexingbergstein of *Jism* magazine, who wants to know if jazz "as we know it" is dead. An imaginative if occasionally purple improvisation follows, after which he says cavalierly, "Well, I guess that all depends on what you know." Bowie then returns to the trumpet with a parade figure (AACM musicians are singularly march-conscious), some torrid Harry James balladry, raspberries, growls, a bop riff, and a mocking wah-wah rejoinder.

Dada obtrudes everywhere, and the drolleries suggest an anthropological awareness that supersedes cognizance of the black-music tradition. *People in Sorrow* (1969), which may well be the Art Ensemble's masterpiece, builds from primeval indirection to flowering melody, from amorphousness to arching structure. It begins with several seconds of silence, timidly intruded upon by minimalist fragments and percussive sounds that softly trace the central melody. About two-thirds through the first side, we hear unintelligible voices and the creaking of a rocker in the blistering country sun, after which a percussion interlude reintroduces the primary theme, quietly but firmly asserted. The melody, reminiscent of Hale Smith's "Feathers," blooms on side two, with sundry and increasingly dynamic variations. Nothing is sacred to anthropologists, except perhaps for human history itself, and the Art Ensemble, always hovering between burlesque and pathos, has dallied with bebop ("Dexterity" and Bowie's Gillespie-like solo on "Montiverdi II," which has New Orleans changes), shuffle blues ("Old"), rhythm and blues ("Bye Bye Baby"), African chants ("Bap-Tizm," and the Miriam Makeba-like opening of "How Strange"), street-corner chants ("Certain Blacks"), rock ("Rock Out"), decorous soul ("Theme de Yoyo"), hard bop ("Ohnedaruth," another good extended quilt), Albert Ayler in the vicinity of Anton Webern ("Lebert Aaly"), gospel ("Old Time Religion"), and audio theater ("Spiritual"). They've also crafted such provocatively indigenous pieces as Mitchell's "Unanka," Favors's "Tutankhamen," and the quartet's "Proverbs I," which Mingus appropriated as "Canon" for his *Mingus Moves*.

The AACM was beset by tragedy in 1969, when two promising twenty-four-year-old members, Christopher Gaddy and

Charles Clark, died within a month of each other. The shock of their deaths suffused the organization with impatience; no longer willing to wait for the world to come to them, the Art Ensemble, Anthony Braxton, Leo Smith, and Leroy Jenkins embarked on a lengthy tour of Europe, where they won international recognition. The Art Ensemble recorded most of the pieces mentioned above in Europe, and found its fifth member, percussionist Don Moye.

Meanwhile, the release of additional albums by Jarman, Abrams, and Braxton further established the diversity of the AACM musicians. Joseph Jarman's "As If It Were the Seasons" is a twenty-four-bar song employing three octaves, and is played on recorder, cello, soprano sax, and alto sax before Sherri Scott sings it twice, alone and with violent counterpoint. She's not the coloratura the music demands, but the performance integrates voice in a fresh and unusual manner. Jarman's saxophone solos, never as eccentric as Mitchell's or as stiffly virtuosic as Braxton's, are always accessible, no matter how frenzied, by virtue of their dynamic clarity; his compositions occasionally recall Satie, Debussy, and Stravinsky. Jarman's impact on the Art Ensemble was characterized by an increased accent on theater and sustained sound mosaics, and a marked decrease in the abrupt juxtapositions perfected by the ensemble when Mitchell was in control. Abrams suggests that if Jarman were given the opportunity to record his ambitious orchestrations, as Braxton has, they would be as impressively received.

Abrams conceives of his own recordings as projects, each designed to address a specific musical problem. His cover painting on *Levels and Degrees of Light* includes a pit colored with square patches in the manner of Paul Klee, and intimates the static, hallucinatory quality of the music. Voice is used differently on each of the three selections, for wordless vocalizing, choral recitation, and poetry. The haunting title selection is best, thanks in part to Penelope Taylor's fine contralto. Abrams is heard on clarinet, searing, even cramped in tone, buffeted by and echoing through the crescendos and diminuendos of Thurman Barker's drums and Gordon Emanuel's vibes. On "The Bird Song," however, the temptation to build a bleeding sonic boom through the use of echo proved irresistible, and the individual contributions are distorted and nullified, though the colors are frequently arresting.

Abrams's thirty-minute piano solo, "Young at Heart," fancifully integrates a panoply of piano techniques into a sustained improvisation—something Jaki Byard (whom Abrams much admires) and Giuseppi Logan previously attempted. His third album, *Things To Come from Those Now Gone,* is a hodgepodge of projects, touching upon neobop, wordless vocalizing (Ellingtonish in character but rather banal in execution), and balladry (charmingly conceived). Abrams tethers the seeming polarities of funk and freedom in his electric piano contribution to Eddie Harris's "Turbulence," and demonstrates his increasing authority as a keyboard stylist on *Sightsong,* an album of duets with Malachi Favors, and *Duet 1976,* where he complements Anthony Braxton. One of his most successful recorded performances as composer and instrumentalist is "Bud P.," a dedication from 1978; its two themes suggest the moodiness of Bud Powell's ballads and the crashing rhythms of his fast pieces, without derivative references. It shows Abrams to be one of those rare bandleaders who can create an exciting density of sound with only two horns, and illustrates his theory that an improvisor must work with the specific material of a piece to avoid clichés.

Anthony Braxton's *For Alto,* a double-album's worth of alto saxophone solos, was recorded in 1969, and boldly called attention to the capabilities of the saxophone as an independent concert instrument. Within the AACM, Roscoe Mitchell preceded Braxton in working along these lines ("Thke"); moreover, unaccompanied horn solos, which have their jazz origin in the two- and four-bar breaks common to jazz ensembles of the '20s, were previously explored by Louis Armstrong, Coleman Hawkins, Sonny Rollins, John Coltrane, Eric Dolphy, and Lee Konitz. But *For Alto* opened the floodgates, and within seven or eight years, unaccompanied horn recitals were a commonplace in New York's lofts. One of Braxton's best solo performances, "For Cecil Taylor," is a blues-drenched tour de force, recorded with a pint of echo, and redolent of Dolphy's sonority. In Europe, Braxton inaugurated recitals that influenced numerous musicians, notably Steve Lacy, who found the solo form ideal for his waspish investigation of note rows and static rhythmic figures. At the same time, Braxton's association with Circle (Chick Corea, Dave Holland, Barry Altshul) took his name beyond the parameters of new music, and led to Holland's excellent album *Conference of the Birds;* his "See Saw" solo is Konitz-inspired with a Benny Carter sourdough edge.

In other contexts, Braxton's music has been disappointing. His heavy involvement with the fashions of the European avant-garde seemed to stifle the exuberant vitality of his best work; his vulnerability to received ideas made ambitious concepts seem mere exercises. This was also true of Jarman and Abrams on occasion, but whereas they could usually counter the sterility of bad composition with authoritative improvising, Braxton's soloing was marred by rhythmic unease, often manifested in relentless patterns of staccato eighth notes. His finest work as composer is *Creative Music Orchestra 1976,* a wildly ambitious and fruitful mélange of big-band jazz, parade music, and stillwater, "open ended" improvisations, revealing a sense of humor and an ability to reinterpret old forms with a lively ear. The album's ironic send-up of a march is just the kind of wry, unexpected gambit Braxton does best. Its jubilant theme, more appropriate to a German beer garden than a military review, modulates to a repeated oompah figure, as though the melody had been wrung out. Into this berserk stasis comes Leo Smith, playing only the timbres of the trumpet that are of no use in a march; a familiar riff for the reeds precedes George

Lewis's rippling trombone and Braxton's deliberately misanthropic clarinet. The march returns with a flourish and waddles merrily along.

When the AACM travelers returned from Europe, they were no longer satisfied to remain in the Midwest. As Abrams put it, the move east was motivated by a desire to "follow up some of the business we've generated—if we don't, then other people will take advantage of these things." Leroy Jenkins, who organized the Revolutionary Ensemble with Sirone and Jerome Cooper, was one of the first to settle in New York. A proficient violinist who combines blues tonalities with the fevered rhapsodizing of a nineteenth-century romantic, Jenkins was trained in the European tradition ("All my teachers were black frustrated concert violinists") and inspired by Heifetz, Stern, and Oistrakh before discovering Eddie South and Stuff Smith. Unlike Braxton and Leo Smith, who listened to Webern, Xenakis, and Stockhausen, Jenkins's classical background was Beethoven, Mozart, Mendelssohn: "The only modern composers I know are in jazz."

Before it disbanded in 1977, the Revolutionary Ensemble was an uncommonly tight unit, the sum of contrasting yet congruent parts—Sirone's earthy bass and crackling trombone, Cooper's meticulous drum patterns and piano, and Jenkins's ravishing violin. It could be pastoral and urban, derivative and distinctive, bluesy and classical, baroque and austere, and though the trio's first record was named for Viet Nam, its subsequent, nonprogrammatic endeavors were more successful: in particular, *Revolutionary Ensemble*, which includes a Jenkins ballad, a Sirone pastel, and a Cooper march. In 1975, Jenkins composed and conducted a stirring piece for eighteen musicians, under the auspices of the Jazz Composers Orchestra; *For Players Only* seemed an early summation of the AACM's influence in New York. The players were apportioned by sections—reeds, brass, rhythm, and strings—to the four corners of an auditorium, with the conductor situated in the middle, and the audience in cir-

cles around the podium. In conducting collaborations throughout the room, devised not in notes but in the improvisational
personalities of the participants, Jenkins was the ultimate con-
trapuntist. "We don't make money in the short run," Jenkins
said, "but we're the bread and butter of jazz. Jazz is a music of
musicians, not producers."

Leo Smith's odyssey began in Mississippi, where his stepfather was a blues singer named Alex Wallace. He moved to
Chicago in 1967, became vice-president of the AACM a year
later (Bowie was president), toured Europe, and moved his family to New Haven, where he practiced, wrote and published
three pamphlets on theory and notation, and operated Kabell
Records. His early influences were Miles Davis and Don Cherry,
but when Mitchell brought him into the AACM, his devotion
was such that he played seven nights a week, composing regularly and having the results promptly performed: "It was like
being a court musician." Smith eschews the term jazz in favor
of Creative Music, the alternative to composed or classical
music. Once we've reduced music to those two spheres, he suggests, we can get to the actual work without lugging along a
vocabulary of meaner catagories. He is opposed to rigid song
forms, including the blues—"they have been done away with
and replaced by structures."

Those structures can seem quite vague to the initiate. For
the first album by a group he calls New Dalta Ahkri, *Reflectativity*, a trio—Smith on trumpet and percussion, Anthony
Davis on piano, and Wes Brown on bass and Ghanaian flute—
brush-colors two lengthy pastorales with an appealing, punctili-
ous reserve. There are no sustained solos, and discrete ideas are
offered against a vista of silence, passed among the three with
an abiding sense of tradition and immediacy. The music is im-
maculate in conception and performance. It's difficult to distinguish this kind of expressiveness from self-indulgence—the result either holds you or it doesn't. I find New Dalta Ahkri
generally convincing. Anthony Davis, perhaps the most talented

musician who came under Smith's influence in New Haven, gave an example of the problems posed by impressionistic structures: "It's challenging to come up with something different each time, but Leo alters the conditions. On a piece called 'Play Ebony, Play Ivory,' he said, 'In this section, I want some free-stride piano.' " Smith released two other records on Kabell, one of solo trumpet and the other a quintet edition of New Dalta Ahkri (with Oliver Lake and Paul Maddox added); he has no qualms about vanity recording—"Most people who put out their own records have given up the idea that you are only important if someone else records you."

The most successful band of AACM members since the Art Ensemble is a trio called Air, with saxophonist Henry Threadgill, bassist Fred Hopkins, and drummer Steve McCall. They can be ethereal at one moment and noisy as street traffic the next, elegantly swinging or obsessively free. Although a strongly disciplined unit, Air's members often give the impression of three individualists marching in different directions; aggressive tensions, established at the outset of each performance, are sustained by the maverick ingenuity of the players. Hopkins gets a dark, lacquered sound from the bass, and plays breathlessly fast configurations, in which sliding pitches, double stops, and loud fretting action contribute to the bustle. McCall often seems his opposite, breathing easy and deliberating over the drums. He will begin a solo with a lyric sally on the high-hat, doodle impressionistically on the cymbals, explode a montage of bass drum and snare patterns, and just as suddenly recede to a nearly inaudible episode with mallets; he galvanizes the band. Threadgill plays alto, tenor, baritone, bass clarinet, flute, and hubkaphone, which is a double-decker row of hubcaps that he strikes with mallets. Although his tone on flute is clean and bold, I prefer him on the saxophones, where the tonal and rhythmic influence of Sonny Rollins and the procedural concepts of Ornette Coleman are occasionally intimated. Air's first records were made in Japan, but the group's wide-ranging interests were most ably represented on its American releases, especially *Air Time,* where jazz and third-world musical traditions prove to be quite compatible, and *Air Lore,* an enchanting and fully realized investigation of works by Scott Joplin and Jelly Roll Morton.

Of the younger AACM players to stake out New York, the most promising are Chico Freeman and George Lewis. Freeman, the son of Chicago's veteran saxophonist Von Freeman and a former student of Muhal Richard Abrams, was voted into the AACM in 1972; the following year, he won two awards, including best all-around soloist, at the Notre Dame Jazz Festival, and his band won three more. He is a commanding saxophonist, volatile and satisfying in a variety of contexts, and a composer capable of conjuring simple but memorable themes. His debut albums, *Chico* and *Kings of Mali,* as well as Don Pullen's *Warriors,* are exceptional showcases for his expressive virtuosity, and *Spirit Sensitive* finds him exploring standard ballads with gracefulness and maturity. Lewis also studied with Abrams and became a member of the AACM while majoring in philosophy at Yale. The complete trombonist, he's ventured into the tailgate lore of classic jazz, the multiphonics pioneered in Germany by Albert Mangelsdorff, and just about everything that lies between. Lewis, who has recorded with Roscoe Mitchell and Anthony Davis and has toured with Count Basie and Anthony Braxton, displays remarkable timbral variety in his nimble solos. His recordings include *The George Lewis Solo Trombone Album,* a tour de force, and *Homage to Charlie Parker,* a tribute that avoids specific references to Parker's music in favor of a static, electronic opening (recalling Miles Davis's "He Loved Him Madly") and teasingly brief improvisations by Douglas Ewart, Anthony Davis, and Lewis.

According to Leo Smith, "The importance of the AACM today is that it never ran out of steam. It represents the control of destiny for the music and the artist." For a while, it seemed doubtful that the AACM could secure its musicians a fair hearing, but as the 1980s loomed, the problem was academic: the music had transcended the boundaries of loftdom, and many of its best proponents were recording for well-known labels. Still, opportunities for work were anything but constant, and the likelihood of a band's staying together for much longer than a particular engagement was slim (the Art Ensemble and Air notwithstanding).

One thing is clear: the energy and accomplishment of the AACM players were contagious enough to ignite New York's musical community. The Chicagoans introduced new instruments and unusual instrumental combinations, formats, styles, and techniques. Whether or not they can sustain themselves, they have proved to be a sustaining power for the music. They responded intelligently to the problems posited by the tradition, and reached conclusions that influenced its future. Abrams's estimation was modest and reasonable: "You know the AACM is just a drop in the bucket, but I think we've added some quality criteria to those which already exist. The advanced compositional techniques and improvisation is like a model for a minute—just for a minute, 'cause you know how it changes—but it'll be an example. A lot of people will pick up on the example and do very well with it. A lot of people that are not AACM people. Now, who those people will be a couple of years from now, who knows?"*

1977–80

---

* A point of clarification: Several musicians who worked with AACM musicians were not themselves members, among them Sirone, Jerome Cooper, Anthony Davis, and Wes Brown. Their contributions were indicative of the organization's impact.

Breuker Battles the Bourgeoisie

Americans are in the habit of dismissing European jazz as a hapless emulation of the real thing, ancillary at best and naïve in the main. This dismissal is not without justification, for, with the exception of the Belgian guitarist Django Reinhardt, Europeans have had small impact on the development of jazz. Slavish trad, swing, and bop bands proliferated on the Continent between the '30s and '50s, but even an occasional pocket of gifted practitioners—for example, such early Swedish modernists as Lars Gullin, Stan Hasselgard, Arne Domnerus, and Bengt Hallberg—seemed insubstantial and shadowy. More recently, a few European virtuosos have begun to exert considerable influence on their instruments; Albert Mangelsdorff's system of harmonics has made him the most widely studied trombonist since J. J. Johnson, and the accomplishments of pianist Martial Solal or bassist Niels Pedersen or saxophonist Evan Parker are impressive, if isolated.

Still, the universality of jazz, as first prophesied by Ernest Ansermet in 1919, is a decisive phenomenon in this century's music, and it was inevitable that Europeans eventually assimilate its language to express their own cultural and political imperatives. An extraordinary flurry of activity in Holland, West

Germany, Poland, Japan, and elsewhere during the past fifteen years suggests that European jazz has taken a bold step forward; the most rewarding evidence I've found is a series of records by the Dutch saxophonist and composer Willem Breuker and his Kollektief. His is an internationalist music, neoclassical in shape, conservative by most avant-garde standards, and intensely political. It is also flush with melody, confidently played, and trenchantly funny.

Like that of most European countries, Holland's jazz life was originally boosted and somewhat defined by the presence of visiting Americans, in this case Coleman Hawkins, who played with Theo Masman's Ramblers Dance Orchestra in 1935 when Hitler banned blacks from Germany, and Benny Carter, who two years later led the first interracial big band in jazz at a Dutch resort. They were powerful influences for more than a decade after their visits, but by the '50s the cool school was in vogue, and Dutch jazz was symbolized by bandleader Wes Ilcken and his wife, Rita Reys, a fine singer who combines Ella Fitzgerald's swing with a huskiness reminiscent of Anita O'Day. In the mid-'60s, Misja Mengelberg, a disciple of Monk, and Han Bennink, a drummer and clarinetist, both of whom recorded with Eric Dolphy on *Last Date,* were the gurus of modernism. In 1967, they organized the Instant Composer's Pool with Breuker, who represented a still younger and more iconoclastic generation. A year earlier, the German pianist Alex Schlippenbach founded the Globe Unity Orchestra, the most ambitious of the internationalist collectives. Neither group proved satisfactory to Breuker: the ICP was close minded about his theatrical and avant-garde endeavors, the GUO was given to conceptual free-for-alls. In 1973, he formed his Kollektief, a ten- or eleven-piece orchestra with an emphasis on compositional form.

The avant-garde jazz movement of the '60s undoubtedly played a crucial role in allowing Europeans of Breuker's generation to find their own voices. As Joachim Berendt has written, they knew better than Americans that "meaningful and artistic music is possible also outside the realm of functional harmony handed down from romanticism." Albert Ayler's textural innovations had immediate appeal to musicians who were groping for an expressiveness that would break the vise of standard chord progressions. Moreover, the vocalized, unmannerly sounds of the American jazz avant-garde suited a widespread and deeply ingrained desire to thumb noses at the commodity music of the middle class on the one hand, and the mandarins of Europe's musical elite on the other. In "Red Music," the preface to *The Bass Saxophone,* the great Czech writer Josef Skvorecky notes that Goebbels's declarations on the ugliness of jazz "was one reason we whined and wailed, rasped and roared, using all kinds of wa wa and hat mutes, some of them manufactured by ourselves." The Kollektief brings to fruition the political strivings heard so briefly in American jazz ten years ago, when Archie Shepp recorded *Fire Music,* Charlie Haden *Liberation Music Orchestra,* and the Revolutionary Ensemble *Viet Nam.* Yet, for the most part, Breuker's political points are not scored through specific allusions to persons or events: he attacks authoritarianism by subverting its elitist assumptions about art, and stumps for democratic internationalism with a musical syntax that echoes Joyce in its pancultural borrowings, puns, and juxtapositions.

Breuker's music combines harmonies that alternately cleave and chafe, melodies that recall (frequently with direct and extended quotations) numerous musical cultures, ensembles of anarchistic windiness and startling precision. In their theatricality, eclecticism, sardonic humor, and whispers of Weill and Eisler, Breuker's recordings call to mind Carla Bley's *Escalator over the Hill;* on a more general level, an obvious analogy can be drawn to Charles Mingus and the Art Ensemble of Chicago. But what finally distinguishes Breuker from his American counterparts is the use of devices that are determinedly and relevantly European. Like Mahler, whose tunes he occasionally echoes, Breuker believes, "The symphony should be like the world; it must contain everything." His concerts consist of previously chosen pieces and excerpts that are quilted into a single nonstop performance; the variety of references is dazzling.

Live in Berlin (BVHaast), one of his strongest recordings, consists chiefly of excerpts from two amorphous works. "La Plagiata" is a series of frankly plagiarized fragments ornamented and contorted into fresh music; "Anthology" is a catchall for vignettes that mercilessly satirize the postwar European avantgarde as sterile and dogmatic. The eclecticism falls into T. W. Adorno's definition of "literary music": it indulges with knowing credence street music, the European classics, all styles of jazz, dance musics (especially the tango), marches (another coincidental link between the Kollektief and the AACM), and bourgeois pop. The "Oratorium from La Plagiata" includes a solo by Ronald Snijders, an immensely talented flutist who can balance tonal purity and funkiness on the ends of a single phrase, that is based entirely on Chopin's Funeral March and "Tico Tico." I wonder what ASCAP will make of such borrowings.

The album opens with a Kurt Weillish march, precisely intoned and constructed in layers—a rhythm vamp, brass ostinato, and fugal counterpoint from French horn and trombone. Breuker's "Oratorium" solo begins with moaning glissandos and soon undergoes abrupt register and volume alterations, suggesting a lineage between Johnny Hodges and Albert Ayler. His and indeed all the improvisations are lively; these are consummate musicians, and Breuker allows them as much solo space as he takes himself. One of the slyest wags in the bunch is an ex-Dixieland trombonist, Willem Van Manen, who swings jerkily after the orchestra plays a rueful march. "Jan de Wit" could be a collaboration by Weill and Elmer Bernstein (*The Magnificent Seven Go Dutch*), but for a splendidly earthy tenor solo by Maarten Van Norden, and "Jalousie-Song" begins as Gilbert and Sullivan and flails itself into a strenuous romance that would have warmed Nietzsche's cockles. "Jail-Music," a kindergarten march with a few Rebel yells, leads into the "Anthology" excerpt, where hideous dissonances are sustained over jungle drums, and a somber Germanic theme is filtered through a polyphonic tunnel into a pastoral flute solo. For an encore, the ensemble flounces into a glitzy Latin arrangement of the Ruby and the Romantics oldie "Our Day Will Come," which is also sung by the whole group a capella.

The European Scene (MPS) is something of a sequel (both were recorded in the fall of 1975). There are additional excerpts from "La Plagiata," which Dr. Konrad Boehmer describes in the notes as giving "the impression of someone proudly driving around in a stolen and freshly repainted car," and "Anthology": ". . . a culture baby suppressed by two mothers and an authoritarian father finally sees the chance to make the music it likes together with other babies of the same conviction. The scene has a painful ending. The culture baby gets a miserable beating from the father and has to return to the avant-garde piano." The piece consists mostly of a Chick Webb-inspired drum solo, so even with the annotation the joke isn't easily grasped; but the performance is funny all the same. Breuker is almost satanically detached as a composer: he supplants emotion with juxtaposition, toppling authoritarian themes with wicked improvisations, distorting lacy melodies with grotesque timbral deviations. The album ends with his unaccompanied bass clarinet in an uproarious solo that shows he is incapable of taking himself seriously enough to forget there is an audience present. Yet his "PLO March" is as humorless as it is politically naïve.

Breuker has written and recorded two film scores, as well as theatrical music for two of Brecht's earliest plays, *Baal* and *Drums in the Night*. These are generally disappointing, although *Getrommel in die Nacht* (BVHaast) displays his accomplished writing for strings and has some memorable thematic material. The scores have no improvisation, however, and it's puzzling that for an internationalist like Brecht, Breuker failed to employ the Kollektief's greatest virtue—its razor's edge balancing act between written and ad-libbed parts. Incidentally, the Weill influence is conspicuously absent here. There are intoxicating tangos, and a palm-court waltz swooning over ominous drums. Among the best of his more representative recordings are *On Tour* (BVHaast), with "Antelope Cobbler," a combination Scottish jig, jitterbug, and polka, and "Potsdamer Stomp," in which a New Orleans band, grunting over a conga-line rhythm, discovers the rhythm-and-blues relic "Hambone"; and *Live in Shaffy* (BVHaast), recorded under the leadership of Breuker's excellent pianist, Leo Cuypers, and boasting a sumptuously evocative dedication to Roland Kirk, and Breuker's "Ham and Egg Tango," which uses Groucho Marx's "Hooray for Captain Spaulding" as a tag phrase.

I've only scratched the surface. Breuker's records, and those of the equally fascinating Globe Unity Orchestra, are difficult to find, and until an American company secures rights to the BVHaast and other catalogues and issues them in properly annotated editions, few Americans are likely to get a firm grasp on these prolific players. The Kollektief's only New York appearance was in 1977, and additional tours will be necessary to present us with the theatrical correlative to the music. Perhaps the Dutch zeitgeist won't be too much longer in breaking through—Breuker's conviction that his music fights fascism, and his success in getting the Dutch government to subsidize it, might even rekindle similar passions here. But that's not as important as the great pleasure these albums afford, or the qualitative level at which they manifest the determination of highly skilled Europeans to make the jazz language work for them in their own accents.

July 1979

4

Adventures in the Jazz Trade

It's Dizzy Again

In the forty years since he made his way to New York from Cheraw, South Carolina, via Philadelphia, John Birks "Dizzy" Gillespie—whose bulging cheeks and upturned trumpet bell symbolize jazz—has been acclaimed as the world's greatest trumpet virtuoso in or out of jazz ("That man!" conductor Dimitri Mitropoulos once said of him, "When I heard him I was thrilled to death"), as the composer of several innovative jazz pieces that have become standards, as an entertainer of rare comedic gifts, and as a musical pathfinder of incalculable influence. Unlike Charlie Parker, who died at age thirty-four of the effects of alcoholism and heroin addiction, Gillespie has been able to observe his reputation grow steadily from the stormy days of the bebop movement, when he was dismissed as a crack-brained enfant terrible, to the present, when he is cherished as an elder statesman not just of bop but of jazz itself.

During intermission at a Pace University concert in the fall of 1977, a young man took hold of his hand and said, "My grandma's been telling me about you ever since I can remember." Gillespie turned his head thoughtfully, eyebrows arched, epiphany dawning. "We've passed the my-mother-heard-you stage," he said to no one in particular; "now it's 'my grand-mother'!"

Gillespie was celebrating his sixtieth birthday that October, an event greeted with warm congratulations throughout the jazz world. He wasn't the first bop veteran to pass that mile-stone: Kenny Clarke, who helped devise the modern drumming style, is three years older, and Thelonious Monk, the ingenious composer-pianist, is Gillespie's senior by eleven days. But Clarke has lived in Europe since 1956, and Monk has been generally inactive in recent years. Gillespie, on the other hand, maintains a constant regimen of touring and recording, and serves as an ambassador of jazz as well. Moreover, he continues to evince signs of musical growth. His tone has mellowed into an increas-ingly attractive and personal sound, and although he continues to discount his credentials as a blues player, he has become a splendidly authoritative bluesman. His recent compositions, such as "Olinga," while as challenging formally as his earlier classics—"A Night in Tunisia," "Woody'n You" and "Groovin' High"—are cast in a peaceful, meditative mode, more concerned with dynamics and mood than with lightning-fast chord pro-gressions.

Everything about Gillespie, from the ebullience that charges his improvisations to his mock-surly strut and theatrical looni-ness, proves that the cocky irreverence at the heart of all musi-cal movements can be sustained beyond the initial burst of in-spiration. Gillespie's wit, candor, and demeanor are as reassuring of his agelessness as are his imperious high notes and those half-valved pitches that whimper and cajole, scold and preach. Nor has he abandoned the free-and-easy spirit of the jam ses-sion, as attested to by his occasional, unannounced appearances on concert stages and in nightclubs.

Gillespie's present resurgence in the role of patriarch is un-derscored by the fact that, much to his surprise, he finds him-self spearheading something of a bebop revival. At an all-star Avery Fisher Hall concert in the fall of 1975, billed "A Tribute to Dizzy Gillespie," he told the capacity audience, "It's good to see that bop has stood the test of time"; he was cheered for several minutes. A year later, Dexter Gordon, the preeminent bop tenor saxophonist, made one of his rare American visits since moving to Cophenhagen in 1962, and was overwhelmed by the enthusiastic response. The movement, augmented by a steady stream of reissued recordings of bop classics, has been gathering force ever since. In 1976, the Smithsonian Institution's Division of Performing Arts devoted to Gillespie a two-record retrospective entitled *The Development of an American Artist*. In his liner notes, producer and critic Martin Williams wrote, "John Birks 'Dizzy' Gillespie is a great figure in American music, in world music, and perhaps the greatest living musical innovator we have." Bebop is the innovation with which Gillespie is most intimately associated; the word itself probably originated as an onomatopoeic attempt to describe a rhythmic figure, but it came to signify a music that had the effect of dissecting the jazz of the swing era and putting it together again in a new way.

Harmonically, bebop took the large, ineluctable leap from a diatonic, riff-based music of few chords and fewer keys to a labyrinthine chromaticism with elaborate chord substitutions and a marked preference for the diminished scale. Although the fast, angular melodies of bebop sounded chaotic to skeptics, a new virtuosity was required to play them. Gillespie and Parker brought fresh fevers to jazz with their stunning instrumental articulation and range.

The most profound change they wrought was rhythmic, symbolized by the substitution of a fluid pulse, sustained by modern drummers on the shimmering ride cymbal, for the crisply stated sock-cymbal beat of swing; and by the soloists' unpredictable accents and asymmetrical phrasing. One might say that while the swing soloist improvised in a situation governed by time, the bop soloist made himself the focal point around which time coalesced. The new rhythm proved to be the Rubicon that few, if any, of the pre-bop musicians could cross, and it was in large measure responsible for changing the image of jazz from a popular dance music to that of a more exploratory concert music. This was an inevitable step, but it was vexed by considerable racial frustration.

Gillespie, Parker, Monk, and the others came of age in the years of the Harlem Renaissance, when blacks were making great inroads into the nation's cultural life. They were not the first jazz musicians to consider themselves artists rather than showmen (the same could be said of most of their predecessors), but they did resent the banalization of jazz by popular dance bands and novelty recordings. Seeking to bring a new life to jazz, the pioneers of bebop hoped that their high standards, technical bravura, private wit, and implacable energy would guard against decadence, at least for a while. The opposition was vicious. "Bebop has set music back twenty years," a leading white bandleader said. Many people were put off by it, feeling that Modern Jazz was an alien language shared only by a handful of radical black musicians. An older generation felt threatened by the new music; a younger generation preferred the immediate accessibility of rhythm and blues, which was just coming to the fore.

This lack of recognition and understanding, coupled with the widespread experience of racial alienation, led to a climate of self-defeating bitterness among many bop musicians. The situation was made deadly by the massive availability of heroin in black neighborhoods after World War II, and by the disastrous example of Charlie Parker, that authentic musical genius, supreme hipster, and junkie of Gargantuan appetite. Though he warned against drugs, Parker's self-destructiveness was widely imitated.

Still, bop provided the basic mode of jazz expression through the mid-60s, by which time it had become the jazz establishment. Then it ran into trouble not because it seemed foreign but because it sounded too familiar. The revolt against bop was embodied by the free-jazz movement that started in the late 50s, led by saxophonists Ornette Coleman and John Coltrane and pianist Cecil Taylor, which sounded, to the uninitiated, tumultuously discordant and—because it abandoned traditional time signatures—unswinging. Bop musicians were incredulous that they could be superseded by such seeming chaos but, by 1968, it was obvious to everyone that the shape of jazz, as Ornette Coleman once entitled a prophetic album, had changed on at least three levels: The best of the upcoming musicians were joining the new avant-garde; musicians were now using modality, which is to say that they based their improvisations on scales rather than on bebop's chords; and rock was having the positive effect of introducing new colors and instrumental effects to jazz, and the negative one of encouraging cynical commercialism.

From 1963 to 1967, Gillespie led a series of superb quintets, all featuring saxophonist James Moody. He even sparked a new controversy by hiring an electric bassist (Frank Schifano)—something practically unheard-of at that time in jazz circles. The years that followed, however, were bleak. What with the popular hegemony enjoyed by rock and the split in the jazz community between the old and the new guards, many veteran musicians found work scarce. Gillespie remained active, but he recorded infrequently, usually as a soloist rather than at the helm of his sometimes indifferent bands.

Then, in 1974, he signed with Pablo Records, a new company headed by jazz impresario Norman Granz, and began recording prolifically again. By this time free jazz had expanded into a kind of panstylistic eclecticism, attended by a greater respect for older styles of jazz. Shortly afterward, he organized a lean, tightly knit quartet for which he wrote several new pieces and revamped some old ones. In the future he intends to play his compositions with symphony orchestras—the charts are being written by a varied collection of arrangers, including Lalo Schifrin, Quincy Jones, J. J. Johnson, Thad Jones, Michel Legrand, Robert Farnon, Coleridge Perkinson, Gil Fuller, and

Tom McIntosh. With the new interest in bebop, a new vigor
entered Gillespie's playing, and at the age of sixty he was en-
joying a renaissance.

Gillespie and his wife of forty years, Lorraine, live in a roomy
split-level house in Englewood, New Jersey. On their well-
cropped lawn sits a large metal sculpture by Dizzy's neighbor
Albert S. Gross, consisting of two circles sandwiching a stem
that emerges at about forty-five degrees. It was not made with
Gillespie in mind, but one can easily abstract from it Gillespie's
famous forty-five-degree trumpet bell and his hugely distended
cheeks. (When a doctor at Walter Reed Hospital saw a photograph in *Life* of Gillespie's puffed-up jaw, he invited him to
come in for X-rays and subsequently documented the condition
now diagnosed as Gillespie's Pouches.)

When I paid a call, Gillespie was, as usual, in transit. He had
just returned from a tour of Africa, where he had picked up a
virus ("I don't care what Alex Hailey says, I could have left
that over there"), and soon he was supposed to fly to California
to appear on the "Tonight" show. We visited in his basement,
which is outfitted with four tape recorders, a turntable, speak-
ers, an electric and an acoustic piano, a ride cymbal, congas, a
pool table, and a bar. The walls are covered with nearly two
dozen plaques, trophies, city keys, and a large Dizzy Gillespie
bust.

He is a man for whom comfort is a natural condition, and his
serenity is contagious if you adjust yourself to his contempla-
tive, easygoing tempo. His cheeks are leathery in repose, like
tanned hides, and there are touches of gray in his sideburns and
at his temples, but he looks a good deal younger than sixty. He
carries his girth handily, as though it were one of the rewards
of his career. When he is animated by a pleasant thought or
memory, his voice rises half an octave and his eyes sparkle boy-
ishly. A follower of the Bahai faith, Gillespie rarely drinks
liquor. He opened two bottles of a nonalcoholic beer that he

imports from Switzerland and began talking about Cheraw, South Carolina, where he was born on October 21, 1917.

"I've always been a musician, from the time I was eleven or twelve. My father made his living as a brickmason, but he always had a houseful of instruments. He died when I was going on ten, and that's when I started fooling with the piano. About 1928, I think it was, the public school got instruments from the state. All the big guys got what they wanted and there was only a trombone left, so I took that up because I was determined to be a musician. The trombone didn't work out too well, but the boy next door got a trumpet, and he'd let me practice on it. Well, in school, Miss Alice Wilson saw me with the trumpet and she organized a little group aside from the band that played marches. She only played in B flat, though. Every year they had a minstrel show with dancers, singers, comedians, and two guys on the end named Mr. Interlocutor who would jump up and ask a question and get a laugh. Then it would be our turn to play. We were pretty good in B flat, but I couldn't read music. A guy named Sonny Matthews heard about me and sent for me. I took my school horn down there, and we played 'Nagasaki' in C. I couldn't find one note. Nothin'! I was so embarrassed, I cried and cried. Finally I learned how to read by learning trombone from a friend who was taking lessons. We started getting stock arrangements and things, and when I was fifteen, I got a scholarship to the Laurinburg Institute in North Carolina. By then, I could read very well.

"Southern bands used to come through my hometown, and sometimes they'd let me come up and play. There was Doc Pettiford, Jimmy Brown, Smiling Billy Stewart, Capitol City Aces, Killer Jazz Hounds. I was also able to go to the white dances and hear bands like Neely Plumb and the Georgia Tech Ramblers, because I was like a celebrity. I'd bring my cousin or someone and we'd dance—I was a good dancer—and they'd crowd around and throw money at us. I'd just pick up the money and listen to the bands. I remember a boy named

Jimmy Ganey, a white boy, who played drums with Ned Hixon's band. They were hillbillies and they'd try to play stock arrangements. I used to tell him about the drums—I'd say, 'Don't play two, play four.' I was always a student of rhythm.

"The first time I heard Roy Eldridge play trumpet, he was broadcasting from the Savoy Ballroom with Teddy Hill's band. Roy was the messiah for our age, just like Louis Armstrong was the messiah for the one before that. We tried to play just like him, but I never did quite make it. I didn't get to see any of the important bands until my mother moved to Philadelphia in '35. There was a French teacher at the Laurinburg Institute named Mrs. Wilcox, and her brother, Eddie Wilcox, played piano with Jimmie Lunceford. So when I went to Philadelphia and all the bands were playing there, I walked up to Mr. Wilcox and said, 'Mr. Wilcox, my name is John Gillespie and I went to school with your sister.' He invited me into the theater and I met Willie Smith, Trummy Young, and all the guys. Around the same time, I got to see Louis Armstrong at Fay's Theater. He had Snakehips Tucker, the dancer, and Luis Russell's band with him. But as far as clowning, Fats Waller gassed me more. He was funny—good musician and funny, too."

Gillespie earned the nickname "Dizzy" at age seventeen by showing up for his first job in Philadelphia carrying his trumpet in a paper bag. Reports of Gillespie's antic sense of humor were widely circulated when he traveled to Europe with Hill's band in 1937. He was known to play while wearing gloves, or with his chair facing backward, or with his trumpet derby on his head. But he was also recognized as an unusually skillful if derivative musician. He met his wife, Lorraine Willis, in 1938, and a year later landed a job with the Cab Calloway orchestra. This association ended with a widely publicized skirmish (Calloway wrongly accused him of throwing spitballs onstage, and Gillespie drew a knife), but during his two years with the band, Gillespie was heard as soloist, composer, and arranger.

"I still sounded like Roy Eldridge when I was with Cab, but

other things started developing. I became involved with Monk
and Kenny Clarke, and we'd play a lot in the daytime. Every
time I'd find something new on the piano, I'd show Monk, and
when he found something, he'd show me. Roy's playing was
based on the trumpet itself, but my playing started developing
from the piano. It was with Cab that I first met Charlie Parker
in Kansas City. I had a friend, Buddy Anderson, who played
good trumpet with Jay McShann, and we'd jam together in
Kansas City. He wanted me to hear this saxophone player, but
I wasn't too interested because I'd been hearing Don Byas, Lester Young, Chu Berry, Coleman Hawkins, and Ben Webster,
and I said, 'Not another saxophone player!' Until I heard him.
Jesus! Knocked me off my feet. We played all day that day, in
the Booker T. Washington Hotel, Kansas City. Must have been
'39 or '40.

"Actually, Charlie Parker was the architect of the new sound.
He knew how to get from one note to another, the style of the
thing. Most of what I did was in the area of harmony and
rhythm—what the rhythm section was supposed to do. We got
tired of playing the same B-flat seventh chord, so we started experimenting, which was how we got the flatted fifth, which
meant that we could play on two keys at one time. We just
went crazy with it, though, and it became a cliché. Well, we
were playing these substitute chords and we had to have a melody to go with them, so sometimes we'd write a new melody to
fit the new chords. 'Groovin' High' was based on an old song
called 'Whispering,' but where there was originally one chord,
we'd play four. I never thought of it before now, but I used to
hear 'Whispering' on Saturday afternoons in the theater around
home. It was used on one of the western serials—Ken Maynard
or Yakima Canutt or Bob Steele or somebody.

"It's hard to say in words how our music came together.
When I found out how Charlie Parker played, it was just what
I needed to put with my contribution. It wasn't copying, be-
cause anything I brought in he'd add something to, and I'd do

the same. Harmonically, Monk played different from anybody. He was the most original. If you played with him and didn't know the chords, it was shame on you, because he'd embellish and you wouldn't be able to follow. One time I said to Monk, 'Look, what did you get from me? What did you learn from me that you really worked on and made into something else?' He said, 'Night in Tunisia,' 'Salt Peanuts,' 'Woody'n You.' I said, 'I'm not talking about no tunes.' As an example, I told him that he was the first one I heard play a minor sixth with the sixth interval in the bass clef, just like I was the first one in our crowd to play 'How High the Moon'—I learned it from Nat Cole. Now I told Monk that I used that minor sixth in many ways, thousands of times. Well, he couldn't think of anything that he first heard from me and then developed.''

Gillespie is generally thought to have recorded the first indisputably modernist solo on an otherwise undistinguished 1942 release by the Les Hite orchestra. The tune was "Jersey Bounce," and his solo was only sixteen measures long, but its back-of-the-beat phrasing, dynamic range, harmonic resourcefulness, and virtuosic control heralded a new way of thinking about jazz. The new music was refined in private sessions and in the bands of Earl Hines and Billy Eckstine during the next two years, but a recording ban initiated by the striking American Federation of Musicians prevented proper documentation. By 1944, what had essentially been a cliquish way of playing, devised by and for a coterie of adventuresome young musicians, began to exert a more pervasive influence. Bassist Oscar Pettiford organized with Gillespie the first bop band to play on New York's Swing Street, as Fifty-second Street was known in the 30s and 40s. (Plans are under way to implant in the sidewalks of Fifty-second Street between Fifth Avenue and the Avenue of the Americas the names of the jazz musicians who made the street world famous, and Gillespie will be among the first to be so honored.) Several other bands helped disseminate the new ideas in subsequent months. Within a year, many of the new independent labels founded during the recording ban were eager to record Gillespie, Parker, Pettiford, singer Sarah Vaughan (who was to bop what Billie Holiday was to swing), and other proponents of the new style. Musicians all over the country were learning tunes (and memorizing the improvisations played on them) like "Salt Peanuts," "Billie's Bounce," "A Night in Tunisia," "Hot House" and "Groovin' High." But the major record labels ignored bop.

When Gillespie organized his first big band to accompany the Nicholas Brothers, the legendary dance team, on a tour of the South, he encountered hostility from black audiences. "We were playing 'Salt Peanuts,' and they wanted to hear all those blues guys." The experience was a disaster, but in 1946, Gillespie's second big band had the opportunity to record such ambitious works as "Things To Come" and "Emanon," proving itself to be one of the most exciting orchestras ever assembled. During this period, Gillespie began actively incorporating Afro-Cuban rhythms into his music.

"I didn't start playing congas until [conga virtuoso] Chano Pozo joined the band, but I always did like Latin rhythms, and played the maracas. We had a saying in those days, 'Give me some skin,' and Chano couldn't speak English too well, so to him skin was lard. That's how we got the name 'Manteca,' which is Spanish for lard. 'Manteca' was a collaboration. Chano came to me and said he had an idea with the bass starting off, and then the trombones coming in, then the saxophones, and then BAM! After he did all this, in typical Afro-Cuban style without harmony, I said, 'We need something else.' I started writing an eight-bar bridge, but I couldn't resolve it so it became a sixteen-bar blues. I think 'Cubana Be/Cubana Bop' was the best collaboration by three people in music up to that point. Chano Pozo had the idea of the opening, an Afro beat. George Russell used to be a drummer, so he put the drum part behind the beat and started developing the music for about twenty-four bars. And then the melody—I wrote and arranged that, that was my contribution. Then there was a montuno that Chano and I did, and finally George Russell took what I had written and developed it to the end. That was the first modal writing in jazz."

Gillespie also began earning the reputation of a stage clown. His dark glasses, goatee, and beret became the superficial symbols of bop and inspired the hipster uniform which the beatniks later adopted. He may well be the last great entertainer to emerge from the jazz tradition. In the late 40s, his shenanigans disarmed skeptical audiences and helped him achieve a popularity—and notoriety—denied Charlie Parker. "I'm never at a loss for what to do on stage," Gillespie says, "because I came up with Cab Calloway, Lucky Millinder, and Tiny Bradshaw, and they would show you what you could do on stage."

Some of Gillespie's comic bits are very old indeed. For at least twenty years, he's been telling audiences, "Now I'd like to introduce the members of the band," whereupon he introduces them to each other. It's still funny.

The routine got a big laugh at Gillespie's appearance at Pace University's Schimmel Center. "I want you to see the real me," he told the audience, snapping his fingers, wiggling his hips, and shouting, "Soul!" He introduced a lovely, muted piece called "Brother K" like this: "Dr. Martin Luther King was a great inspiration to many people throughout the world because of his philosophy of nonviolence. We follow that . . . to a certain extent. If someone questions my manhood, I'm gonna have to cut him."

During another night that week, Gillespie was feted with a birthday party at the Village Gate by Cobi Narita's Universal Jazz Coalition. He arrived without his trumpet, wearing a blue suit and a camera, looking like a tourist, and greeted the standing audience with a surreal sermon. "Shut up," he warned, "don't start no shit." Then, like C. L. Franklin, he put fist to chest: "This puts something on your *heart*—do I hear amen?"

He praised the "young dudes" (a Hilton Ruiz band that had been playing "Night in Tunisia" when he arrived), and asked for an amen for them. "Cobi Narita deserves not the purple heart, but the *black* heart—do I hear an amen for that?" After several more amens, he shouted, "Hey, let's have a big hand for the unity of mankind!" Then he got serious to introduce the next musician: "One of the finest instrumentalists I have ever known in the history of my career. I can remember this young man when I was a little boy and my mother took me to Detroit to see him—the master, let's hear it for Mr. Bebop, Barry Harris."

"To be perfectly honest," said Harris, who is twelve years younger than Gillespie, "Dizzy used to babysit for me." DG: "That's 'cause I was goin' with his mother. Wait a minute, I was goin' with his mother to the sanctified church. They *cut* you in Detroit for talkin' about a cat's mother. Come up here and talk, Barry. This is one of the *educated* niggers." Gillespie's rap was one of the better improvisations of the evening, though Harris, whose wit is quieter but no less acerbic, had the final say. Before introducing his band, he said he would play a chorus of a tune by "one of our greatest musicians." Unidentified, it was Thelonious Monk's "Reflections."

Charlie Parker, Gillespie says, could be pretty humorous, too. "He used to do some pretty funny things on the stand. He'd fall in with whatever I was doing. You know, Charlie Parker didn't use narcotics around me. He respected me. Everyone smoked grass, I guess, but I never knew much about the narcotics. I was scared—I had a wife who was my anchor, and I knew I better not get started with that."

Gillespie suggests that the widespread use of drugs was partly due to a confused sense of identity. "Everybody was looking for something. It's like everybody was joining the Muslims to try and keep from being black. Because 'Negro' didn't give you identity. If you say you are Italian or German, that's something you can recognize. But we didn't have none of that, and when you became a Muslim you had identification, a new name. You were no longer just a Negro.

"There is less prejudice in jazz than other aspects of our society, but I found out if you were black you could never get past the stigma of being black—I don't care how far you go. But everybody comes from something, and when you study the history of pre-Christian Africa, you know they had some great civilizations. I wrote 'Kush' about a great African civilization. It's so ironic that I got a doctorate in music and never got out of high school. But those honorary degrees and awards mean something. They mean that somebody appreciates what you're doing, and it gives our kids something—because most of the history they get is about the white man.

"There is some prejudice in jazz, and some of it's reverse prejudice. But that's natural, you see, because jazz *is* our music. That doesn't mean that Stan Getz can't play or Bunny Berigan can't play. But your playing is so much a part of you that your early life has to come out in your music. Every now and then you hear a teety-teety-teety from a trumpet player and you know it's a white musician. But music is music—you're dealing with the same notes."

The perennial young Turk is past sixty, but Dizzy Gillespie is not looking back. "I just helped establish a particular style in our music—it's no big deal. I feel lucky to reach this point. I feel that my playing changes all the time, but it gets harder every day. You'd think the trumpet would get easier, but it doesn't. The more you know, the more you know what you can't do. You discover new things all the time, and a good audience inspires you. So does unity among the musicians. You never know what you're going to do until you're up on the stage."

In a typical performance, Gillespie's tone alternates between rich buoyancy in the upper register and velvety understatement in the middle; his phrases are long, darting, and replete with unpredictable harmonic turns. Gillespie is also a masterful percussionist, and when he isn't soloing, or conducting the ensemble with his agile hips, he is often seated at his conga drums, creating polyrhythms.

There is frequently a fifth musician sitting in on the engagements Gillespie plays in New York. Jon Faddis, a gifted twenty-five-year-old trumpet player originally from Oakland, California, in some ways epitomizes the renewed interest in Gillespie's music. While it is true that most of the jazz-trumpet stylists who've come along since Gillespie are indebted to him directly or indirectly, Faddis is the first firebrand in years to pattern his style precisely on the master's. Gillespie, who calls him "my musical son," first heard Faddis play in San Francisco ten years ago, and they got to know each other when Faddis moved to New York in 1972. Gillespie sees a parallel between their relationship and that of King Oliver and his young protégé in the '20s, Louis Armstrong: "Jon used to play my things, but he's playing a lot of his own now, becoming more himself. Yes, sir, the music just goes around and around, evolving all the time."

June 1978

Adventures
of the Red Arrow

No one knew where he would strike next. It was the cool evening of the cold war, 1958. By day, the mild-mannered major general scoured the country seeking revenge on the interest-grappling banks, the insurance monoliths, the larcenous at heart. From out of the prairies, he pulled up in a newly rented car. The bank managers were delighted to be of service to the grayed, bespectacled general—even as he presented for cashing his monthly paycheck, almost $2000.

But by night, in the quiet of a motel, he whipped off the uniform, washed the gray from his hair, and removed the specs, to stand revealed as . . . the Red Arrow! Who knows what greed and gullibility lurks in the soul of man? The Red Arrow knows.

Meanwhile, trombonist J. J. Johnson was listening to the ten Charlie Parker sides that would be collected as *The Essential Charlie Parker*. He was asked to submit comments on each selection, to be printed on the jacket. On hearing "Swedish Schnapps," his response was, "By the way, what ever happened to Red Rodney?"

Listen, gentle reader, to his story.

The Bar Mitzvah Present

Red Rodney, the forty-seven-year-old trumpeter who once soared in the shadows of Charlie Parker's wings, has returned to jazz. For years, he'd been making a lot of money playing in Las Vegas pit bands—accompanying everyone from Elvis Presley to Barbra Streisand—and on TV shows filmed in L.A. The commuting wore him out, and the bad music drove him crazy—"All you play is fast dumb riffs, over and over, da dada da dada." Two years ago, while doing the Flip Wilson show, he reached down for a mute and "it was like being hit by a hammer." He suffered a paralytic stroke, couldn't walk or talk for a year, while the hospital ate up his cash. He was a vegetable, but he was determined to walk, talk, and play again. This time, however, it would be *his* music; the important thing was to be, once again, the best trumpeter he could possibly be.

As he recovered, two events brought him some attention, after nearly twenty years of obscurity. A loosely researched Parker biography, Ross Russell's *Bird Lives!*, devoted a good deal of space to the redheaded kid whom Bird hired to replace Miles Davis, and one of his own best records, *The Red Arrow,* was re-released by Onyx. A comeback seemed possible.

Rodney, a gentle, cherubic man still sporting a bright auburn head of hair, was passing through New York, en route to a European tour with George Wein's concert package, *Charlie Parker Remembered,* featuring Dizzy Gillespie and other giants of the bop era. He wanted to tell his story.

Born Robert Roland Chudnick in Philadelphia, in 1927, he had already marched in the drum-and-bugle corps of the Jewish War Veterans when he received a trumpet for a bar mitzvah present. He didn't know what jazz was, but like anyone growing up then, he listened to the big bands—Artie Shaw, Benny Goodman, Tommy Dorsey. He enrolled in the famous music course at Mastbaum, where his classmates included John Coltrane, Buddy DeFranco, Johnny Coles, Jimmy Heath, and Buddy Savitt.

At fifteen he was playing with local groups, but when the war broke and the draft started eating away at the big bands, a good trumpet player was always in demand. Red would play the Steel Pier in Atlantic City on weekends, and bandleaders passing through would hire him for the duration of their stay. Benny Goodman took him on for a month, and there was a tour with Jerry Wald.

From Harry James to Dizzy Gillespie

"Harry James was my first big influence, naturally, like any white trumpeter of age thirteen or fourteen." He listened to all the "known" players, like Ziggy Elman and Bunny Berigan, but Harry was his main man. As he learned more, he discovered "how tremendous Roy Eldridge was." And there were others, especially Hot Lips Page and Charlie Shavers. But then came Diz.

In 1945, at eighteen, Red joined the Elliot Lawrence orchestra on the CBS radio station in Philadelphia. It was a good studio orchestra, and the air shots and publicity helped get his name known. But the best thing about the daytime broadcasts was that he was free to play evenings in a jazz club called the Down Beat. One night, Dizzy Gillespie came in. Red was mesmerized. "He fascinated me. I heard what I wanted to hear and what I wanted to sound like." Red didn't understand what Gillespie was doing harmonically until Howard McGhee, another trumpeter who had fallen under the Gillespie spell, came through town and explained it to him. He became friendly with Gillespie: "It was wonderful just being with him, listening to him, hanging out with him." He knew his musical direction lay in the new sounds which would be known as bebop.

Bird

"Dizzy kept telling me about this saxophone player I had to hear. We had Sundays off in Philly, so one Saturday night after the job, he took me up to New York with him and I met Charlie Parker. When I heard him play, I near fell out the window. Oh my God! Everything came together at one time. I knew then. I knew where it was and who was it and what I had to do. Godalmighty, we hung out right off. I came over every weekend after that. Bird was very encouraging. I really believe he liked me personally. I don't know why—I loved him!—but he liked me."

Red was playing by ear; he didn't know chord changes, but he was determined and eager to be influenced, and it came easy. All the while, he was becoming recognized on his own. He had recorded and toured with Claude Thornhill, Gene Krupa, and Woody Herman. The solo he played on Herman's "Lemon Drop" attracted attention, and he had a big record with "Perdido," on which he introduced a countermelody that many musicians still use. Yet he did not have *too* high an opinion of himself. He knew he was getting to be a good player, but he didn't think he was ready to go with Bird when the master offered him Miles Davis's seat.

At this time, he was back in Philly. He had been on the road with Woody while his marriage was falling apart, and when his oldest son was born, he decided to come home. His wife left anyway, but shortly afterward Parker called about the job. "I'd love to," Red told him, "but there are so many guys who are more deserving than I am." He was thinking of Kenny Dorham and Fats Navarro, but Bird insisted, so he took the job.

Junk

It was 1949, and Charlie Parker's heroin addiction had already assumed legendary proportions. Wherever the band traveled, the Mooche was there to provide the scag, and the hangers-on rolled up their sleeves wanting to brag they had turned on with the Bird. Rodney was clean; he didn't want to mess around with that. But he was beginning to feel lost. For one thing, the critics ignored him; for another, he was accused of being a junkie anyway. It seemed a natural conclusion: Red had just come from a stay with Herman's Second Herd, which was crawling with users, and his association with Parker confirmed the guilt.

Looking night after night "at this colossal genius standing next to me," he thought, "Would I be nearly so great if I entered into *that* world?" He wondered, and a couple of times he sniffed, figuring sniffing's not going to be anything. The first time he got sick, but when the sickness passed, there was relaxation: tension gone, fears allayed. He played high that night and well, but in retrospect, he insists, "I would have played well anyway. You know how you go along and then all of a sudden, bump, you rise to another plateau, and you work real hard and then, bump, you rise to another one? Well, that period when I joined Charlie Parker, I was rising to another plateau. That's what it was, not the junk."

He kept sniffing. Bird hollered and threatened him, even refusing to turn on with him. "Do as I say, not as I do," he would insist. Red didn't know he was hooked until one night when the band was playing Philly, and he decided to stop. The sickness started, and he thought it was the flu, unwilling to accept, in his mother's house, that he was a junkie. He phoned Bird, "Man, I can't play tonight, I am sick as a dog." Bird already knew. He came over, gave Red a taste—for the first time—and cleaned him up. Everything was fine. They left for work together.

For the time being, it was a habit he could afford. It cost twenty to thirty dollars a day, and Red, in addition to playing with Charlie Parker, was getting a lot of studio work. It was a magic time.

On the Road

Red Rodney sinks back in his chair; his pink eyelids wearily envelop his eyes. He resembles those Hollywood child stars who eerily retain their youth in faces like waxen masks. In an off-moment, though, when they forget to hold themselves, their years swell up and ravage the mask. Red's boyishness is fighting fatigue; his paunch is still undecided between baby fat and stratified age. His voice is a little groggy. Then he pops up, his head drawing out of the shell, his arms and chest coming alive. "You can imagine what it was like traveling all over the country with this genius!" His eyes glow when he remembers Charlie Parker. Bird was "a very modest, humble human being," he says. Oh, he could get angry and demand that people do things for him and give him money when he needed it, but, in general, he was "warm and humane and cared deeply for the other person."

The weirdest road incident came about in 1950, when agent Billy Shaw arranged a southern tour for big money. "You gotta get rid of that redheaded trumpet player; we can't have a white guy in a black band down south," Shaw insisted. Bird said, "No, I ain't gonna get rid of him, he's my man. Man, ain't you ever heard of an albino? Red's an albino." Shaw knew Red was Jewish—he'd heard him speak Yiddish to Parker, much to the delight of the saxophonist, who called Rodney "Chood," a contraction of Chudnick and Jew—and raised hell. Bird said, "Leave it to me." Red knew nothing of this conversation. When the band arrived at the first gig, Spiro's Beach in Maryland, he was surprised to see a sign reading, "The King of Bebop Charlie Parker and his Orchestra featuring Albino Red, Blues Singer." Bird said, "You gotta sing the blues, Chood baby." "But I don't know any blues." "Sing 'em anyhow." He did. The other guys chanted behind him like a choir, and the audiences loved it. In three weeks, nobody ever questioned the masquerade. "They were very polite," Red says.

Swedish Schnapps

Parker saved his life once. Red was living at 201 East Fortieth Street and was sick. He was trying to kick the habit. He didn't think he'd be able to make the upcoming gig at the Village Vanguard, so he called Parker and told him to get Kenny Dorham. A couple of hours into the dawn, he called him again. "Man, I'm awfully sick. Could it be this?" Parker said, "Well, I don't know, I'll be over to see you anyway." Bird hadn't hired Dorham, figuring he could do what he'd done in Philly—give Red a taste and clean him up. He arrived at the apartment and snorted him . . . nothing. He gave him a big shot . . . nothing. He said, "Get your clothes on, man, I'm taking you to a hospital." Red stood up and passed out. Parker carried him down and hailed a cab for Columbus Hospital. When Red came to, his ruptured appendix was gone and Parker's face was the first thing he saw. "Well, guess I'll *have* to hire a trumpet player now," Bird said, smiling.

Red spent six or eight weeks recuperating in a Catskills resort owned by (tenor saxophonist) Allen Eager's mother. He played three hours a night with the band. When there were no customers, they played jazz, and Eager sat in. He was lounging in the swimming pool when the loudspeaker erupted, "Emergency call for Rodney!" It was Bird: "Hey, we gotta record date this afternoon and I want you down here." Red protested; it was impossible. Parker said, "Norman Granz is here and he's gonna have a plane for you." Granz told him to go to Grossinger's, where a chartered plane would be waiting. The plane flew to the airport, where a helicopter stood by. That day they made "Swedish Schnapps" and "Si Si."

A Visitor

Rodney was with Parker for another year after that session, a good year. He'd stopped trying to kick: "If you kick too hard, you'll stub your toe." The end came when Bird with strings became popular. Parker had tried to keep him on—Rodney was paid a couple of times without having to play—but there was no room for a trumpet in the new set-up. After a brief stay with Charlie Ventura—until *that* band broke up—he returned to Philadelphia. One afternoon the doorbell rang. A young black boy put out his hand and said, "My name is Clifford Brown and I'm a trumpet player. I'd sure like to speak with you and study. I'd like to take lessons from the man who plays with Bird." Red didn't teach, but the kid was so sincere and had so disarming a smile, he invited him in. After an hour's talk ("I could see from his questions, he was no ordinary kid"), Red asked him to play: "He knocked me out *then!* He was tremendous. He already had that gorgeous sound and was just getting his ideas together. I told him, 'There's nothing I can show you, you just have to keep playing like you are.' " They became friends; whenever Red played Philly, Clifford would come to hear him. When Clifford went with a local band, Chris Powell and the Blue Flames, Red proudly proclaimed, "Another year and this kid's gonna take New York." Which is what happened: "From the very beginning, everybody knew. He was that great."

The First Bust

The divorce had come through, and Rodney was settled in Philly, leading a small band including tenor saxophonist Buddy Savitt and a local pianist named Jimmy Golden. The whole band was using, everybody knew it, and one night the cops came in and pulled them off the stand. They were beaten and thrown in jail. "I always got beat up terribly though I never gave them any back talk. Man, I was respectful, I called them 'mister' because I was afraid of them. But I always got knocked around. In '63 two cops in Vegas knocked my teeth out because I couldn't answer some questions. They beat me so bad, an FBI agent came around and got me to file a civil-rights complaint, but they couldn't make it stick. What can you do?"

He was sent to the federal narcotics hospital in Lexington, Kentucky, for four and a half months, the regular cure. The first few weeks, the withdrawing period, were a drag, but the rest wasn't so bad. There were some great musicians there, and he met his second wife there. They married shortly after being released, but not before copping some junk. There would be three more stays in Lexington.

More Bar Mitzvah Presents

Charlie Parker died in 1955 at thirty-four; Clifford Brown was killed a year later at twenty-five. The music scene was drying up for bop: "I think one of the reasons was that we refused to entertain. We thought we were too hip for that and the people stopped coming. We were wrong." Back in Philly after another trip to Lexington, Red Rodney was having trouble with the vice squad. Though temporarily clean, he was subjected to a shakedown nearly every night. He went to see the head narcotics-and-vice cop, Captain Murgatroyd, who operated a kosher catering establishment on the side. He said, "Cap, your men are killing me. Every time I get a job, they get me knocked off and here I am clean with a wife and a baby." Murgatroyd stood up and declared, "You *are* clean, kid, and I'm gonna help you." He introduced him to his partner in the catering business with the words "Here's your new bandleader." That weekend Red played two bar mitzvahs and a wedding. At the office, a sign was posted: "Red Rodney Orchestras."

After nearly a month's abstinence, Rodney now had a license, no less than the captain of the vice squad, so he got hooked again. Murgatroyd didn't mind. The music was unbearable, but the money was pouring in. "I played very little jazz during this period, '56 and '57. Occasionally, I'd get a big-band gig for a school, but it was a flop. I'd have a good band but they didn't want to hear it. Yet I was coining money hand over fist playing shit. It can be done out there. If I'd stayed with this big office, I'd be a millionaire today. Even though it was crap, I used all the good musicians and made them a living." For a while, Bernard Peiffer, the French pianist, was a regular; Savitt and Billy Root were also mainstays. In no time, Red Rodney was a pillar of the community. He'd have three bands working society gigs. The first, with Red, would get $1500, the second $800, and the third $650. If he promised to show up for the ceremony of one of the bar mitzvahs he wasn't working, just to participate in the candle lighting, he'd get a little more. His popularity remained undiminished, even though he always showed up a little late, after hitting up.

His habit was running several thousand dollars a week. He was busted a number of times, sometimes with his wife, but usually he paid off the cops who pulled the bust. A new narcotics squad was now in competition with Murgatroyd's boys. But no sweat, if he couldn't pay the cops, he could always pay the judge through his lawyer. "Murgatroyd was good to me. I tried to pay him but he never took a dime from me. I hear he's a rich man today from taking everybody else's money. Fact, I played his niece's wedding—an Irish Catholic wedding in a Jewish catering house—thinking it was my treat, but he insisted on paying me. Figure that out."

Grapes of Wrath

In 1958, fed up with "the society bit," Red Rodney sold his burgeoning business to another bandleader for twenty-five thousand dollars and headed out for San Francisco. "It was a mistake, San Francisco is a terrible place for music." There was no jazz work, and for casuals, he was offered a fraction of what he was paying his own men in Philly. The money was running out, so he became a securities expert. "I didn't know a thing about securities, but I let them do all the talking and they thought I knew everything. I can't tell most of it, because the statute of limitations hasn't run out yet, but I can tell about General MacIntyre."

The General

With the ingenuity required to negotiate a difficult chord change at an impossible tempo, Red Rodney was planning capers. Prime territories were San Francisco, his home base, and Las Vegas. The previous year he had recorded his two best albums, not realizing they would serve as his farewell to music for some time. Now, at thirty, he surveyed his life and made a decision. He thought, "Here I'm going to jail for three and six months and being treated like a dog for using stuff. If I'm gonna go to jail, let it be for something big." The Red Arrow was not destined to be a mere thug. He would bilk only the rich to forestall becoming one of the poor. "The idea was to take the companies that take us off every day."

One afternoon, he noticed a captioned photograph in the newspaper. General Arnold T. MacIntyre had been appointed disbursement officer. "Hey," he thought, "I look like this cat!" Around the same time, a hooker friend showed him the paycheck she'd lifted from a colonel. Rodney bought it from her and, after researching the average monthly salary of a major general, turned it over to his printer for duplication. He also purchased a major general's uniform. Armed with a roll of credit cards made, by his printer, of teak wood, and twenty checks, each for one thousand eight hundred forty-some-odd dollars, Red Rodney, alias General MacIntyre, the disbursement officer, traveled around the country. Uniformed, his hair dyed gray, wearing glasses, he'd walk into a bank, ask to speak with the manager, and unroll the stream of credit cards, not letting anyone examine them too closely. In this manner, he supported himself handsomely for a year.

He was working Las Vegas a lot, thinking it would be a good

place to settle when he kicked. In a Reno paper, he read about the Atomic Energy Commission in Mercury, Nevada. Seems the payroll for the Nellis Air Force Base, $180,000, was being held there. The Red Arrow was loaded to the gills with guts. He was shooting methedrine to get up and heroin to stay down. He decided to go in and get it.

He drove up to the Atomic Energy Commission in a rented car and asked to see the commander of the place, a colonel. When the colonel saw the major general, unexpected and wanting to inspect the premises, he quaked and gasped and sputtered. "Weeeeee! I got this turkey," the Arrow thought. "He must be doing something wrong, he's more nervous than I am." The colonel unctuously offered the general his quarters. "No, I can stay at the Bachelor Officers' Quarters." "I wouldn't think of it, General." He ushered the superior officer into his office to examine the books in privacy. The Arrow saw the safe. "How the hell am I gonna open it?" he wondered. The colonel opened the safe, removed the books, and, leaving the safe open, walked to the door, saluted, said, "At your service, General," and split.

"Hmmmmm," the Red Arrow thought, saying a silent prayer for the movies he'd seen about army protocol. Truth to tell, he was scared to death. He walked over to the safe . . . and the money was gone! (Later he learned the money had been moved to the Nellis base ninety minutes before his arrival.) However, there was a briefcase with $16,000 in it. He took ten, hoping it wouldn't be missed for a while. He also took a bundle of securities. The Colonel wasn't around, so he asked the sergeant at the gate for a lift into town. Town consisted mostly of Beverly Harrell's whorehouse, where, he explained to the sergeant, he would be staying the night. With the sergeant watching, he had to walk into the whorehouse. He and a whore were shown to a room. As she removed her blouse, he noticed tracks on her arms. "Hey, c'mon, let's turn," he offered. "What the fuck kinda general are you?" she asked. "A dope-fiend general!"

The Chase

The Red Arrow doubled back to Mercury to retrieve his rented car, drove it up the highway to Goldfield, checked it, and rented another. He switched back to his Red Rodney persona. On the road, he pulled over to look at the securities. There were Reynolds securities and government parchment-paper stock and, say! what's this? Two pieces of paper with gobbledygook written on them. He didn't know what they were, but they frightened him. Then anxiety subsided. "If these papers are what I think they are," he mused, "they could be my ticket to freedom or some kind of deal." In San Francisco, he tucked them in a safe-deposit box. The FBI was combing the Coast for the guy who had ripped off the Atomic Energy Commission.

The Red Arrow had made a mistake. When the Feds traced his steps to the whorehouse, the whore told them about the junk. Now they knew: the description, the MO, and the junk all pointed to Red Rodney.

They didn't catch him for a while. He played a few gigs in Vegas while keeping a motel room in S.F. He was scoring every day and had one more general's check. He put on the uniform, not realizing the banks had been alerted. When the manager began to stall, he knocked him down and ran out of the bank. A passing FBI car, not even on the case, saw the incident and followed him to his motel. In a few minutes, the place was surrounded.

In the county jail, everyone called him General. Cops and Feds threatened to take him through city court, state court, and federal court. It was a bustling, noisy situation when two Internal Security agents from Washington walked in. Everybody else walked out. The agents grinned. "Listen, Red," one agent said. "You pulled a beauty, but, ah, you had two pieces of paper with the securities." "You mean the gobbledygook? Yeah, I got 'em, what is that?" "Look," the other agent said, "we know you're not an agent, we know, we dug the caper you pulled, it was beautiful. Give us back the two pieces of paper and we'll do this favor. We'll put everything into one. We won't charge you with impersonating an officer, just interstate theft of forged securities."

"Can I have that in writing?"

"We can't put it in writing, you have to take our word. Otherwise, we'll charge you with espionage."

"You got it, gentlemen."

The government kept its word. While Red was waiting in a federal tank to go to court, the agents brought in the Colonel from Mercury. He'd been demoted to major. He became hysterical: "That's the sonofabitch," he yelled, "I'd recognize him any day! He has red hair now, but he was gray then!"

Father Flotsky's Triumph?

"If you ever have to do time," Red Rodney advises, "do it at Fort Worth." He remembers the experience fondly, because he was so busy. Of a five-year stretch, he served twenty-seven months, and used the time to get a college degree and practice his horn. He had to work only one hour a day in the laundry—it was his job to take care of thirteen nurses' uniforms. But didn't he feel cooped up, deprived? "Oh no, not there, because I had a nice room. God! Fort Worth is a beautiful place; it's better than Lexington. Minimum security—they don't have a cell in the place."

However, before Fort Worth, there was Leavenworth—all cells—for a six-month stay. It seems his files had been mixed up; so for half a year he waited there to be sent to the hospital. At Leavenworth, he worked in the writ room, where guys with sixth- and seventh-grade educations studied and learned the law. Rodney became fascinated with them and started college immediately: "All the law is is precedents; it's much easier to be a good lawyer than a good jazz musician, much easier."

He changed in another way—once in stir, he knew he would

never again get messed up with junk. He needed the prison term to kick—he couldn't do it himself—but once inside he didn't even need prison therapy for encouragement: it was time to quit, and he did. After finishing college, he still had four months to serve, so he took the Berklee correspondence course in musical arranging.

The Trial

From Fort Worth, Red went back to Vegas and settled in for a life as a studio musician. He was working the Tennessee Ernie Ford TV show when Melvin Belli appeared as a guest. Red became friendly with Belli and his law partner, Vincent Hallinan, and expressed his desire to go to law school. They helped him enroll in Lincoln Law, a nonaccredited school. The bar association, which passes on every student's eligibility, approved Rodney *every term*. He completed the four-year course in three years, graduating second in his class, though he modestly points out, "In all fairness, mostly cops go to a nonaccredited school." During the last year, he quit playing to devote full time to his studies, and supported himself by selling television sets in a San Francisco department store. On completion of the course, Belli hired him as a private investigator—the bar exam lay ahead. As a P.I., Red wrote briefs, researched cases, and visited the victims of accidents to get them to sign with Belli's office.

Then the bomb fell. He was called into an office and told he would not be allowed to take the bar exam because of moral turpitude. The law of California prohibited a felon from taking the exam. "Well, how come you let me study all this time?" Red asked the judges. The judges weren't exactly sure, though they noted how commendable it was for him to go to school and do so well, and so on. Norman Granz, the jazz promoter, introduced Red to his friend Stanley Moscowitz, a Supreme Court justice. Moscowitz sympathized with Red, assured him he had a good case, and promised him help. Red knew that the highest court in California was his only chance. Finally, the day came for Chief Justice Trainor to read the decision. He said: "This is the law of the State of California and I am going to uphold it. However, anyone who is able to rehabilitate himself, study a subject, pass an examination, and show that his character has been improved should have the opportunity to do so." Trainor wanted to go on record as being against the law he was now upholding. The vote was five to one, with only Moscowitz supporting Red.

Red was embittered. The only way out was a presidential pardon, and Nixon had just taken office. There was no way. He cooled himself down and went to Las Vegas to start working again.

Amerika

Las Vegas, the land of gold. In one of the casinos Red put sixty cents down on a Keno game. A few minutes later, he was $12,500 richer. He bought a house. In 1954, while playing with Benny Carter at the Moulin Rouge, he and several band members had bought some land. Red's chunk had cost $400. He sold it now for $50,000. And every cent of it went to the hospital when he suffered his stroke. It was the stroke that convinced him to return to jazz. Before, he had been making $300 or $400 a week for three hours' work a night; he was nervous about giving up that kind of security. But Vegas started drying up the same time he got sick. The lounges were converted to Keno parlors and, besides, he had had a bellyful of show business.

After his recovery, he began working on restoring his chops, a process that will never end. To make things worse, two cops had knocked out his teeth. His new teeth are a little too long and will have to be filed down. He's still brimming with musical ideas, but his endurance is limited. At home, he's unsure whether he can build a new career, but in Europe, the work offers have been so consistent, he extended a month-long visit to five months.

L'envoi

"I have no regrets whatsoever because I've lived a full life and I never hurt anybody. I suppose there is a little guilt in the *act alone*—you know it's the wrong thing to do—but when I compare it with what's happening today, then, no, it's really not wrong, it was fun. And I paid the dues. I paid more dues than the sonovabitches who almost stole the country are going to pay. The wrong turn I made was in getting disgusted with the music business and with jazz. That was a wrong turn more than the criminal acts. But the business was so bad, and the black and white scene started to get bad and I couldn't stand that. I figured, let me get away from it all. Well, that I regret, walking away from my talent. I've made money; money is not the answer. More than anything, I just want to reestablish myself in jazz, try to play, and make a living, that's all."

January 1975

Long Tall Dexter
Bites the Apple

Dexter Gordon is back, and his magnetism and strength can hardly fail to buttress a scene grown weak-kneed with commercialism and increasingly devoid of rigorous swing. He is back from his adopted Copenhagen with his wife, Fenja, and two-year-old son, Benjamin—named after fellow expatriate-tenor Ben Webster—for a ten-week tour of the country, including his first New York club appearances, two nights at Storyville and a week at the Village Vanguard, since 1969. Anticipation has been running hot and heavy; the capacity audience at Storyville, despite a rainstorm, was so shamelessly elated—after the last of three exhausting sets it stood roaring for five minutes—that one could easily forget that it would be coterie and not mass audiences greeting his return.

It has not always been like that. Asked why he's been away so long, he says, "Nobody asked me." In previous years, he did perform in Los Angeles and Chicago, but "that's because most of my contacts are on the West Coast, that's really my home." He comes back to the United States for the Christmas holidays, partly to escape the Scandinavian winter, and while he is invariably welcomed with choruses of good-to-have-you-back, the enthusiasm was rarely translated into opportunities for work. Incredible, but true. I reminded him of the 1969 New-port Jazz Festival when George Wein ushered him off the stage after two numbers, to the dismay of those of us who had jour-neyed far to hear two expatriates, Gordon and Don Byas (who also played two numbers), and Dexter said, "Yeah, mention that! I certainly felt like playing more than that." At a more recent Newport–New York festival, he was given similarly short shrift at a Lionel Hampton reunion concert. "Well, that's Lio-nel," he says, smiling.

A number of things have conspired to reemphasize Dexter Gordon's presence in the world. Most long-term expatriates are quickly forgotten here, but he has always managed to sustain a moderate American audience in addition to his more clamorous European following. For one thing, he is one of a handful of soloists whose playing has changed and grown for more than thirty years. He is frankly contemptuous of players who haven't kept up with the music and are playing the same way they did during the '40s. For Gordon, "keeping up" means an open-mindedness to new directions in harmony and tonal concep-tion, not transitory fads and trappings. He continues to play the blues and I-got-rhythm configurations, favorite ballads—he has developed into one of our finest ballad interpreters—and his own uniquely witty and jumping originals. In the late '60s, Col-trane was suddenly gone, Rollins was on a sabbatical, and Getz was growing mawkish. The most striking of the avant-gardists, Albert Ayler, was killed, while the best modern and neomodern tenors seemed exiled even in America: Wayne Shorter content to deliver Joe Zawinul's Weather Report, Hank Mobley rarely playing at all, Archie Shepp in college, Jimmy Heath and Al Cohn on view only intermittently. Gene Ammons died, James Moody went to Las Vegas, Sonny Stitt lost his consistency, Sonny Rollins discovered crossover. Zoot Sims remained con-stant but was out of favor. Dexter Gordon—who was, in any case, one of the strongest tenor saxophonists of any generation—began to loom as the last of the tribe.

Gordon's attractiveness is built on his music but is not confined by it. He is one of the few charismatic men in jazz. His very image on a bandstand is reassuring, and perfectly complements the deep sanguinity of his sound, the expressiveness of his ideas, the galvanizing effect of his swing. He is six-feet-five with a powerful frame and a face that combines distinguished handsomeness and childlike glee. He introduced each selection at Storyville in a clear, serious voice, ignoring the requests chattering back to him, and responded to the wild applause following each selection by smiling broadly and holding his mighty Selmer horizontally aloft.

His sound is incomparable—capable of robust clarity on fast tempos and dark sobriety on ballads. He can honk so powerfully in the lower register, you expect walls to crumble before him, and his husky cries in the hidden register can be chilling. It is a sound with depth and authenticity, something you want to reach out and touch. His phrases combine laid-back Lester Young riffs with his own distinctively forthright melodies and boppish fillips, which he inserts with body English, the right foot climbing up the left leg.

If Rollins's humor tends toward the sardonic and parodic, then Gordon's might be described as intellectually impish. One of the numerous lessons he learned well from Lester Young—whose very name causes Dexter's eyes to widen, his palms to turn upwards, and a low "ayyyyyy" to emerge from his throat—is to know the lyrics of the songs he plays: "It gives you a fuller understanding of what the song is about." He introduces ballads by reciting a few lines of the lyric, and his song quotations are often motivated as much by the lyric content as by the musical appropriateness. Gordon wasn't the first to color his solos with quotations—Armstrong did it occasionally, and Tatum, all the time—but he developed it into a fine art. On a thirty-two-bar original called "Fried Bananas," I jotted down the following references: "Stranger in Paradise," "Day-O," "Dr. Hackenbush," Sonny Boy," and "It Could Happen to You."

The pug-nosed kid in "Polka Dots and Moonbeams" turned out to be "Mona Lisa." The compatibility between such levity and the enormous intensity of Gordon's improvisatory thrust illustrates the central paradox of bop, that it is a music where relaxation and tension are inseparable. You begin with tempos that are outrageously fast, chord sequences designed with bravura, and melodic labyrinths, and then you have to improvise a convincing story without seeming to be pressured or hurried or desperate. Swing becomes syncopated cool.

Gordon was born in Los Angeles fifty-three years ago; he started on clarinet at thirteen, switched to alto two years later, and to tenor two years after that. He describes L.A. as being isolated in the '30s. "It was almost like living in Europe. Only the biggest bands came out, like Dorsey, Hines, Duke, Louis, but there were some good locals, like Hampton and Marshal Royal. All my lunch money went to used 78s." In 1939, he heard the Basie band with Lester Young. "Prez! He had that special thing that floored me. I tried to play like him. He was the first to play color tones, like sixths and ninths." Gordon was very much under the Young influence when he joined Hampton's band, where his fellow tenor was Illinois Jacquet: "We were both listening to the same thing, but he leaned more to Herschel [Evans, also of the Basie band] and I leaned more to Prez. At that time Hawkins was the dominant figure with purists—Lester, with his light sound, wasn't considered in the same class. But he had such spirit and joie de vivre."

The two main schools of the tenor sax are those founded by Hawkins and Young, and Gordon is frequently mentioned as the first man to combine aspects of both into a distinct style, which in turn influenced the three major tenors of the '50s: Coltrane, Rollins, Getz. Actually, it was Herschel Evans, a Hawkins disciple, who first attracted Dexter, since Hawkins was in Europe until 1939, while the Basie band was ubiquitous. It wasn't until he heard Hawkins in New York that Dexter realized that part of his greatness was an ability to hear the younger players and "keep up." Comparing Hawkins and Young, he notes, "Hawk was going out farther on the chords, but Lester leaned to the pretty notes. He had a way of telling a story with everything he played, simple and direct. The cats at the corner candy store would make up lyrics to Prez's solos and jam."

In 1941, Dexter was sitting in Hampton's orchestra for a Battle of the Bands at the Savoy. The opposition was Jay McShann. "I dug his alto player, he had a lot of Lester in his playing, and also Jimmy Dorsey." Jimmy Dorsey? "He was a master saxophonist, Bird knew that." The altoist was Charlie Parker, of course; he provided the third major ingredient in Dexter's evolving style. "He was playing so much saxophone, new tunes, new harmonic conceptions, he extended the chords, altering them fluidly. Prez stayed around ninths—he must have listened to Ravel and Debussy—but Bird went all the way up the scale." Gordon became a part of the new movement dubbed bop. "We used to go by Dizzy's house and he'd be playing piano and changes; it was like a little school 'cause cats went up there all the time. I didn't like Monk at first because he wasn't an impressive pianist like Bud Powell; later on, of course . . ." He met the other tenors who had come up the same way, listening to Prez and then Bird, like Wardell Gray and Gene Ammons. "Ammons was playing like Ben [Webster] when he first joined the Billy Eckstine band. After I joined, the mutha changed his style in a minute."

Before Eckstine, however, there was a stay with Louis Armstrong's big band. Louis had walked up to him in a club in L.A. and said, "Hey, gates, I like your tone, kid, you got a nice tone." The next night, Teddy McRae, the band's straw boss, hired him. Dexter was unhappy with the '30s arrangements Armstrong used, and the spiritlessness he perceived among the band members, but he loved Armstrong. "When we left L.A., going on the road, I had a dozen Prince Albert cans of good Mexican pot. Every night at intermission, Pops and I would go

out and smoke. After a week, he didn't bring his shit anymore—
I wouldn't tell him, but it was lemonade. I said, 'Damn, Pops,
I notice you don't bring out that New Orleans Golden Leaf.'
He said, 'Man, that's like bringing hamburger to a banquet.' "

By the late '40s, Gordon had developed the most influential
new approach to the tenor. He had also become involved in a
series of immensely popular tenor battles. It began with Eckstine
singing, "Blow Mr. Gene, blow Mr. Dexter, too." In addition to
Ammons, he subsequently took on Teddy Edwards, Budd Johnson, baritone saxophonist Leo Parker, and, most rewardingly,
Wardell Gray. At the same time, he composed an impressive
number of riff tunes for recording sessions on Savoy and Dial.
Jimmy Heath has described Gordon as the central influence on
the second wave of modernist tenorists, because even Young
seemed dated to them by 1949. One of the musicians most profoundly touched by Gordon's music, particularly his harmonic
inventiveness, was John Coltrane, by only three years Gordon's
junior. By 1960, Coltrane would build a new lexicon on Dexter's foundation, using Indian and pentatonic scales, chord patterns within chords, and phrase permutations, which Gordon,
like Hawkins learning from Parker, would investigate and in-
corporate into his own playing.

But first there was a near-barren decade. By 1950 a new
school of tenors had come on the scene. Ironically, they were
as beholden to Lester Young as was Dexter, but their style was
called cool. "We used to jam together—Zoot, Al Cohn, Allen
Eager. Zoot and I worked in a club in Hollywood for Norman
Granz. He was playing Lester and I was playing Lester, but
there was always a difference." Gordon was no longer as fashionable; worse, he was busted for narcotics and served two
years at a minimum-security prison called Chino, appearing in
the movie filmed there, *Unchained*. (There is a scene where
Dexter is playing in the prison band, but what you hear is the
overdub of a studio musician.) He recorded a couple of albums
in 1955 and wasn't heard from again on records until 1960,

when Cannonball Adderley produced an album called *The Resurgence of Dexter Gordon*. He was soon cast as the lead musician and composer for a West Coast production of *The Connection*, and, more significantly, embarked on a series of seven albums for Blue Note, making clear his increased command in every aspect of his music: they are among the finest recordings by any tenor saxophonist. Pressed to name one album he would recommend to someone who didn't know his music, he offered *GO!*—one of two Blue Note sessions with the late Sonny Clark— "Isn't he beautiful? He was my man."

He was clean, and inspired. But there was no work, and in New York he was denied a cabaret card. He first went to Europe in 1962 after meeting Ronnie Scott, proprietor of a jazz club in London. Scott promised him a month in London and a tour of the continent. "I didn't intend on staying, it just happened. I was working all the time and having a ball in this new environment. Before I realized it, a couple of years had gone by and I was considered an expatriate." He returned for six months in 1965, "but the scene was disillusioning." Again, there was a period of scant recording—until 1969, when he signed with Prestige. He eventually settled in Copenhagen, married, and began recording with the new SteepleChase label, which allowed him to realize the ambition of performing with a string orchestra. He is especially proud of the resultant album, *More Than You Know,* and rightly so. He plans to stay in Copenhagen—"I have roots there now"—where he plays with both local and visiting American musicians, and performs a good deal on television and radio. On the basis of his current success, he also plans to tour the United States every year.

November 1976

The Whiteness
of the Wail

In alto saxophonist Art Pepper, the jazz mythographer finds
not only a prototype for the psychoses and guilts, the triumphs
and losses of the white hipster jazz musician, but a colleague as
well. For Pepper is one living legend who takes his status seriously, like Sarah Vaughan, who, when asked by a sycophantic
Sammy Davis how it felt to be a legend, replied, "Well, I get
up in the morning, look in the mirror, and shout, Hey, I'm a
legend!"—only Pepper means it for real, and with something
like astonishment at having survived to tell the tale. He's eager
to tell, to provide an iconography of the talent and the waste,
the music and the junk (which he calls "a kind of cultural tradition"), the scuffling for work and the shuffling in prison yards
(for more than a decade), the despair and the eventual rainbow
sign: "It looks for me like life begins at fifty," he's written, "and
I never thought I'd live to see fifty, let alone start a new life at
this age."

Pepper has outlived his own worst fantasies and is looking
back at them boldly but cautiously, fearful perhaps that they'll
overwhelm him after all. He's no longer the handsome Pepper
who once adorned record jackets like a late-'50s movie star—
Steve Cochran about to metamorphose into Warren Beatty; he

looks diminished, staring through a fog on the cover of the 1976 release *Living Legend,* his first album in sixteen years (as he mused several times during a heralded Village Vanguard engagement, seemingly awed by the fact). In the picture he wears a Texas Lutheran College sweatshirt with the arms cut off, revealing four fearsome tattoos, one of which looks like a skull with a toupee. His hair is slicked down, framing a less certain face than the one we knew from the classic *+Eleven* album, glassy eyed and worn. His gossipy liner notes avidly recount his tribulations. In the notes to a subsequent album, *The Trip,* he compares the bull sessions at San Quentin to the process of making a jazz solo—in both instances, one takes the improvised "trip" of an imaginative storyteller. In the '50s, you were discreet about "personal problems" like serving time and taking junk, but junk finds its victims outside of jazz today, so the survivor's song recalls another age.

And it's comforting to find in Art Pepper the Homeric muse. Part of the myth of the hipster musician is that he makes it to the other side but, like Orpheus, can't or won't return. Or at least this is the myth of the white fan who seeks in jazz the intimacy of blackness, fearing it all the same. In the Midwest during the '60s, I heard several stories about pilgrims who made the journey to Charlie Parker's Kansas City neighborhood or gravesite and never lived to tell about it. For some reason, the stories seemed believable then and were accepted for their cautionary value, i.e., get as close to the music as you can, white boy, but don't go beyond the music. Terry Southern may have understood this aspect of the white Negro as well as Norman Mailer when he wrote a story about a cornball Charlie who wants to meet the only Charlie who counts and gets bopped on the head in an alley. A couple of years ago, Allan D. Coleman, who has written widely on photography, published a little book called *Confirmation.* It consists of twelve pictures of a tombstone: "Son Charles Parker Jr. August 29, 1920–March 23, 1955." There's also a page of text describing his trip to Kansas

City to see the confirmation of Parker's death, and therefore of his life. For a touch of local color, one "young and limping" black is quoted as saying to another, "Char-l-e-e-e Parker! Dat man could make his hawn talk!" It doesn't matter that no one on earth speaks like that; the point is the otherness of that dark and inviolable world. (Of course, the tombstone may not be a confirmation after all, since Bird really died March 12.)

Our fascination with the great white bebopper—of whom there is none greater than Art Pepper—is part envy and part admiration because he got close to the secret world of black culture—that world of genius and fire and bared emotion that promised salvation. He could speak Bird's language; moreover, he could make from it his own language. Pepper speaks much about the cry in his music, the happiness in the sadness, or the sadness in the happiness: it is the gift of swinging with melancholy that the best white jazz musicians have offered (Beiderbecke, Teagarden, Russell, the Four Brothers reed section in Woody Herman's Second Herd, Gil and Bill Evans) and that helps explain why the black musician who cloned the most white players was Lester Young, the most melancholy and secretive of swingers. The important thing about the good white jazzmen is not that they appropriated the black American's music—a narrow and paranoid sentiment that denies the individuality of all jazzmen, white and black—but that so many of them chose a black aesthetic as the best possible source for self-examination. Those who dug deepest avoided minstrelsy and went beyond mere technique. They offered the jazz listener the only quality no black jazzman can offer—the pursuit of the white wail, a revelation of Caucasian inwit through the black idiom of the blues: a personal search fraught with peril. For in mastering a foreign musical syntax, they have straddled the racial division of American life, crafting a music that is not only of itself, but about itself. The fan's guilt-ridden correlative is the folk story in which the white yokel timidly trespasses in the dark culture, armed with a collection of hip records and a sentimental love for blacks. Oh, what did I do to be so white and blue?

For some, the musical route was not sufficient. Junk provided a keener initiation; it was another step in the excommunication from home that had begun with the original commitment to what James Jones liked to call "an outlaw music." Here, finally, the pathology of the white musician seems to attain equal footing with that of the black musician, who also took junk to get closer to an illusory "cultural tradition," though some blacks must have felt it was a cultural imperative. Billie Holiday once said that in her youth whorehouses were the only places where whites and blacks got together—the shooting gallery was another. Pepper's legend encompasses that hipster's myth of black-white contentment as well. He made his first record twenty-five years ago with Hampton Hawes, the funky bebop pianist who, like Pepper, contradicted most generalizations about West Coast jazz; they were reunited for Pepper's resurgence on *Living Legend*. Here was a salt-and-pepper team with so much blues in common, even racial pedigrees could be discounted. (Hawes, a smart and funny man who died in 1977 gave us his own mythography in a remarkable book, *Raise Up Off Me*, and Pepper is about to do the same. His liner notes and nightclub patter reveal a man who can't stop talking.*)

What a shock it must have been for white musicians when the racial/junkie/musical brotherhood fell apart. By the mid-'50s, it was no longer enough to share the music or a needle. Pedigree won out after all. If the white musicians could accede to the studios, those lucrative Muzak factories into which pale-face dilettante jazz artists frequently passed, then at least the black artists would maintain the purity of the race in the jazz world. Suddenly,. white musicians were poor relations, and many of them, who could have handled any adversity but re-

---

* Just how eager Pepper was to tell all became clear in late 1979, when his autobiography, *Straight Life*, was published. It is almost fanatically confessional, and one of the finest of all jazz autobiographies.

jection from their adopted family, gave up and went back to the sticks.

Many have expressed the dismay of disenfranchisement. Here's Pepper, in the notes to *Early Art:* ". . . musicians were starting to be afraid to let you sit in, afraid you'd steal their jobs. The warmth and beauty left jazz. It became more difficult to play. It was less enjoyable. And then mistrust showed up in the music. There used to be a healthy spirit of competition. You'd go up on the stand with, say, Sonny Stitt, and you'd try to outplay him, and he'd try to outplay you, but it would all be done with good feelings, in the right spirit. Around the mid-'50s, it got to be more like a battle to the death." Even Europe was no help here: In the '60s, famous black musicians reluctantly fired white sidemen because the European promoters wanted "authenticity." Ted Curson paid dues throughout the '60s for carrying an integrated band. Maybe that's why the mutual testimonies by the four musicians on the jacket of *Living Legend* (Pepper, Hawes, Charlie Haden, and Shelly Manne) are so moving; everybody loves everybody again and it's cool to worry about the music first and later about the politics.

It used to be said of Pepper that his direct source material was Charlie Parker and Lee Konitz, a sensible blend of insuperable black brilliance and soul with undeniable white originality. Parker's breathtaking facility was in the immediate service of his emotions, while Konitz, comparatively timorous though resolute, seemed to be thinking out loud, maintaining a cooler temperature for swing. To have combined those two into yet another original voice was to accomplish the most pressing task of the white hipster musician, the balance of both objective (black) authenticity and personal (white) sincerity. In Leonard Feather and Ira Gitler's *The Encyclopedia of Jazz in the Seventies,* we learn that Pepper now considers his real models to have been Lester Young and Zoot Sims, a similar combination, though swing rather than bop oriented. It's a revealing admission, I think, for part of the originality of his sound may reside in his transference of tenor stylings to the lighter horn—this seems especially true of his early recordings (now on Blue Note and Savoy). Even now, many of his ideas suggest Young's and Sims's phrasing grafted to Parker's rhythms. The third influence he mentions, the one that accounts for his present style, is John Coltrane, proving that the most cognizant players (black or white: think of Dexter Gordon and Jackie McLean) are best tuned into the evolving lexicon of the art. His present work is alive with splintered tones, modal arpeggios, furious double-timing, and acerbic wit. He continues to play from deep inside.

What do fan mythologies have to do with Art Pepper, whose appearance at the Vanguard was his first solo flight ever in New York (he had been here previously only as a sideman with Stan Kenton and Buddy Rich)? Probably not very much, and I wouldn't bring it up if Pepper could restrain himself from fashioning his own myth. He talks constantly at the gig, assuming our intimacy with his problems, assuring us of his gratefulness; and since he's right, of course (we do know all about him and are rooting for him for reasons that can never again be *entirely* musical, even if our interest in what he says stems from his immersion in music), we respond in kind. Ornette Coleman, who had played with him in L.A., came in on opening night and noted, "Art sounds good and the audience is making him feel good and that's important." It's reassuring to know that behind the legend is the substance that prompted the sentimentality and admiration that fostered the identification. He refers to his past with a tale-spinner's wonder, like someone amazed he could have experienced it and survived; but he plays like a knowing athlete, trained and poised. Jazz legends never die; they become self-fulfilling prophecies.

July 1977

Jazz Musicians,
Consider Wes Montgomery

In 1944, Wes Montgomery was nineteen years old and living in his hometown of Indianapolis with a day job and a new wife. Inspired by the recordings of Charlie Christian, Montgomery bought a guitar and amplifier, determined to teach himself Christian's solos, though he was unable to read music. After a month's practicing with a plectrum, he plugged in to the amplifier and discovered that the volume was too loud for his family's comfort. He compromised by throwing away the pick and plucking the strings with his thumb. This gave him a uniquely mellow sound, especially at the fast tempos he mastered. Almost as an extension of that dulcet, singing tone, he began to work in octaves—voicing the melody line in two registers. Still unable to read, and never willing to pursue technique for its own end, he eventually devised a structural basis for soloing, beginning with supple single-noted lines, progressing to octaves and finally to dense and intensely rhythmic chords.

Four years after buying his guitar, Montgomery went on the road for two years with Lionel Hampton. Tired of traveling and lonesome for his family, he returned to Indianapolis, took a day job, played at night, and spent most of the 1950s as a local attraction. (There was a West Coast recording with his brothers, but it received little attention.) He was thirty-four when Cannonball Adderley, in town for a concert, heard him and ecstatically called Orrin Keepnews of Riverside Records, urging him to sign Montgomery to the label. He must have been convincing, because Keepnews flew to Indianapolis with a contract.

From the beginning of his belated "discovery," the critical reception ranged from euphoria to hyperbole. No one had ever heard a guitar sound like Wes Montgomery's. The decade had its share of gifted guitarists—Tal Farlow, Barney Kessel, Kenny Burrell, Jim Hall, and others—but the consensus on Montgomery was "not since Charlie Christian. . . ." The records, however, did not sell, and Keepnews, who had a deepening friendship with the guitarist, told him, "A year ago you were unknown and broke; now you're a star and broke, and that's real progress." By 1963, Riverside was going broke, so it is a singularly frustrating irony to Keepnews that one of the last albums he produced for the label was a "commercial" Montgomery date with strings, which was poorly promoted and little heard.

Riverside went under in '64, and most of its artists—Julian Adderley, Thelonious Monk, Bill Evans—had little trouble in finding interested labels. Montgomery went to Verve, where Creed Taylor presided, and made an exciting record with a brass-laden orchestra called *Movin' Wes*. It was, by jazz standards, a commercial success, as was its sequel, *Bumpin'*. Creed Taylor realized something about Montgomery's talent: it was his octave technique and lyrical sound, not his audaciously legato eighth-note improvisations with their dramatic architectural designs, that appealed to middle-of-the-road ears. So he set Montgomery on a course of decreasing improvisation and increasingly busy overdubbed arrangements, while the octaves, once used so judiciously, became the focus of his new "style." The next record, *Goin' Out of My Head*, was a huge, Grammy-winning success. Montgomery's feelings about the album are suggested by Mrs. Keepnews's memory of Wes "slipping the

record to me because he was ashamed for Orrin to hear it."
When Wes belittled the record to Orrin, Keepnews told him,
"You should shut up, as much as you've made from it. I can
hate it, but you can't."

In 1965, Montgomery spent a year touring with the Wynton
Kelly trio. (A few years earlier, John Coltrane had asked him
to join his band, but although they teamed up for a gig in San
Francisco, Montgomery turned him down.) Verve recorded the
Kelly-Montgomery group live and released a superb album
called *Smokin' at the Half Note*. Aside from that disc, the
Montgomery-Taylor relationship, which moved to A&M records,
proceeded inexorably from Taylor's cost-accountancy approach
to producing music. Don Sebesky, a hack arranger with a talent
for blending received ideas into an eclectic goulash, was hired
to write and overdub strings and woodwinds arrangements on
the tracks Montgomery recorded with rhythm. The material
was occasionally good but more frequently not. *A Day in the
Life* became a pop hit and one of the best-selling jazz albums of
all time. With each A&M release, Montgomery became more
encumbered by pretentious arrangements. It is the highest possible tribute to the man's genius that he managed to inject so
much feeling, such unmistakable soul, into situations that
clearly displeased him. One has only to compare one of the
better tracks from this period, "Up and At It," an exercise in
restraint in which he builds his solo on a single, infectious riff,
with the 1960 "West Coast Blues," to see what was lost.

But Montgomery, in his early forties, the father of six, was
earning the kind of money he had long deserved, and in a period when jazz was supposed to be dead or dying, even the critical response was generous. Montgomery, however, was clear
about the distinction between his new recordings and those he
had originally been acclaimed for: "There is a jazz concept to
what I'm doing, but I'm playing popular music and it should
be regarded as such." In nightclubs, he continued to play crea-

tive music, with the inevitable inclusion of a couple of hits during the evening. His talent had not withered; if anything, it had grown. In 1968, the Kansas City Jazz Festival presented several famous musicians—the Adderleys, Clark Terry, Bobby Rosengarden—as guests on a program devoted to local players. For the most part, the Kansans had more to say than the visitors, and by the time Montgomery was scheduled to appear, several of us were about to leave, not wanting to hear a rehash of "California Dreaming" and "Goin' Out of My Head." But the temptation to hear him was irresistible, so we decided to wait. Surrounded by four rhythm players, his regular group, he immediately shot off a single chorus of "Goin'," and followed it with the most fiery, exquisite set of guitar music I've ever heard. What a feeling there was in that huge auditorium. Clearly, he had compromised only on disc and would eventually be recorded more seriously. Creed Taylor wasn't an idiot, after all, and Wes was only forty-three.

He died a month or so after that concert, of a heart attack. His last recordings, posthumously released as *Road Song*, were the most deplorable, bathetic Sebesky travesties to date—an album of baroque arrangements. (Sebesky later credited that idea to Taylor.) The Montgomery industry was just getting under way: Verve released an album of unissued Half Note tapes by the Kelly-Montgomery quartet with superimposed string arrangements. Montgomery's legacy played a large role in allowing Creed Taylor to establish CTI Records, and presumably left his wife and children secure. The cost, however, was the mastery that inspired his odyssey in the first place. There are precious few first-rate recordings to illustrate the work of "the greatest guitarist since Charlie Christian." (*While We're Young* on Milestone is the place to start.)

This was not a case of the artist whoring in order to support serious recording. As Orrin Keepnews has suggested, why couldn't A&M allow Montgomery to make a recording according to his own standards for every two or three he made for the company? Is the answer Creed Taylor, or the industry, or a failing of Montgomery's?

There are many similar tales to be told. Capitol's malevolent control of Nat Cole's career so successfully impugned his jazz reputation that few people are aware of his greatness as a modern pianist—one whom Dizzy Gillespie has called a favorite accompanist, and Oscar Peterson, a primary influence. The same year that Verve overdubbed strings on old Montgomery tapes, Capital issued an album of Nat Cole trio selections from the '40s with superimposed strings. His masterpiece of 1956, *After Midnight*, languished out of print for twenty years, and when the singer's wife wrote his biography, the "complete" discography was shorn of any recordings not made for Capitol (and a few that were).

Of the '70s sellouts, mention must be made of Charles Lloyd, a virtuoso saxophonist, who seems actually to have lost his talent. And what of Eddie Harris, who wrote "Freedom Jazz Dance" and who in 1968 was willing to drive to a small college in Iowa to jam with Ted Curson, whom he had never met? Will Herbie Hancock's *Headhunters* survive as well as *Empyrean Isles?* And could anyone have imagined in 1970 that Miles Davis would someday be satisfied with his playing on *Agharta?*

No one twisted Wes Montgomery's arm to make commercial records, and, indeed, I think he was absolutely right to cash in on his talent—better he than an imitator. What is unforgivable is that Creed Taylor did not respect Montgomery's artistry enough to ensure its preservation. By 1967, *any* Wes Montgomery record would have made money, just as the success of "Ramblin' Rose" could only have increased the sales of a more significant Nat Cole recording.

The rise of the corporate producer during the past decade has been a tragedy for creative music. From the time when Creed Taylor's ostentatious signature began appearing on albums, and Bob Thiele's photo became a feature of every

Impulse record, and Teo Macero released Miles Davis and Thelonious Monk albums with *his* name but not those of the supporting musicians, the myth has grown that the producer is the key to a good recording. This may apply to some areas of pop music, but in jazz, where individuality is everything, this kind of arrogance amounts to an extension of the "invisible man" syndrome.

In *Invisible Man,* Ralph Ellison gave us a black underground hero whose humanness was simply not seen. In the record industry, black music similarly takes on the quality of transparency. RCA's response to the masterpieces Ellington entrusted to the label in the mid-'60s has been to make them unavailable—not because they do not sell, but because they do not sell as well as Charley Pride. One of the best records Ellington recorded for Columbia in the '50s was a frankly commercial effort called *Bal Masque.* Producer Irving Townsend, not satisfied with the sparkling wit Ellington managed to inject into songs like "Who's Afraid of the Big Bad Wolf?", decided to intersperse applause between the tracks to simulate a *bal masque* atmosphere. This in itself was not unusual, but he also had the temerity to superimpose crowd noise—tinkling glasses and conversational hubbub—*on top of the music.* One has to wonder to what extent the music existed for him. Just as one has to wonder whàt producer Norman Granz really heard in Charlie Parker, since he insisted on saddling him with inappropriate sidemen, dull dance-band arrangements, and "oooooh"-ing voices. In the late '60s, Basie toured the world with a bruising big band, but Decca would pay for it only to record hack arrangements of Beatles songs, and as accompaniment to Jackie Wilson—resulting in the worst record either of them ever made. A few years before, Sarah Vaughan's record sessions for Mercury frequently consisted of her singing first takes of material she was introduced to in the studio, because her producer was anxious to discourage creative improvisation.

If there's anything to be learned from Montgomery's story, it is that musicians must accept their relationship with the record industry as a basically adversary one, an analogue to the relationship film directors have with studio moguls. Jazz musicians have long been exploited by the companies, though most of the great ones have learned to use them to their own advantage— Ellington's example in this area is without peer. Too many artists of rich ability, however, have been reduced to quaking whores reporting to cost-accountant pimps.

The solution to exploitation may lie somewhere between the one-shot, independent labels proliferating in the past few years and Stan Kenton's Creative World, the most successful and ingeniously marketed independent. Kenton's business acumen could serve as a model for ambitious, business-minded musicians. A label with a crew of the best new musicians of the '70s could not fail to achieve a measure of success and influence comparable to that of Blue Note and Prestige in the '50s.

The situation has never been worse than for the twenty-year-old New Music. The first generation of avant-gardists was exploited by ESP, Shandar, and BYG; and now a slightly younger generation has fallen into the hands of Columbia's former head philistine, Clive Davis. The much touted Freedom series consists largely of recordings made in Europe, some as long as ten years ago, which Arista now distributes here as a less expensive means of filling out the catalogue than actually going into the studio and recording new music. It is another one of those back-of-the-bus affairs because no acoustic jazz, other than Anthony Braxton, is allowed on the Arista label itself. But then Davis is the man who boasts in his autobiography of making Miles Davis a star under duress, and who fired from Columbia, in one afternoon, Charles Mingus, Bill Evans, and Keith Jarrett—before Jarrett's only Columbia album had even hit the stands. When Jarrett became a star attraction, Davis reportedly offered him an enormous sum to come to Arista. Jarrett refused. [In 1978, Davis did a partial about-face in forming a subsidiary called Novus, dedicated to avant-garde jazz. It's a valuable catalogue with superior distribution to that of the smaller companies, but its segregation from the parent label (one Novus artist referred to it as back-of-the-bus) and the exclusion of all other schools of jazz speak volumes about Davis's paternalistic attitude.] Davis is one of the more flamboyantly unthinking of the record moguls, but he's not unique, and he's not the worst. Jazz musicians suffer iniquities at most of the labels; it's a rare musician who feels that he or she hasn't been mistreated by the bigger companies. Disillusionment is widespread, and scars are deeply felt.

At a time when mafia-big business comparisons turn up as cocktail party bromides, it must be noted that it isn't always easy to distinguish between the actions of the bootleggers and those of the legitimate record companies. A writer can take a bad manuscript and throw it away without worrying that an editor will raid his garbage and publish it. But because until 1972 the copyright laws pretended that jazz did not exist, musicians are not protected from similar theft. Prominent labels frequently issue, without the permission of the artist, music formerly considered substandard that now competes in the stores with the artist's new material. Don't mention the union—the union knows nothing.

The onus of righting this kind of exploitation is in the musicians' hands, and they would do well to think hard about questions of artistic and financial control. I don't think the price of selling out is ever cheap. Should George Benson walk away from the lucrative circumstances under which his talent has been misused by several companies? No one but Benson has the right to answer that question. But perhaps further implications of the question can be gleaned in the story of the genius guitarist from Indianapolis. Because if Benson should get run over by a truck tomorrow, it would be difficult to justify, on the basis of available recordings, my conviction that he is potentially the greatest guitarist since Wes Montgomery.

June 1976

Bensonality

The night before the scheduled interview, George Benson's manager called me from Los Angeles to warn me about the subject of money: A sensitive area, he said; lay off, he implied. Benson turned out to be not all that sensitive—the manager was just worried about his image, he explained. And although I had no intention of bringing it up, with so many musical questions prepared, it soon became clear that the subject was not only unavoidable but something of a tonic chord.

Money, after all, is at the root of Benson's sudden stature in the record industry. His Warner Bros. album *Breezin'*, recorded in January 1976, is the first certified platinum record (over a million copies sold) ever by a musician identified with jazz, and the label's first "Number One with a Bullet" in two years (although other records, such as Fleetwood Mac, have outsold it). The bandwagon is rolling; a perfectly absurd indication was the upcoming CBS Rock Music Awards, in which Benson contended as Best New Male Vocalist, although he had been singing on record longer than anyone in the established-talent category. Benson has become so valuable to so many people that he has to worry less about how much money he makes than about how much he loses if he fails to stay *de rigueur*.

And that is why you needn't expect him to take advantage of his success to record the kind of music he readily admits to preferring, and which critics, for whom he has little use, have continually reminded him is his strong suit: 4/4 jazz. "You can't convince a record company to throw away a million dollars. On *Breezin'*, they're going to gross $6 million. Now, would you like to be the one to go and tell them. 'Well, this time George is going to make a record but we're not going to make as much money on it, 'cause this is going to be a jazz record dedicated to the state of the art'? That's asking them to make a $5-million donation to art music.

"Yes, I could do it, I have momentum now, but I've done that on records and they didn't sell. Man, there are guys out making better records than I could and they're not selling. I mean it isn't all about money, don't get me wrong, but if this is the one chance I have in my life to leave anything to my children, then I'm not going to throw their future out the window. I can always play jazz music—I'm not dead and I'm not going anywhere—and I hope one day I will. It's been my dream to do something that is really considered jazz. But my first interest is in making the listener happy, and if kids can't hear it, I don't care how good it is, you can't sell it to them."

Breezin' is not a disgraceful record, just insipid. As Benson characterizes it, "it's pretty much right down the middle of things. It wasn't dedicated to twelve-year-olds and it wasn't dedicated to the super hip." Benson's leisurely, well-played, but not especially vigorous solos lie supinely across the fashionable rhythms of the day, all clinging to a 2/4 feel. The strings—arranged by Claus Ogerman, whom Benson appreciates for knowing "how to stay out of the way"—serve the double function of giving the record modern appeal as far as airplay is concerned, and accenting the dreamy, lyrical mood beloved by those who like their romanticism massaging rather than gripping. One is reminded of the "Music for Lovers" records that Bobby Hackett made with Jackie Gleason in the '50s, though Hackett didn't get a piece of the action.

In some ways, however, *Breezin'* is Benson's most representative recording since the jazz/rhythm-and-blues sides he made for Columbia in the mid-'60s. For one thing, his septet was recorded "live" in the studio; only the thirty-one-piece string ensemble was overdubbed at a later date. His previous efforts for A&M and CTI were made by tracking, a process in which the soloist, rhythm section, and various sweetening backgrounds are recorded separately. "I can't play to a track," Benson says. "You hear a 500-piece orchestra in the earphones but you're looking out at a lonely studio with nobody there but you. Those records didn't have spontaneity; that's why they weren't successful."

There is a great deal of improvisation vying with *Breezin's* enervating combination of strings, simplistic material, and middle-of-the-road attitudinizing. It's not the kind of improvising that made early recordings like "Benson's Rider," "Willow Weep for Me," and "The Cooker" memorable, with their lean, hungry dissonances, offhanded energy, whistling articulation, and arpeggiated flourishes. But it does allow him to handsomely underscore the romantic qualities he considers basic to his personality.

If the sweeteners numb the immediacy and punch of Benson's playing, especially on "So This Is Love," where his long, modal phrases are particularly affecting, there is no denying the easy charm with which he imbues a basically unchallenging situation. "So This Is Love," "Breezin'," and "This Masquerade" were all knocked off in single takes. He hated the title selection the first time he heard it, "because there was no challenge to my mentality; it's like playing 'Mary Had a Little Lamb.'" After repeated listenings, however, he found something in the tune he felt he could work with. The track most responsible for the album's success is "This Masquerade," on which he sings with a lithe, sometimes keening, use of melisma, and scats in unison with his guitar lines. It was as a singer that he first earned a reputation.

As a child, he attracted some attention singing and playing uke in Pittsburgh, where he was born in 1943. His stepfather, a competent guitarist who never played professionally, idolized Charlie Christian, and Benson soon displayed a love for the guitar, and for Christian in particular. After he won a contest at a street dance in '53, a man approached his mother about becoming George's manager. They traveled to New York, where Benson was introduced to some people in the record business and cut a few sides for RCA's subsidiary Label X. As he was only eleven, there was to be no promoting, so he returned to school. At eighteen, he was leading a rhythm-and-blues band when he heard a record by Hank Garland. Garland was a country-and-western studio guitarist who made one excellent jazz record in 1961. "At that time most of the guitarists after Charlie Christian seemed very subdued, laid back, dark toned, as if those were things that went along with jazz guitar. Garland played with fire that was missing from the others." With his interest in jazz renewed, both by Garland and his discovery that year of Charlie Parker, "who made me think differently," he was ready to accept the job organist Jack McDuff offered him.

This time when he played New York, he stayed.

He was working in a club on 125th Street when comedian Timmie Rogers told him he knew someone who would go crazy when he heard Benson play. The someone was John Hammond, who, on Rogers's advice, cut short his vacation to catch the last night of Benson's gig. "I had heard that John Hammond hated rock 'n' roll and on this job the man hired me with the stipulation that if I played one jazz song, the gig was over. You see what I'm up against?" Hammond was impressed, but he couldn't convince Columbia to sign him as a guitarist. Benson was criticized at the time for his thin, trebly sound; it has since become influential, but then it was considered too rock and rollish. So Hammond convinced the company to sign him as a singer, even though he hadn't sung in years. And that's why he sang three or four short cuts on the albums he made for the label—to fulfill the contract.*

Two albums were released, but "the best album I made is in the can over there." A recurrent theme in Benson's evaluation of his career is that the best records, the most musical ones, invariably end up on the shelf. "I don't cut jazz records, 'cause they put them on the shelf and you can't make a living off records that don't come out. A & M has records on me in the can that are fantastic. I've got some tapes that I cut live in a club in Harlem for Creed Taylor that are phenomenal. But he gave them back to me, said the company doesn't want them."

Creed Taylor became his producer in 1968, when Wes Montgomery died and Benson was tapped as a "replacement." It was not a harmonious relationship. He had no control whatever over the finished product: Until *Breezin'* he was never invited to a mixing, and so his sound was frequently buried and distorted. He resented the tracking process, the vulgar whiteface cover art on his *White Rabbit* album, the arrangements by Don Sebesky, whom "you can't make a sideman," and the records that didn't come out. "I did a record for CTI with Cedar Walton. They never released it, because it was too musical, too good. Cedar wrote the tunes so you *know* it was excellent. You're never going to hear them. They'll probably put it out sometime all messed up because The Man didn't like it."

Benson has often felt hampered, if not downright paranoid, about establishment figures in the music business, from producers to critics, from disc jockeys (who used to advise him to stop singing) to the manager who convinced him to turn down an offer to join Miles Davis in the late '60s. "I wanted to join his group for the experience, to learn something, but my managers and producers said, 'Hey man, you're gonna be bigger than Miles Davis, don't do it.' Oh, sure, I regret it. It's like

---

* This, of course, is Benson's story. Hammond subsequently denied signing Benson as a singer.

getting an offer to go to Juilliard and having to turn it down." Benson reveres Davis most for his uncanny ability to make dramatic changes in his music at the most propitious times. Out of their friendship came one selection on the *Miles in the Sky* album. Other tracks stayed on the shelf.

"Miles," Benson says, "is still trying to make this simple music interesting, but he's smart and knows when to change, and he's still making the big money doing *what* he wants exactly *the way* he wants." Benson's respect for Davis's determination obscures the different kinds of commercial compromise each of them represents. Davis, and Herbie Hancock as well, moved their music into the commercial sphere without sacrificing command. Benson is a musician who has habitually laid his talent at the door of mandarin producers. Not only does he allow "environment" to shape his musical attitudes, but he is proud of his virtuosic ability to do so. "I don't think, 'Well, now I'll do this or that.' Like everyone else, I let life take me where it leads. Whatever's available to me in the studio is what I use. Once I find out what I have, I never play past them, because I will not play against another musician."

And again: "I'm like the tree in the wind. You can still be the tree but you have to be flexible. You still maintain your musicianship—that's something I'll never give up, all my records say I'm a musician—but if you keep fighting, something's gonna knock you down."

Perhaps the limberness of his branches can be attributed to the fact that he considers himself a guitarist and refuses any further categorization. He is unhappy with critics who have confused the styles of jazz and rock with phrases like "jazz-rock" and "crossover." For him jazz is pure and simple, 4/4 swing music, as exemplified by his favorite drummer, Jo Jones. When he plays in that context, it is as "a member of another organization," such as in the Public Broadcasting television John Hammond tribute, when he had the opportunity of playing with Jones and Benny Goodman, whose sextet recordings with Charlie Christian still represent a summit for Benson. He also participated in a Helen Humes album Hammond produced in 1975, but, 'You see what happens to those things? I loved it but how many did it sell? That was a great record and we could do a better one, but what did it mean? The few people you do make it for don't even buy the records; they get them for free."

The fact that jazz doesn't sell makes it impractical for him to play it, he argues. "Why shouldn't a man do what he's capable of?" he asks, referring to earning power rather than to artistic ability. We know how sternly Duke Ellington might have answered that question; Ellington advised that "a musical profit can put you way ahead of a financial loss." But Ellington—and Davis and Hancock—came from middle-class backgrounds as I did, and maybe you had to share George Benson's hungry days to appreciate his response to success. "Want to hear me play jazz?—pay me. Give me a million dollars and I'll make the greatest jazz record you ever heard, 'cause that's what I'd lose by playing it."

Which brings us back to the imperatives of money. The present popularization of jazz consists largely of taking soloists with distinctive, but flexible, sounds and pressing them, like rose petals, between the leaves of studio-contrived, pop-chart-tested formulae. Some of these nominal leaders are little more than hyperbolized studio hacks. Benson is a lot more than that. *Breezin'* is a good deal better and freer than the vast majority of records in its genre; as a leader, he has put together a rigorous sextet, combining musicians who would prefer to play jazz with those who are at home with rock. Almost symbolically, he uses both acoustic and electric-keyboard players, and assigns guitarist Phil Upchurch the wah-wah filler so that he won't have to do it.

Benson sees his own success as a beacon for younger jazz players, especially blacks whom producers have tried to squeeze into blues-related roles. "I'm using my artistry to show kids who have been told not to listen to jazz. You had musicians who came out of the jazz era recording for Motown records and selling a hundred million copies and creating the number-one sound in the country. But the kids don't know that, they don't know that it's not the Jackson Five playing the music behind them. Those were jazz people and we never got the credit. Now we're stepping forward and getting the credit."

He remembers his last conversation with Wes Montgomery. Wes was unhappy because he didn't like the music being issued under his name. "But then when we finished talking, he got into his new car, better dressed than I'd ever seen him. Only a couple of years before, I drove my stepfather 200 miles to see him, because he wasn't convinced that Montgomery was as good as Charlie Christian. There were three people in the joint; Wes had a raggedy old car, and was eating in those funky, jive restaurants that probably took his life."

As Benson walked me out of the spacious home that he and his wife and three sons have lived in for ten months—and which he soon expects to sell for something bigger—he reminisced, "When we first came to New York, I was promised a job and it didn't happen. My wife cried and I never will forget it. I told her, 'Don't worry, baby. We're gonna make it.' And you see, ten years later. . . ." He spread his hands and smiled.

August 1976

The Avant-Gardist Who Came In from the Cold

1. Allow the Love To Take Shape

On a windswept morning in January 1975, I went up to the Whitney Museum to watch the Cecil Taylor Unit rehearse a new work, "Ila Ila Tado," to be performed that evening. Although the Unit had frequently been augmented during the years, its basic components were Taylor's piano, Jimmy Lyons's alto sax, and Andrew Cyrille's drums. For close to an hour, Taylor and Lyons dueted while Cyrille leisurely set up his traps. Cecil's head was all but wrapped up: a beige knit hat was pulled over his ears; dark glasses connected it with an imposing handlebar mustache. His hands leaped and skittered across the keyboard; his small, wiry frame undulated with the music. Lyons was intent on the sheet music propped on his saxophone case and leaning against the piano. The interplay took on a call-and-response pattern. At one moment, Lyons faltered; Taylor repeated the passage, the altoist picked it up, and they were off again. For a slow movement, Cyrille provided a gong accompaniment, then moved to the drums to provide the music's third textural level. The three rose to a crescendo before winding down to a shimmering meditation: then quick silence. Taylor said, "Let's do the chant thing," and they retired to a corner to practice the chants that would begin the evening's performance. Weeks later, at his Canal Street loft, Cecil told me, "There's no talking at the rehearsals. I present the material and we start playing."

Cecil Taylor, at forty-three, has been an American cult figure for twenty years. He has an international coterie of followers who consider him a towering figure in contemporary music, a genius. In the United States, however, his existence has been precarious, not in terms of economics—although the economic factor makes it difficult for him to work with large-scale ensembles—but in finding artistic acceptance. Recently, a prominent figure in the rock world offered to present him in a major concert hall, but only if he would put together a funk group. Taylor regards cultural oppression as far more debilitating than economic or social oppression, and when one hears an Ellisonian echo in his talk, it is the hard-won response of a keen intelligence sensitive to an impossible situation: "By being in America, or by being in the West," he says, "you are invisible, you are not seen."

And yet, if Cecil Taylor's career has often seemed like a gamble against implacable odds, it is now evident that he has won. It has never been possible to write about him dispassionately, but suddenly one no longer needs recourse to noisy rhetoric: the accomplishment speaks for itself. Taylor is a prophet—not because he was ahead of his time (whatever that means), but because he was so attuned to his time, to the traditions behind him (European, African, and American) and the values before him, that his vision became the path the rest of us had to follow. Those encountering his music for the first time in 1975 found the experience a good deal less disconcerting than it was for those who discovered him a decade ago. The music of Cecil Taylor, as well as that of his contemporaries—Eric Dolphy, John Coltrane, Ornette Coleman, Albert Ayler—is unmistakably part of our world. So the tragedy is not that he is "unpopular," but that we fail to recognize him for what he is.

While meticulously brewing a pot of tea, Cecil Taylor gave a rapid and thorough review of *The Wiz*, which he had seen the previous night. After the show, he had gone dancing. "African musicians danced and played music but they also did other things important to their communities. We live our lives; it's important for me to get around, to go see *The Wiz* and go dancing rather than practice twelve hours a day. I'm feeling a lot of things I didn't know I could feel. One is really always practicing." Cecil has long been fascinated by dance, but his investigation into the nature of African culture began more recently. The decoration of his spacious, walk-up loft reflects both interests. The first time I met him—in 1968—he was reading Peter Gay's *Weimar Culture*. I don't know how he felt about that book, but in reacquainting myself with Cecil for this piece, I was reminded of Gay's portrait of a period in German culture when the Jew, the outsider, became the insider; when the oppressed became the tastemakers for the oppressors. Cecil is acutely aware of the impact that black culture has had on the very backbone of American life: I also remember proudly showing him my very hip jazz-record collection and being crestfallen when he asked me to play something by James Brown.

He was born in 1933 in Long Island City to a black middle-class family. "Rhythm is life the space of time danced thru," he has written, and his consuming interest in dance may stem from the time, at age five, when his mother encouraged him to study tap. "I loved it but it depends on how a child is led into things. When my mother died, I stopped practicing the piano because, in a certain area, she represented the idea of discipline. But there's another problem with dancing. When you play an instrument, the instrument becomes the body and you are involved with the instrument. When you dance, your body is the instrument and there is the possibility of the audience disturbing the kind of self-consciousness that allows you to do certain things. It took me a long time to get to the point where I could just do what I want to do on the dance floor."

His shyness, evidenced in that statement, has been misinterpreted by some as aloofness toward his audiences. It's true he doesn't hop out onstage with "Howdy, folks, the Unit would like to play a little thing we do hope you'll enjoy," but neither does John Cage. Yet who consistently gives more of himself on stage than Cecil Taylor? His tenacious refusal to compromise his talent is not a reproach to the audience, but a sign of respect. "The absolute choices an artist must have are not to be bargained with. You prepare and you present. The audience, whether it knows it or not, also prepares."

A graduate of the New England Conservatory of Music (where he had to put up with teachers—he calls them "clerks"— who belittled his interest in traditions other than the European), he was dismissed by some critics, early on, for trying to marry the ideas of the European avant-garde with jazz. Actually, the synthesis he was working toward was even more complex: "The more I play, the more I become aware of the non-European aspects of the music." The striking originality of his conception is rooted in his acknowledgment of the various traditions to which he has been exposed. He doesn't refute the word "jazz," but he wonders at its implications. Since he puts little stock in the notion of American classicism, he traces many of his "methodological procedures" to Africa. When the slaves were brought to America, their cultural history was wiped out and replaced by "another school resulting in a nonhistorical continuum. Therefore, one doesn't recognize the continuance of methodological procedures" from Africa in the jazz tradition. Instead, "we have a tendency to talk about Europe because you have a whole body of literature giving philosophical moment to a conception of ordered music which is retained through symbols."

Although Taylor believes the "continuum of black feeling

and thought in America" has been at least partly sustained by a system of racial oppression that has kept blacks isolated, he sees the cultural oppression as "so great that no one ever thinks of black people as having a culture. And most black people don't think of themselves as having a culture." When the leader of a string quartet congratulated him on a performance, mentioning Mozart and Ravel's "Sonatine" in the course of an effusive compliment, Cecil's response was "Why don't you talk about Ellington and Bud Powell?"

Taylor's conversation tends to be discursive. He doesn't lose sight of what he wishes to say, but he has so much to say that he can look at a subject from several points of view, all commingling. This characteristic is reflected in his poetry, which at first seems highly elliptical but on closer inspection reveals, in its carefully threaded images, a fragmented vision like the reflections in a shattered mirror. At times, his music also seems to be sustained by an occasional "Ah! and here's something else!"

"Musical categories don't mean anything unless we talk about the actual specific acts that people go through to make music, how one speaks, dances, dresses, moves, thinks, makes love . . . all these things. We begin with the sound and then say, what is the function of that sound, what is determining the procedures of that sound. Then we can talk about how it motivates or re-generates itself, and that's where we have tradition." Taylor speaks of the relative traditions of Leontyne Price and André Watts, representing a continuance of the Euro-American con-ception, as opposed to Billie Holiday and McCoy Tyner, "trained musicians of another kind." The indifference of black Americans, no less than white, to that other kind of tradition has multiple manifestations. He recalls Ellington wanting to perform his sacred mass at the church he attended as a child and being told, "We don't have that kind of music," and the opposition toward Aretha Franklin singing at Mahalia Jack-son's funeral. He invokes Jesse Jackson saying, " 'Black people blahblahblah,' and who does he have to play at his exposition? Cannonball and Roberta Flack" (whom Taylor considers compromised artists). He compares the treatment of the Ellington and Armstrong funerals in the *Amsterdam News,* New York's black paper, with the coverage in Paris and certain English papers. He concludes, "Black people do not have a pantheon for Ellington; there is no area in which black artists can operate with the support of black money."

At the same time, he notes the irony of this tradition's achievement of success through imitation. He once told the critic John Litweiler, "One difference between [Gladys Knight] and an imitative artist such as Janis Joplin is that imitation is self-destructive." Yet he is now less dogmatic about certain aspects of commercial success. As a very young man, he stopped listening to Ellington: "I couldn't tolerate any necessities that were not absolutely musical, and Ellington decided he was going to make his band economically solvent. I didn't accept that. I was saying Artist! Artist! Artist! right?—but at the same time, I was being supported by my father." When his father died, he decided to take a job washing dishes to maintain what he shrugs off as a "certain kind of thing."

Like Miles Davis, Cecil Taylor is willing to talk freely about other musicians and becomes especially animated discussing those he loves, like Ellington and Erroll Garner. Early in his career, he recorded Billy Strayhorn's "Johnny Come Lately" and a number of standards. I asked him if he would ever again play music he hadn't composed. "No, that's why I like to buy a lot of other people's records. I thought about doing an Ellington thing I heard recently on one of those fantastic records: Gonsalves does this solo called 'Happy-something' ["Happy Reunion"] and then Ellington plays this solo which was probably written by Strayhorn ["Lotus Blossom"] and it is just beautiful. But I've learned something about the process of art—and this is why Donald Byrd is so full of shit, and the others who take Stevie Wonder's songs and readapt them. You know, if you love someone, you learn things about that person, but you don't become them. For instance, I've always loved Erroll Garner and I used to write these very elaborate piano pieces in which I would attempt my interpretation of Garner, say in 1950. I discovered it didn't sound so much like Erroll Garner as it sounded like me, whatever that was at the time.

"Garner is always staggering when you listen to those introductions because to me, *they* are the compositions. The other things are charming. Similarly, if Sonny Rollins would just investigate those cadenzas, it could be a very interesting area. Let the other musicians who joined him deal with the construction of those cadenzas; he wouldn't have had to think about anything else. I remember hearing Garner on a bill with Charlie Parker, when I was seventeen or eighteen, on Fifty-second Street. Bird went out for the intermission and was talking to someone on the curb. Garner started playing and I watched Bird; he listened, stopped talking, and just ran back to the stand, picked up his horn, and started playing."

Taylor's affection for Garner may seem surprising, but a comparison of the two is illuminating. Each approaches the piano as a percussion instrument. Garner's steady left hand will play a counterrhythm to the series of octaves his right hand dances out, paralleling the drumlike manner with which Taylor often orders his music. Garner and Taylor are among the few modern pianists who make a major stylistic point of dynamics ranging from fortissimo to pianissimo. When Garner segues from a stentorian introduction to an almost inaudible melodic statement to a vibrant set of variations, there is a thrill in his unpredictability and constant thoughtfulness. Similarly, much of the delight in Taylor's effulgent leaps across the keyboard, his tumbling bass salvos and wind-hammer pointillistic jabs at the higher register, stems from their contrast with the near-muffled lyricism he will then gently coax from the piano. Finally, they share an inexhaustible fund of energy.

"I had a marvelous time talking to Erroll Garner last summer when we were on the same plane to France. He was *very* interesting. The kind of conversation I had with him could never have happened with Miles Davis, whom I also admire. It's interesting, because in his own way, Erroll Garner is as successful as Miles Davis and he will probably live a lot longer."* Again, Taylor revealed a hint of self-effacement: "The way his demeanor was with people on the plane and to me—I really didn't think he remembered me or knew me—it was just a completely different kind of thing."

Perhaps Cecil Taylor's music is most readily distinguished by its freedom from predetermined harmonies and rhythms. But freedom is illusory and must ultimately be defined by the personalities involved. When Cecil refers to the tradition of his music, he is speaking really of several interlocking traditions, those of the piano and alto, of the piano and drums, of the piano *as* drums, of the drums and alto, of the trio format. Thus the success of a Unit performance is linked to the long-term commitment of the participants: Lyons has been with him regularly since 1961; Cyrille, who first played with him in 1958, has been a regular since '63. Similarities with Ellington in this area are obvious.

I asked him how much of a Unit performance was notated. "Ahhhh, what do they say about things like that?—'I thought you'd never ask.' And at the same time I dread your asking me, because it means going into the whole concept of notation. I might begin by saying that the eyes are really not to be used to translate symbols that are at best an approximation of sounds. It's a division of energy and another example of Western craziness. When you ask a man to read something, you ask him to

* He didn't; Garner died January 2, 1977. Yet it's interesting to note that Davis retired from music several months before Garner's death, and by mid-1980 was still unheard from.

take part of the energy of making music and put it somewhere else. Notation can be used as a point of reference, but the notation does not indicate music, it indicates a direction."

Taylor defines improvisation as "the ability to talk coherently to yourself through the symbols," an achievement learned simply by practicing. "That's really frightening to people who write compositions, because this means that you're prepared to make instant compositions." In a sense, improvisation—"one of the primary building blocks of this music"—represents to Taylor the primacy of feeling over logic: he considers invalid the tendency to subordinate emotion to the mind in art.

Music, then, is feeling. "One of the things that turned me off European music is that I'd get the scores by Boulez, Stockhausen, Pousseur, and Ligeti, and I would look at them and say, 'My, this is interesting.' And I'd listen to the music and it didn't sound particularly good. I don't listen to artists who only want to create something that is interesting. To feel is perhaps the most terrifying thing in this society. This is one of the reasons I'm not too interested in electronic music: it divorces itself from human energy, it substitutes another kind of force as the determinant agent for its continuance. And I'm saying that heat and the energy from people is related to the sun which is related to the reason why plants grow."

Out of the traditions of the instruments and of improvisation itself grows a "feeding process," which is a "determinant agent" for his music—traceable, Taylor insists, to Africa. For, clearly, Western ideas about notation do not explain the phenomenon of the Ellington band. "How did that band exist?" Taylor asks. "Because we know that what was written on certain scores could not possibly have resulted in the sounds that were made."

Therefore, he concludes, "there's something else. The determinant agent of this music has to do with ancestor worship, it has to do with a lot of areas that are magical rather than logical. A group exists in this music in terms of a feeding process. It has nothing to do with energy except that one tries to keep one's body in shape. It has to do with a language of sounds that are exchangeable depending upon one's knowledge of the tradition."

The feeding process is illustrated every time Taylor, Lyons, and Cyrille play. Cyrille's versatility and quicksilver reflexes are unceasingly engaged in a stormy drama with the pianist. Lyons, who prefers a fat, middle-register sound to extensive overblowing effects, has an even more difficult role, negotiating a path between the two and transferring Taylor's melodies to the saxophone. He follows Taylor's lead, working closely with him rather than resorting to private contortions. His persuasive timbre suggests that it alone can provide the proper texture; that a tenor would be too dry, a soprano too sharp.

The magical qualities in the relationship between these three men are, according to Taylor, "unique to this music and can be traced back to when Africans cut down a tree to build a drum and did a dance around the tree to bless themselves for taking a life and at the same time to consecrate it because of the change in function that the skin of the tree would have." Tracing the feeding process not nearly so far back, I remembered a story about the early Basie band. Harry Edison complained to Count Basie that without sheet music he didn't know what he was playing. "When the band ends," he said, "I don't know what note to hit." Basie told him, "If you hit a note tonight and it sounds right, just play the same note tomorrow!" The tradition Cecil Taylor has inherited is one of unending discovery.

The jazzman may be the last American hero. He has to fight for his sound, his vision, his tradition. His victories are mostly private and frequently pyrrhic: most of the great innovators never reached fifty. Cecil Taylor is the most vital of contemporary musicians. His music satiates, transmuting the sanguine into the ecstatic, the fearful into the devastating. If his art has an unavoidable political edge, it is because, like all great art, it sears the pretenses of comfort with intimations of mortality. "The great artists," he says, "rather than just getting involved with discipline, get to understand love and allow the love to take shape."

2. Search for a Common Language

Carnegie Hall has been the stage for several pacesetting jazz concerts since Benny Goodman's extravaganza of 1938, but few held greater promise than one in 1977 entitled "Mary Lou Williams and Cecil Taylor Embraced." It was doubly innovative for bringing together two outstanding keyboard artists in a program of duets, and for dramatizing the search for a common language in jazz piano.

During the years of bebop, when traditionalists and modernists were pointlessly entrenched in a bloody skirmish, the ever sensible Williams remarked, "I see no reason why there should be a battle in music. All of us aim to make our listeners happy." Her own magnanimity was well established. Following a remarkable swing-era career, during which she virtually created the sound of the Andy Kirk orchestra, Williams came to New York and played an active role in the obstetrics of bop, modifying her own already advanced style. The '40s proved to be as productive for her as the '30s had been: she organized a superb but inadequately recorded all-women quintet, she wrote arrangements for Duke Ellington, and her "Zodiac Suite" became the first work by a jazz musician to be performed by the New York Philharmonic.

Williams retired from music for a few years, making her return at the 1957 Newport Jazz Festival as guest conductor-pianist with the Dizzy Gillespie orchestra. On the same program there was an introverted, resolute pianist of twenty-four named Cecil Taylor, whose music, serious demeanor, and refined New England accent made the recent swing–bop controversy pale into history. Taylor's achievement in bringing conservatory techniques to bear on jazz improvisation was suffered, even respected, but not much subscribed to. His melodies and harmonies were asymmetrical; his rhythms did not snap into an even 4/4. Moreover, in 1957, there was little evidence to support the conceit that his way was the way of the future. (John Coltrane was playing "Bye Bye Blackbird" with Miles Davis; Charles Mingus had a small coterie; Ornette Coleman and Eric Dolphy were still unknown.)

Mary Lou Williams was not enchanted by Taylor's music on first hearing, but she has come to know it increasingly well in recent years. Taylor is a frequent visitor at the Cookery when she plays there; in 1975 they performed opposite each other at the Whitney Museum's Composers's Showcase. At a press conference for the Carnegie concert she said Taylor represents the best in the avant-garde because he knows the tradition—thus, the mainstream declared solidarity with the avant-garde. But the concert did not actually conclude with the triumphant physical embrace one might have expected. After the last selection, Taylor disappeared, while Williams returned for three encores. The audience (considerable in size) cheered resolutely, but Taylor was gone, and there was not a little disappointment and confusion. Significant events beg to be summarized with sentimental symbols; a juicy hug and a fastidious encore would have done the trick. Instead, we were left wondering what went sour.

Rumors of discontent had circulated during rehearsals: he was overpowering her; she wanted a rhythm section, he didn't. Bass and drums were present for part of each set, and though it might be unfair to call Bob Cranshaw and Mickey Roker Mary Lou's henchmen, it seemed as though she had enlisted their support to contain the predatory avant-gardist. The rhythm section provided a change in color, inspired Williams, and gave an unexpected shape to Taylor's own percussive patterns. But it also underscored their fundamental disagreement.

Harmonically, Williams can play as outré as Taylor; melodically, they get along fine. It is in the area of rhythm that healthy tensions turn to real friction. To Williams, an architect of the Kansas City beat, swing has the distinct demarcations of bar lines. For Taylor, the relentless ching-a-ching is intrusive and obstructive. Roker made only a cursory attempt at accompanying Taylor. (I wondered how Andrew Cyrille, who has played with both, would have handled the problem.)

I found the encounter more successful than not. The structure of the program was intriguing; there were several flashes of mutual recognition and genuine empathy. Each was in good form individually, and during those peak episodes when they connected, they managed to complement each other's best qualities. Williams's spare, bluesy ministrations were a vivid landscape for Taylor's aharmonic loop-the-loops.

The first set was continuous. It began with a rocking, spiritual-like piece started by Williams and amplified by Taylor, followed by a quite charming rag. Taylor soon shot off into the upper register with a characteristic flurry, while Williams coolhandedly searched for propitious moments to jump in. The predetermined format tended to fragment his solos, with the not unattractive effect of making them highlight passages: He was never given more than a few minutes to flex his muscles before getting strong-armed into the next movement. Some transitional block building ensued, leading to an apparently serendipitous Taylor train rhythm, with colorful comments from the second piano. Roker and Cranshaw entered, precipitating an assertive boogie-break and solo by Williams, whose strength of touch was much in evidence. Free interplay preceded a lyrical wind-down.

The second set opened with a curiously delicate ballad, probably by Taylor, romantic in character. The second and last piece of the set was the most successful—an angular, Monkish theme stated by Taylor over a strong rhythmic pattern by Williams. Here the intensity was buoyant—he proferring fevered riffs, she giving pointillistic encouragement. For a while, the common language was essentially percussive. But then Taylor bounded into his own world, entranced and intractable, and Williams was back on the outside looking in. Retaliation came quickly as Roker and Cranshaw rejoined them, initiating a straight four. This was the chance for the lady to strut her stuff, and she did so jubiliantly, with Taylor laying out. Her cohorts were rewarded with solos, after which all three turned silently to Taylor, the stranger in a strange land, who responded lustily for (a mere) ten minutes. All four united for a finish that Taylor seemed to regard as premature. They bowed and walked off, but only Williams, Cranshaw, and Roker returned to play "A Night in Tunisia," "I Can't Get Started" (a highlight, for which she was unaccompanied), and a blues. "Where's Cecil?" someone yelled from the balcony.

Taylor's disappearance fed speculation about a rift between these two volatile personalities. Indeed, one had noticed with some discomfort the contrast between Williams's wary attentiveness and Taylor's self-involvement, and perhaps that conflict was why the evening wasn't as transcendent as had been hoped.* Still, something valuable was achieved—a freewheeling, occasionally inspiring if too infrequently electric meeting of minds. A stronger case was made for the flexibility of Mary Lou Williams than for that of Cecil Taylor, but they did find levels at which they could communicate effectively without patronizing each other. *Note:* The concert was recorded by Pablo Live and issued as *Mary Lou Williams & Cecil Taylor Embraced.*

3. An Entangling Alliance

Given the continuing hold of elitism on the arts in this bastion of democracy, some creative collaborations are bound to gleam as much with metaphoric resonance as with the promise of sat-

---

* Months later, Taylor explained that he left according to plan, so that Williams could play a few pieces alone.

isfactory work. I was delighted to learn that Cecil Taylor and Mikhail Baryshnikov planned to fashion a dance together, for in a decade swamped with meretricious fusions here was a mating born of aesthetic curiosity, one that promised a genuine challenge to the assumptions of two presumably rockbound traditions. A not unpleasant fragrance of borrowed prestige added the tinge of irony, as the latest in a line of conquering Russians brought before America's cultural commissars the most innovative American pianist of the past quarter-century. What would they make of their native son?

It wasn't only my sense of mischief that was roused, nor even my sense of justice—although news of the collaboration immediately brought to mind an evening eleven years ago when members of a college music department insisted that Taylor was a charlatan, that he could not really play his instrument. I anticipated the breaking of new ground. No jazz musician save Ellington has been as intimately involved with dance as Taylor, and not even Ellington had so scrupulously studied the Bolshoi tradition. Taylor's obsession with dance and Baryshnikov's vaunted adventurousness suggested a favorable chemistry. Yet while the collaboration had already proved fruitful to the participants, other chemistries were in the air when I went to Philadelphia on August 9, 1979, to cover the third performance of the piece. The twelve-minute pas de deux entangled the American dance establishment, the Russian star, and the jazz interloper, and if the bottom line was mutual respect, a barely sublimated stratum of paranoia and egotism had to be cut through. Even the genesis of the piece was murky with contradiction.

So far as Jim Silverman, Taylor's manager, knew, the process began when Baryshnikov asked Richard Tanner, a dancer with the New York City Ballet, to choreograph a pas de deux for himself and Heather Watts; Tanner's roommate, Shelley Freydont, a dancer with the Louis Falco Company, told her boyfriend, saxophonist Alan Braufman, who told Silverman, who called Tanner with the suggestion that Taylor write the music. According to Tanner, it was *his* idea to use Taylor, and Freydont encouraged him to arrange a meeting. Tanner says that Baryshnikov had heard of Taylor and approved the idea. According to Silverman, Taylor was flattered and excited by the prospect of such a collaboration, and at his first meeting with Tanner both men worked at impressing each other—Taylor by invoking great dancers he'd seen before Tanner was born, and Tanner by attempting to execute a few Taylorisms on his Steinway.

There were immediate problems concerning money and rehearsal time. Originally, the piece was commissioned for the International Dance Festival in Chicago, and paid for by Geraldine Freund. Both Baryshnikov and Peter Martins, the principal dancer with the New York City Ballet, liked it and wanted to retain it for a show they were organizing called Baryshnikov & Friends, which would play the Hollywood Bowl and Philadelphia's Robin Hood Dell West. Since the company's budget had been worked out a year earlier, Martins agreed to finance Taylor's participation out of his own pocket. Prior commitments made rehearsal time scarce: Taylor and Tanner first met on June 1; they rehearsed June 2–7, 19–21, and 23–27, and debuted in Chicago on June 28. The audience was cold and indifferent, but afterward, Baryshnikov made a point of telling Silverman, "Now listen, I want to do this thing some more." He then left for China with Bob Hope, and there were no more rehearsals until just before the August 3 performance at the Hollywood Bowl, to an equally cold audience of 18,000.

By the day of the Philadelphia engagement, there was discontent on all sides. Baryshnikov had hurt his foot in Los Angeles and expressed dissatisfaction with his performance; Taylor felt that he had not been treated with due respect in the promotion; and Martins resented having to pay for Silverman's transportation and hotel bills. Tanner felt the tension mounting and became distraught when he learned that Taylor would not arrive in Philadelphia in time for an afternoon rehearsal. When Taylor arrived for a 6 p.m. run-through, Tanner met him at the train station. "Are we still speaking?" he asked. They kissed and hugged, and Taylor told him, "That shit has nothing to do with us."

As the rehearsal started, Baryshnikov and Heather Watts were on stage in sweat-pants, much as they would be dressed for the actual performance. There were two pianos on the stage, one prepared for the three-and-a-half-minute opening section in which Taylor plays on the strings (Tanner's idea) and a nine-foot Steinway for the rest. Taylor, dressed in a white hat, shades, sports clothes, and sandals, manipulated the strings with mallets, a hotel key, and other implements, as the dancers went halfheartedly through the movements. At one point, Baryshnikov danced Watts offstage and Tanner had to resituate the movements. When they finished, the audience of ushers in yellow shirts applauded, and Tanner said, "Well, the crew likes it."

I asked Baryshnikov how he liked it: "It's very different, obviously. You're more dancing in the music than for the music. I don't think it's ever been done before. It isn't 1-2-3-1-2-3 or 1-2-3-4. It gives you another dimension about dancing to music, because you're improvising the time. Not the choreography, because the steps are there, but the time. Of course, I'd heard a prepared piano before, but never anything like that. When we started to work together, I listened to his records—very challenging and inventive. It's three people working very closely together. We start and stop together but in between there are sections, and we look to each other. Cecil knows a lot about dance."

The particular challenge of the piece is this: Taylor has composed a specific musical work, but he is relatively free to retard or accelerate tempos and dynamics. Taylor explained the first stage of the collaboration with Tanner: "Dick said, 'Write some music and I'll choreograph.' I said, 'Well, that's one way of doing it. Another is for you to make a movement and I'll find the right sounds.'" This intrigued Tanner, who found himself having to meet three objectives: movements suitable to the two dancers; a dance suitable to the kind of music Taylor plays; and a performance that wouldn't be structured or counted. "We'd kind of do things with counts," Tanner said, "but leave it loose. We'd sort of fit what they were doing into his music. Misha and Heather were fascinated by that because completely different things happened. They felt they were improvising—it was the same steps, but nothing rote about it. The movements came first, in pieces, and Cecil would watch and try stuff. But then we very quickly rearranged the pas de deux around the music—it was the same steps and movements but a different feeling, and it changed a great deal. Cecil takes the tempo where he wants it to go. If he plays violently, they dance violently; if he lays back, they lay back. When to start the next step is up to them. Also, he has a good eye and knows dance. I started out thinking he was fascinating, and wound up thinking he was just brilliant. It was riveting to see the way he discarded certain ideas and retained others."

After the rehearsal, Taylor returned to the hotel in a limousine provided by the dance company. He was impressed by such amenities, which aren't usually forthcoming in the jazz world, and seemed nervous. The performance was two hours away, and as part of his ascetic preparation for a performance, he hadn't had a cigarette all day. He was tight: "It's very interesting, that's all. I'm learning a lot. There are certain problems and I'm dealing with them and learning." There was discussion of the rehearsals and the stiffness of the dancers—"I mean how much rehearsal do they need? And they're still marking it!" There was uncertainty about the order of the program. Silverman said, "They keep changing it. When we got to L.A., they changed the order about five times between the afternoon we got there and the next day." A friend of Taylor's asked him if there was a picture of him in the program. "It couldn't hold it," Taylor said, yawning, making light of something that distressed him a great deal.

Here was a collaboration between colossi of different cultural spheres, and Taylor felt he was being treated as an accompanist. He realized that Baryshnikov was the drawing card, but what did that have to do with fair billing for a work of art? There was no Taylor biography in the program, nor was his name announced at the performance; the piece was listed incorrectly as *Eatin' Rain in Space*. The full title is actually *Tetra-Stomp: Eatin' Rain in Space*. "I have nothing against having my name in lights," he said. Tanner sympathizes: "He had every right to be upset."

Taylor had dinner in his hotel room. At about 8:40, the driver of the limo came into the lobby and called him: "Mr. Taylor, this is the chauffeur, Harold, I thought you were supposed to be down here at 8:30." "You thought, huh?" Taylor said. For some reason, Harold was amused by Taylor's arrogance. On the way to the amphitheater, Taylor was more relaxed. He expounded on the waning reputation of the Bolshoi, noting that there were supposed to be a couple of young Russian dancers who would very likely supplant Baryshnikov as quickly as he had supplanted Nureyev. He spoke of Baryshnikov's forthcoming position as the artistic director of the American Ballet Theatre, his agreement to play the life of Jimmy Cagney, and the rumors that he would make a total career switch from dance to acting. America was still looking abroad for cultural benediction, he surmised in reference to the worshipful attitude toward Russian dancers. He admitted letting his paranoia get out of control when Baryshnikov missed their first rehearsal and, pointing out that choreographer-dancer Diane McIntyre and three of her colleagues would attend the concert, added, "There are four black women in the audience who danced with me at the Studio Museum in Harlem on December 31, not for twelve minutes but for two hours. What Baryshnikov and the others trained like him do, they do *well*, but they should know that if Diane McIntyre came up she'd kick their ass for thirty-five or forty minutes and she would be *in-ven-tive* in *her* language." Still, he admired Baryshnikov and particularly Watts ("She's been very open from the beginning"): "I enjoy it, I learn, and, in the end, I feel good after."

The dire responses of the audiences in Chicago and Los Angeles did not have an apparent effect on the principals. Baryshnikov had told me earlier, "What do you expect? If 300 out of 2000 like it, it's okay with me," and Tanner would later confess, "I always assume that people won't like it." But there were riled tempers all the same. As Taylor arrived at his dressing room, Peter Martins pulled Silverman aside: "Who the hell do you think you are? I'm paying you for professionalism. It's 9:10, you were supposed to be here at 8:50." Silverman argued that Cecil was ready now, didn't have to put any makeup on. As it turned out, the pas de deux, scheduled for 9:30, went on fifteen minutes late anyway.

From the first strokes Taylor applied to the strings of the prepared piano, there was an excitement in the audience. People who had already heard Tchaikovsky, Scarlatti, and Ricardo Drigo, and would subsequently hear Gershwin, Stravinsky, and Chopin, moved forward in their seats. Taylor pulled glissandos from the strings, scratched them with a key and coat hanger, and malleted them for rhythmic patterns, while the dancers addressed each other with jerky, marionette-like movements. When Taylor switched to the Steinway, the music floated breezily, then strengthened in density, bubbled with characteristic parries and angular pauses. Like all of Taylor's music, it was rich and dramatic. The dance movements were busy and eclectic, combining stiff-legged leaps, coquettish passes, and romantic glides. About two-thirds through, there were brief solo sections for Baryshnikov and Watts, and then a finish that I found wonderfully intense. Having seen a rehearsal, I knew that the objective was now for the dancers to wind down in tandem with Taylor, that the movements and the music had to converge within a loose and hazardous framework. It was mesmerizing to watch Taylor and the dancers exchange looks and conclude as one—a dampened piano chord sounding as Baryshnikov fell backward over Watts's chest. But I wondered if that tension existed for someone watching the work for the first time, and if the nature of the piece didn't demand a second and even third viewing for one to appreciate its improvisational challenge.

The audience erupted with the largest ovation of the evening. Baryshnikov and Watts raised their right arms in deference to Taylor, who alone acknowledged the applause without smiling; as it continued, he broke into a grin as well. Backstage, Taylor, bathed in sweat, was high and expansive. He stalked the room, nodding his head, eager to talk. He greedily lit his first cigarette of the day, his hands shaking, and proceeded to chain smoke one after another. "In a way it was the best performance so far. Much tighter." "And they danced better," someone volunteered. "Un-hunh, and it was fun," he said. "A craft is a craft." He talked about the different disciplines involved: "Jazz isn't supposed to have methodological constructs, but dance is set movements, and moving is a kind of religion. So finally, everyone gets pissed off because they want to control the movements." Someone raised the problem of credits, and he sloughed it off. "This is a worthwhile project, you push the other stuff aside." Well-wishers noted how much he was working now, and he said, "No one ever works too much. You work enough to know that that's what your life's about." About the audience's enthusiasm, he noted, "It was nice. But this is the East Coast, they should know what's going on." Of Baryshnikov, he added, "He's a demon, very clever, political, polite—it's 'Hello Cecil' when we start, and 'Thank you, Cecil' after. I think Baryshnikov is really exciting when he's dealing with things he didn't hear in Russia." The sounds of Gershwin filtered through the ceiling, and Taylor grimaced at the simpy arrangements.

Upstairs, Watts and Bart Cook were finishing a pas de deux while Baryshnikov exercised in the wings; then he and Martins ended the program with a series of exchanges to Chopin. Taylor came upstairs for the final curtain calls, and shouts from the audience proved that a number of people were well aware of who he was, despite the absence of a program note. As he hurried out into the waiting limousine with Baryshnikov, there were almost as many cries of "Cecil, Cecil" as of "Misha, Misha!" Champagne bottles chilled in Taylor's suite, where he was joined by a small coterie of friends and former students. He lounged in a chair, smoking continuously, a television silently flickering in the background. He was in good spirits, listening intently to his visitors' comments; reminiscing a little. Diane McIntyre, a charming, soft-spoken, witty woman, arrived, and after a few pointed questions about the work's procedures, delivered a spontaneous criticism so lucid that I was too spellbound to write any of it down. She hoped there would be subsequent performances to get it right; no one was sure there would be.

The present contract is fulfilled, with only tentative plans to do the ballet in Fort Worth and Memphis in fall 1980. Tanner doubts if the New York City Ballet has the interest or funds to present it in New York, though Joseph Papp expressed some interest in producing it one night when *A Chorus Line* is dark. It's pretty much up to Baryshnikov and Martins. However many times it may yet be performed, and however successful it might become, the impact is less likely to be felt in dance than in the specific careers of those involved. Tanner says, "It may be totally new for classical ballet, but I'm assuming that Merce Cunningham and John Cage worked that way." I don't know if they did or not, nor am I qualified to evaluate *Tetra-Stomp: Eatin' Rain in Space* as a ballet, but it seems unlikely that experiments of this sort will ever attain a significant place in classical ballet, if only for commercial reasons. The immediate returns are sizable all the same, and they are not all metaphoric. The experience has affirmed Taylor's sense of his music's adaptability, and of the challenge of brevity; he speaks of devising shorter pieces, and is participating in increasingly diverse situations, including a collaboration with Max Roach. Baryshnikov speaks of learning a new dimension in "dancing to music" from this collaboration, and it's safe to assume that any improvisational powers he's gained will be invaluable in re-creating so street-wise a dancer as Jimmy Cagney. Martins has expressed some interest in dancing the role when Baryshnikov joins the ABT. But perhaps the real importance of the collaboration lies not in what it bodes for the future, but in the fact that it came off at all. A fusion that might have seemed preposterous a decade ago was handled as naturally as, ah, eatin' rain in space.

1975–79

Discography

This is neither a comprehensive discography nor a consumer guide, but merely a list of the better recordings discussed in the text. A relatively lesser artist might therefore be represented by more albums than a major one—though an occasional album has been added to bring a performer's work up to date, or to fill in a gap. When an album has been included for a particular selection (usually one that I mentioned in passing), that selection is identified. I've tried to stick to records that are in print, but have not always been successful in doing so.

ETHEL WATERS: *Oh Daddy!* (Biograph BLP 12022)
 Greatest Years (Columbia KG 31571)
 On Stage and Screen (Columbia CCL 2792)
BESSIE SMITH: *Any Woman's Blues* (Columbia G 30126) ("Kitchen Man")
BILLIE HOLIDAY: *The Golden Years* (Columbia C3L 21) ("My Mother's Son-in-Law")
BING CROSBY: *Rare Early Recordings* (Biograph BLP-C13)
 A Legendary Performer (RCA CPL1-2086e)
 Bing and Al, Volume One (Totem 1003)
 The Best of Bing Crosby (MCA2-4045)
THE DOMINOES: *14 Hits* (King 5006X)
 Featuring Jackie Wilson (King 5007X)
ELVIS PRESLEY: *Golden Records* (RCA LSP-1707e)
OTIS BLACKWELL: *These Are My Songs* (Inner City 1032)

BOBBY BLAND: *Here's the Man* (Duke DLP 75)
  Spotlighting the Man (Duke DLP 89)
  B. B. King & Bobby Bland (ABC DSY-50190/2)
SARAH VAUGHAN: *How Long Has this Been Going On?* (Pablo
  2310-821)
  Live in Japan (Mainstream 2401)
EDDIE JEFFERSON: *The Main Man* (Inner City 1033)
BETTY CARTER: *What a Little Moonlight Can Do* (ABC Impulse ASD-
  9321)
  The Audience (Bet-Car MK1003)
FRANK SINATRA: *The Essential Frank Sinatra* (Columbia S3L 42)
  Songs for Swinging Lovers (Capitol SM-653) (Three selections
  have been lopped off and the sound ruined on this reissue.)
  Trilogy (Reprise 3FS 2300)
JACK TEAGARDEN: *King of the Blues Trombone* (Epic JSN 6044)
BOBBY HACKETT and JACK TEAGARDEN: *Jazz Ultimate* (Capitol TT933)
BENNY GOODMAN: *A Jazz Holiday* (MCA2-4018) (Features Teagarden
  and the Venuti-Lang Orchestra.)
JOE VENUTI: *Stringing the Blues* (CBS 88142) (with Eddie Lang)
  Joe & Zoot (Chiaroscuro 128) (with Zoot Sims)
  Alone at the Palace (Chiaroscuro 160) (with Dave McKenna)
COUNT BASIE: *The Best of Count Basie* (MCA2 4054)
  Good Morning Blues (MCA 4108)
  Sixteen Men Swinging (Verve VE2-2517)
HARRY EDISON: *Sweets, Lips & Lots of Jazz* (Xanadu 123) ("Hold the
  Phone")
DONALD LAMBERT: *Harlem Stride Classics* (Pumpkin 104)
  Meet the Lamb (IAJRC 23)
EUBIE BLAKE: *Rags to Classics* (EBM-2) ("Charleston Rag" or "Echoes
  of Africa")
JAMES P. JOHNSON: *Father of the Stride Piano* (Columbia CL 1780)
JOHN HAMMOND: *Spirituals to Swing* (Vanguard VRS 8523/4) ("Caro-
  lina Shout")
PROFESSOR LONGHAIR: *New Orleans Piano* (Atlantic SD 7225)
  Live on the Queen Mary (Harvest SW-11790)
  Crawfish Fiesta (Alligator 4718)
CHARLIE PARKER: *The Very Best of Bird* (Warners 2WB 3198)
  The Savoy Master Takes (Savoy SJL 2201)
  The Verve Years (Verve VE-2501; 2512; 2523)
  At the Pershing Ballroom (Zim ZM-1003)
  Summit Meeting at Birdland (Columbia 34831)

SONNY ROLLINS: *Taking Care of Business* (Prestige 24082)
Easy Living (Milestone M-9080)
Don't Stop the Carnival (Milestone M-55005)
ARTHUR BLYTHE: *The Grip* (India Navigation IN 1029)
Bush Baby (Adelphi AD 5008)
Lenox Avenue Breakdown (Columbia 35638)
In the Tradition (Columbia JC 36300)
ERIC KLOSS: *One, Two, Free* (Muse MR5019)
THE HOUSTON GRAND OPERA: *Scott Joplin's Treemonisha* (Deutsche Grammophon 2708 083)
DICK HYMAN: *Scott Joplin: The Complete Works for Piano* (RCA CRL5-1106)
IRVING BERLIN: *There's No Business Like Show Business* (Book-of-the-Month 60-5256)
JOAN MORRIS: *The Girl on the Magazine Cover* (RCA ARL 1-3089) (Berlin songs)
FRED ASTAIRE: *The Astaire Story* (DRG Archive DARC-3-1102) (several Berlin songs)
DUKE ELLINGTON: *Concert of Sacred Music* (RCA LPM-3582)
Second Sacred Concert (Fantasy 8407/8)
Third Sacred Concert (RCA APL1-0785)
Carnegie Hall Concerts January 1943 (Prestige 34004)
CHARLES MINGUS: *Passions of a Man* (Atlantic SD 3-600)
Mingus Revisited (Limelight LM 82015) (originally released as *Pre-Bird Mingus*)
Presents Charles Mingus (Candid BR-5012)
Newport in New York, Vols. 1 & 2 (Cobblestone CST 9025-2) ("Lo-Slo Bluze")
Let My Children Hear Music (Columbia KC 31039)
ORNETTE COLEMAN: *Skies of America* (Columbia KC 31562)
Dancing in Your Head (Horizon SP-722)
Body Meta (Artists House AH 1)
DON CHERRY: *Old and New Dreams* (ECM-1-1154)
JAMES BLOOD: *Tales of Captain Black* (Artists House AH 7)
ROSCOE MITCHELL: *Sound* (Delmark DS-408)
Congliptious (Nessa N-2)
L-R-G/The Maze/SII Examples (Nessa N-14/15)
LESTER BOWIE: *Numbers 1 & 2* (Nessa N-1)
MUHAL RICHARD ABRAMS: *Levels and Degrees of Light* (Delmark DS-413)
Young at Heart/Wise in Time (Delmark DS-423)

Sightsong (Black Saint BSR 003)

Lifea Blinec (Novus AN 3000)

ART ENSEMBLE OF CHICAGO: *People in Sorrow* (Nessa N-3)

Phase One (Prestige PR 10064)

Nice Guys (ECM-1-1126)

ANTHONY BRAXTON: *For Alto* (Delmark DS-420/421)

Creative Orchestra Music (Arista AL 4080)

AIR: *Air Time* (Nessa N-12)

Air Lore (Novus AN 3014)

LEROY JENKINS: *Revolutionary Ensemble* (Inner City 3016)

For Players Only (JCOA 1010)

LEO SMITH: *Reflectativity* (Kabell K-2)

Spirit Catcher (Nessa N-19)

GEORGE LEWIS: *Solo Trombone Record* (Sackville 3012)

Homage to Charles Parker (Black Saint BSR 0029)

CHICO FREEMAN: *Chico* (India Navigation IN 1031)

Spirit Sensitive (India Navigation IN 1045)

WILLEM BREUKER: *Live in Berlin* (BVHaast 008)

The European Scene (MPS 68.168)

DIZZY GILLESPIE: *The Development of an American Artist* (Smithsonian P2 13455)

The Gifted Ones (Pablo 2310 833) (with Count Basie)

Jazz Maturity (Pablo 2310 816) (with Roy Eldridge)

RED RODNEY: *Bird Lives!* (Muse 5034)

The Red Arrow (Onyx 204)

DEXTER GORDON: *Go!* (Blue Note 84112)

More than You Know (SteepleChase SCS-1030)

ART PEPPER: *Living Legend* (Contemporary S7633)

Today (Galaxy GXY 5119)

WES MONTGOMERY: *While We're Young* (Milestone 47003)

The Small Group Recordings (Verve VE2-2513) (Includes *Smokin' at the Half Note.*)

GEORGE BENSON: *Benson Burner* (Columbia 38569)

Breezin' (Warners BS 2919)

CECIL TAYLOR: *Cecil Taylor & Mary Lou Williams Embraced* (Pablo Live 2620-108)

3 Phasis (New World NW 303)

Spring of Two Blue-J's (Unit Core 30551)

Index